Crime Reduction Partnerships

Crime
Reduction
Partnerships

Second Edition

Colin Rogers

OXFORD
UNIVERSITY PRESS

OXFORD
UNIVERSITY PRESS

Great Clarendon Street, Oxford, OX2 6DP,
United Kingdom

Oxford University Press is a department of the University of Oxford.
It furthers the University's objective of excellence in research, scholarship,
and education by publishing worldwide. Oxford is a registered trade mark of
Oxford University Press in the UK and in certain other countries

First Edition published in 2006

Second Edition published in 2012

Impression: 1

Photodisc / getty; Brand X Pictures / Punchstock; Brand X Pictures / Punchstock; ImageState /
Punchstock; loopa / iStockphoto.com; Photodisc / Punchstock; Justin Kase / Alamy; David Coder /
iStockphoto.com; DigitalVision / Punchstock; Dominic Harrison / Alamy; Up The Resolution
(uptheres) / Alamy; Photodisc / Punchstock

British Library Cataloguing in Publication Data

Data available

ISBN 978–0–19–965926–5

Printed in Great Britain by
CPI Group (UK) Ltd, Croydon, CR0 4YY

Preface to Second Edition

It is now some six years since the Crime Reduction Partnerships book was first published. During that time we have seen many changes in the way in which the police and their partners work together to tackle community issues and problems including not only crime and disorder, but now such problems as terrorism.

Importantly, during this time there has been a radical change in policing philosophy introduced by the election of the Conservative–Liberal Democrat Coalition Government which has refocused somewhat the aims and objectives not just of the police and their partners but other criminal justice agencies as well.

Coupled with the introduction of legislation such as the Police Reform and Social Responsibility Act 2011, various Terrorism Acts and the proposed changes to Anti-Social Behaviour Legislation, all to be delivered within the framework of 'The Big Society', the time seems right for an updated version of this book.

It has always brought me considerable pleasure when people comment that the book is readable and understandable, and it is with this in mind that the second edition is produced.

I am grateful to Lucy Alexander at Oxford University Press for all her help and assistance with this edition, and of course any mistakes unwittingly included are mine alone and I accept full responsibility for them.

Dr C. Rogers
March 2012

Preface

The original idea for a book on crime and disorder reduction partnerships came from a conversation I had with a senior police officer (now a Chief Constable). I was a sector Inspector in the basic command unit that he was in charge of and both of us had identified a gap in the knowledge of practitioners within the field. This ranged from a basic understanding of why they were required to take part in the process to the more complex concepts, including strategy, audits, and the problems of introducing change into any organization.

I had been involved, in a practical sense, in setting up one of the first community safety partnerships in the area and had worked at incorporating many differing agencies into it. I had also been responsible for evaluating its success, in company with academics from a local university. Such was my interest in the area of crime and disorder reduction partnerships, it subsequently became the subject for my doctoral thesis.

What was apparent was that practitioners, not just police practitioners I may add, were attempting to carry out their function with little or no knowledge or awareness of the issues surrounding this approach to policing. I use the term 'policing' in its original and widest sense here, where many agencies are responsible for upholding the fabric of society. It was indeed a major change in the way the police organization carried out their duties. No longer were the police alone responsible for dealing with crime and disorder, but everyone had a duty to carry out this function.

Cultural and organizational resistance to this change surfaced on many occasions and had to be dealt with in a manner that meant those who opposed the partnership approach felt included and could appreciate its benefits. Hence the main reasons for this book—to raise awareness of the partnership approach, to become an informative resource for police and other practitioners, and hopefully to help break down barriers that may still exist.

Problems still surface in the partnership approach to dealing with crime and disorder. The exchange of information, for example, a problem highlighted by the Bichard Inquiry, is still to some extent a thorn in the side of many partnerships. This problem will, with the involvement of the ACPO guidelines in this area, hopefully recede in the future. Cultural and organizational differences still need to be addressed as well as, in some parts of the country, co-terminosity of boundaries between local authorities and Basic Command Units.

That said, in many parts of the country there exist excellent examples of partnership approaches that have been and still are tackling crime and disorder in an efficient and effective manner. Dissemination of this good work should be a vital ingredient in any strategy so that 'what works' in one area might be seen to work in another. This does not imply that a one-size-fits-all approach will work. After all, the term 'community', always a hotly debated concept, in one location might mean a different thing altogether in another and people react differently to an initiative tried elsewhere.

I have attempted to write the book in a style that is easily accessible for practitioners. People who may not have the time to sit and read for many hours, but who need to understand quickly what the ideas are behind situational crime prevention for example, will hopefully find this a useful approach. It is also written in a style that most readers can easily understand based not just on my academic research and work, but also on my involvement as a former police officer.

I have tried to limit the book to the issues that seem to be more relevant to practitioners in whatever role they occupy in reducing crime and disorder. If I have neglected something that is deemed to be important, then I would welcome constructive feedback, so that, if the need arises, future editions may be amended. Certainly, new legislation such as the Serious Organised Crime and Police Act 2005 may necessitate future amendments.

As the chapters in this book were coming together, the shocking events in London on 7 July 2005 took place. Terrorism and other global crimes have become more prominent in the public's consciousness, with the subsequent demand for more law enforcement. Some people may believe that this will be to the detriment of crime and disorder reduction partnerships as the focus becomes more international rather than local. On the contrary, events seem to suggest that our local communities hold the key to prevention, in many instances, of even the most catastrophic and barbaric acts of terrorism. Local knowledge, information, and intelligence are vital to understanding what is happening within our country. The National Intelligence Model, more than ever before, relies on local input from Basic Command Units, who in turn are involved in major information exchanges with a number of key agencies engaged in crime and disorder reduction. Partnership inclusion of the many diverse members of our communities may well prove of benefit in the fight against terrorism.

Acknowledgements

I continue to thank the people who have supported me in the process of writing the first edition of this book, and now the second edition. Many thanks should still go, I feel, to two friends who started me on my academic path some years ago, and without whose sage advice much of what I had hoped to achieve would never have materialized. David Smith, mentor, friend, and the person responsible for introducing the Police Studies Degree at the University of Glamorgan, and Professor David Hillier of the same institution have been invaluable in providing help and guidance over the years, and I am forever grateful.

Also many thanks must go to the people at Oxford University Press for their belief and support, and in particular to Lucy Alexander who has guided and assisted me and supported me through all the trials and tribulations of writing this second edition!

I also wish to express my thanks to Keith Prosser for his help with the first edition of this book.

Finally, a very special thank you must be registered to my family for all the love and support they have given me over the years, particularly during my academic oil-burning period! To Alison, Mathew, and Alice, many thanks—this book would not have been written without you.

Contents

Abbreviations

ACPO	Association of Chief Police Officers
APA	Association of Police Authorities
ASBO	Anti-Social Behaviour Order
BCS	British Crime Survey
BCU	Basic Command Unit
BVPI	Best Value Performance Indicator
CDRP	Crime and Disorder Reduction Partnership
CJS	Criminal Justice System
CPS	Crown Prosecution Service
COP	Community Oriented Policing
CPTED	Crime prevention through environmental design
CRAVED	Concealable, removable, available, valuable, enjoyable, and disposable
CRP	Crime Reduction Programme
CSP	Community Safety Partnership (CDRP equivalent in Wales)
DAT	Drug Action Team
FPN	Fixed Penalty Notice
HMIC	Her Majesty's Inspectorate of Constabulary
HVP	High Visibility Policing
LSP	Local Strategic Partnership
NCIS	National Crime Intelligence Service
NCPE	National Centre for Police Excellence (formerly CENTREX)
NCRS	National Crime Recording Standard
NIM	National Intelligence Model
NRPP	National Reassurance Policing Programme
PAT	Problem Analysis Triangle
PCC	Police and Crime Commissioner
PCSO	Police Community Support Officer
PITO	Police Information Technology Organization
PNC	Police National Computer
POA	Problem-Oriented Approach
POP	Problem-Oriented Policing/Partnerships
PPAF	Policing Performance Assessment Framework
PSA	Public Service Agreement
RAT	Routine activity theory
RCT	Rational choice theory
RSL	Registered social landlord
SARA	Scanning, analysis, response, assessment
SBD	Secured by Design

SCP   Situational Crime Prevention
TIC   Taken into Consideration
TPI   Targeted Policing Initiative
TT&CG Tactical, Tasking, and Coordinating Group
VIVA   Value, inertia, volume, and access
YIP   Youth Inclusion Programme
YOP   Youth Offending Panel
YOT   Youth Offending Team

Special Features

The book has been written from a practitioner's point of view in order to help you access more easily the information contained within it. Further, it is written in a manner that hopefully will help you reflect upon the issues relating to crime and disorder reduction partnerships. Primarily written for the use of the police practitioner, it is hoped many parts will be useful for other practitioners operating within the field. Each chapter is laid out in broadly the same manner and contains all or some of the features shown below.

Chapter introduction
This highlights the main areas of the chapter and provides an indication of the scope of its contents.

Key point box
Where it has been felt appropriate to reinforce an important or pertinent point which has been covered within the text of the chapters, a key point box has been included to reinforce the information. This has been included for ease of reference for the reader.

Scenario box
Included in relevant chapters are scenario boxes that highlight the provision of good practice in certain areas. Readers are asked to consider how these scenarios compare with activities that occur within their own areas.

Summing Up
At the conclusion of each chapter, readers are invited to apply the information and knowledge contained in them to their local crime and disorder reduction partnership. This reinforces the knowledge gained from reading the chapter.

Useful websites
Also at the conclusion of each chapter, and throughout the text, there are links to pertinent websites.. Readers are encouraged to explore these websites in order to reinforce the information and knowledge already laid out in the work.

1

An Introduction to Crime and Disorder Reduction Partnerships

1.1 **Introduction**

Policing in England and Wales has undergone and is still undergoing significant change. So profound is the reshaping of the delivery of policing services that, it could be argued, these changes amount to a paradigmatic revolution. Kuhn (1996), for example, suggests that this type of dramatic change occurs when a new way of working attracts an enduring group of adherents away from competing modes of activity. In this instance, the new way of working for the police was that of partnerships involving the community, outside agencies, and local authorities in an effort to reduce crime and disorder and the fear associated with both. The last few decades has increasingly seen the development of the partnership approach to policing in general and to crime and disorder prevention and reduction in particular. This is in contrast to the previous reactive style of policing in which the police were seen as the only available experts who could tackle crime and control criminals. The situation now arises where practitioners are undertaking functions of crime and disorder reduction work or parts thereof, having little or no understanding of why they are doing the work and, on occasions, how to carry it out effectively.

It is difficult to identify precisely when the debate on policing and crime prevention first used the concept of partnerships. Partnership in this sense refers to a purposeful relationship between the police and the public, or between the police and other agencies in this field. The debate on policing does not appear to have mentioned the concept until the rise of community policing in the early 1980s, since when the idea that the police could no longer tackle crime alone has become something more than a slogan. It was during this time that the Home Office promoted a number of initiatives, including the formation of the Home Office Crime Prevention Unit, whilst various Home Office circulars, including Circular 8/84 (Home Office 1984b), encouraged all agencies to become involved in crime prevention. The then Conservative Government supported the launch of Crime Concern in 1988 and from that time onwards oversaw the development of the Safer Cities initiative, which has been the catalyst for many of the crime prevention partnerships in this country. This was especially so in the case of cities where there was a need for economic and social regeneration and which were likely to be subject to social unrest. A common factor in these schemes was the involvement of police, local government, and other bodies in the form of partnerships, which, it was argued, showed that this was a sound approach for effective community safety and crime prevention work. Perhaps one of the most influential documents to be published during this period, however, was the report of the Standing Committee on Crime Prevention chaired by James Morgan, which had the responsibility for reviewing the development of crime prevention. This report became known as the Morgan Report (Home Office 1991a) and contained many proposals for the structure and coordination of crime prevention strategies, and in particular highlighted the need for the partnership approach, with an increased emphasis on the role of local authorities.

1.2 **A Brief History of Crime and Disorder Reduction Partnerships**

If one accepts the argument that the rise of partnerships in crime and disorder control has been dramatic, then an historical analysis of the origins of this particular approach is necessary for further understanding. Also, an analysis of the component parts of the partnership approach would need clarifying. These usually involve a style of policing which is considered unusual, or different in some way from the normal reactive style of policing, and the use of crime prevention techniques. Crime prevention techniques appear to contain elements of situational crime prevention and include a consideration of repeat victims of specific crimes. Partnerships also purport to include wide consultation with the community they serve.

The last thirty years or so have produced a substantial amount of research and advice to the police service, urging it to tackle problems with the aid of the community and other agencies. Many of the publications urging this approach stem from the Home Office, and a typical example of the mood for change can be seen in the influential Home Office Circular 8/84. The following box sums up the approach.

KEY POINT—THE VIEW FROM THE HOME OFFICE

'Every individual citizen and all those agencies whose policies and practices can influence the extent of crime should make their contribution. Preventing crime is a task for the whole community.'

Home Office (1984b:1)

1.2.1 **Kirkholt and other initiatives**

The message could not have been clearer for police services. Consequently, throughout the country, partnership initiatives were introduced. Initiatives such as the Kirkholt Burglary Prevention Project (Forrester et al 1988, 1990) were promoted as flagships of the partnership approach and the police service was encouraged to engage with other agencies in community crime prevention initiatives. For a number of years the Home Office sponsored and published research into specific areas of tackling criminality that appeared to highlight the successful approach of partnerships involving differing agencies. These initiatives covered a range of offences from burglary (Brown 1997), to public order and annoyance on housing estates (Morris 1996), to thefts against retail outlets (Tilley 1993). The common theme of all this work was the claimed positive results obtained by several agencies collaborating to tackle highly specific crimes. Indeed, such was the faith in the partnership approach that the Home Office published a document that provided examples of partnership initiatives from various locations within this country that were deemed good practice (Home Office 1997a). The intention of this document, it was claimed, was to provide a framework of ideas for those agencies not already engaged in the paradigm of partnership policing.

One of the main reasons behind the introduction of the partnership approach lay in the fact that there had been a rise in recorded crime, coupled with the realization that the police did not have the resources to tackle this problem alone.

1.2.2 Community safety

The publication of the Morgan Report (Home Office 1991a) saw the term 'crime prevention' replaced by the concept of 'community safety' in order to broaden the base of support for such partnerships.

KEY POINT—COMMUNITY SAFETY

'The term crime prevention is often narrowly interpreted and this reinforces the view that it is solely the responsibility of the police. On the other hand, the term community safety is open to wider interpretation and could encourage greater participation from all sections of the community.'

Home Office (1991a:1)

Since the review of the Crime and Disorder Act 2006, Crime and Disorder Reduction Partnerships are now commonly referred to as Community Safety Partnerships both in England and Wales. By using the term community in 'community safety', it was hoped that this approach would be more acceptable to the public at large for, as Cohen (1985) rightly points out, the word 'community' appeals to the individual perceptions of positive feelings. When the imagery portrayed is positive, the term is associated with concepts of 'natural', 'openness', 'integrative', or simply 'in the community'. Therefore, such concepts as community centres, community prisons, and community policing are generally viewed as positive and non-threatening.

Central to the concept of partnerships is the need for a wide consultation process involving the public agencies involved, private businesses, and the community. For partnerships trying to provide this service, the aims of this consultation process can be listed as follows:

- The drive to reach as broad a cross-section of the population as possible. All parties, it is argued, have an interest in consulting as widely and deeply as possible, as failure to do so could mean that prominent crime and disorder problems are not brought to their attention.
- The identification of public priorities to influence the annual policing plan, to assist in targeting valuable police resources to particular community concerns.

- The identification of public priorities for local action, so that local partnerships can be focused on individual community problems such as the perception of youth annoyance.
- To provide the public with information on policing and community safety matters, feeding back information to the public and improving the quality of consultation.

1.2.3 **Response to partnerships**

Partnerships are concerned with the management of providing a service to the community and, therefore, organizational attainments are quite high on their list of consultation priorities. For the public, according to Elliot and Nicholls (1996), the main reason for engaging in the consultation process with policing partnerships seems to revolve around two main areas of concern, namely:

- Obtaining rapid police action on public concerns, so that it is likely that the public do not merely wish to be consulted on their views as their priority will be to get the police to address their problems.
- Obtaining information from the police, such as what the police are doing, how they are performing, and the impact they are having on crime. They may well see consultation as a way to achieve this.

However, the consultation process itself, whilst a positive idea, is far from infallible. Public meetings, where the community is asked to attend to air its views, are not necessarily representative of the community as a whole. Marginalized groups such as gay and lesbian groups, youth elements, and those regarded as outsiders because of minority ethnic background are often not represented at such consultation processes. Consequently, the concerns addressed are those that are normally aired, it could be argued, by locally elected representatives and other community leaders who may not be acting on behalf of the whole community. These issues are discussed at length later in this work.

One of the biggest influences on the formation of the partnership approach to crime prevention, and touched upon earlier, is the Home Office's Standing Committee on Crime Prevention Report *Safer Communities: The Local Delivery of Crime Prevention through the Partnership Approach* (Home Office 1991a). This report, known as the Morgan Report, is so influential in this area that it requires closer scrutiny.

1.2.4 **The Morgan Report**

Circular 8/84: *Crime Prevention* (Home Office 1984b) may be seen as a watershed in crime prevention policy. Its emphasis lay in the principle that crime prevention must be accepted as a significant and integral goal of public policy, both centrally and locally. In this circular, particular stress was placed on the need for a coordinated approach and joint strategies involving partnerships against crime. Although more often rhetoric than reality, around the country the idea of multi-agency 'partnerships' in crime prevention had clearly arrived in Britain.

Effectively, community safety, as a guiding idea, was heralded as a way of moving beyond a situational definition of crime prevention (focusing on the management, design, and manipulation of the built physical environment) to a broader social definition (seeking to change criminal motivations which are perceived to lie within people by affecting the social environment).

By the end of the 1980s the Home Office Circular *Tackling Crime* (Home Office 1989) showed the further development of the partnership and community orientation to crime prevention in the Home Office. Particular attention was given in the circular to the problem of coordination, or rather the lack of it, between agencies making up the criminal justice system. This circular led the way for what was considered to be the key inspiration for much of the subsequent local government, multi-agency, and seemingly social crime prevention schemes of the 1990s, the Morgan Report (Home Office 1991a).

The Report went on to identify six key elements that needed to be addressed, namely structure, leadership, information, identity, durability, and resources, in order to improve the organization and delivery of multi-agency crime prevention.

The Report supported the notion that local authorities be given the statutory duty (and therefore the resources) to coordinate crime prevention/community safety strategies for their locality. The Report also argued that sufficient resources to make this change must be forthcoming from central government. In passing, it may be noted that the recommendations regarding both local authorities' statutory role and resourcing were not taken up by the government during the 1990s, probably due to its concerns over costs and its ideological hostility to local government per se. With the enactment of the Crime and Disorder Act 1998 (Home Office 1999a), a statutory partnership was introduced rather than Morgan's recommendation of a leadership role for local authorities. The Labour Party's proposals, however, as part of this Act, stated that no extra resources would be given to local authorities to meet their new statutory responsibilities for crime prevention. That said, much of the Morgan Report's philosophy of partnerships, multi-agency collaboration, and audits is to the fore in current crime prevention policy proposals (Home Office 1997a, Home Office 2005a).

Hughes (1998) argues that the Morgan Report appears for the most part as a report written by local authority and police officers for executive officers. In particular, the question of how these multi-agency partnership officer groups relate to issues of democratic accountability, he believes, is never fully addressed. Further, it is argued that citizens are being called upon to play a crucial role in crime prevention through their own actions. As in other social policy areas, there is an appeal to the much-vaunted but ill-defined active citizen to play a key role;

in this case in both crime surveillance and 'policing'. The Home Office pamphlet *Partners against Crime* (Home Office 1994a) confidently asserted that the power of partnerships in beating crime was proved, and three complementary partnerships were presented as initiatives to be launched or given further encouragement nationally in 1995. These were the already well-established Neighbourhood Watch schemes, Street Watch, and Neighbourhood Constables.

1.2.5 Public involvement

Much of the central government proposals for 'community' crime prevention suggested that voluntary community action should replace collective provision, resulting in a voluntary surveillance society, whilst the extent to which the multi-agency 'call to arms' from both the Home Office Circular 44/90 (Home Office 1990a) and the Morgan Report (Home Office 1991a) has affected the thinking, shape, and direction of local crime prevention initiatives in the UK is also an important factor. In particular, their research addressed the six elements mentioned previously as crucial to multi-agency partnerships highlighted by the Morgan Report (see **1.2.4**).

Over the past twenty years it has become evident that managing criminal acts has become an increasingly diffuse and diverse problem, with more emphasis on interactive agency work. For Garland (1996), this is a new way of governing crime problems, namely the 'responsibilization' strategy, with the recurring message that the state alone is not, and cannot effectively be, responsible for preventing or controlling crime. Others must be made aware that they too have a responsibility in this regard, and have to be persuaded to change their practices in order to reduce criminal opportunities and increase formal controls. In the context of crime prevention this strategy is clearly associated with notions of partnership, multi-agency, and, of course, self-help. This of course now appears to fit in with the present governments drive for the delivery of public services through the concept of the Big Society whereby volunteers, charities and others are expected to work closely with partnerships which is discussed fully later in this book.

1.3 Further Thoughts on Partnerships

For partnerships, therefore, there is a need for close cooperation to ensure that more crime is reported, rather than remaining hidden and unreported. Further, with this information shared between agencies repeat offences can be easily identified and action taken immediately to prevent re-victimization. Such strategies, it is hoped, place victims' rights firmly on the partnership, and therefore political, agenda. However, this type of approach has failed to transform practices, and victims' feelings about the criminal justice system remain on the whole negative. Whilst many current partnerships' relationship with victims remains in the domain purely of notification and the supply of information to them, it is suggested that victims could play a greater part in the policy formation which guides many partnerships in crime prevention.

1.3.1 Inter-organizational problems with partnerships

For some, therefore, the partnership approach has just become the new buzzword of the crime prevention 'industry'. However, it is no bad thing for the responsibility for the 'crime problem' to be owned by an increasingly diffuse variety of individuals and organizations, even if the make-up of the partnerships is far from ideal. Alternatively, it is the very diverse make-up of many of the agencies that constitute partnerships that can be problematic. Attention is drawn to the inter-organizational conflict and differential power relationships that can occur. Partnerships, especially within the field of crime control and criminal justice, by their nature, draw together diverse organizations with very different cultures, ideologies, and traditions that pursue distinct aims through divergent structures, strategies, and practices. Deep structural conflicts exist between the parties that sit down together in partnerships. Criminal justice agencies have very different priorities and interests, as do other public sector organizations, voluntary bodies, the commercial sector, and local community groups.

Not all agencies and groups are equally powerful and certain agencies tend to dominate the policy agenda, such as in the field of crime prevention. This has been pointed out by Sampson et al. Their comments are seen in the following box.

KEY POINT—DOMINATION OF AGENDA BY THE POLICE

'The police are often enthusiastic proponents of the multi-agency approach, but they tend to prefer to set the agenda and dominate forum meetings, and then to ignore the multi-agency framework when it suits their own needs.'

Sampson et al. (1988:178)

While this approach can cause conflict, agencies involved in partnerships use strategies such as conflict avoidance to contribute to the smooth running of partnerships at a formal level.

1.4 Four Dominant Views

One of the strongest supporters of the partnership approach to community safety was Jon Bright (1991, 1996, 1997, 1999) who argues for the partnership approach by tackling four dominant, prevalent views about crime and disorder reduction.

Bright's views are regarded by many as underpinning much of the partnership philosophy in terms of crime prevention. Briefly, the dominant views challenged by Bright are:

(1) 'Nothing much can be done.' Bright argues that government policies such as quality training and employment programmes support families, improve parenting, and maintain family cohesion. He suggests that interventions such as these can be effective in reducing crime and reoffending.

(2) 'The criminal justice system prevents crime.' Here Bright argues that the formal criminal justice system—apprehending, prosecuting, sentencing, punishing, and rehabilitating offenders—has only a limited effect in controlling crime. Increases in police resources do not necessarily lead to reduced crime, and rates of recidivism following release from prison remain high. This is supported somewhat by the Audit Commission (1996), whose report into multi-agency style policing in Central Scotland found that other factors contributed towards reducing crime figures. In particular, the Audit Commission highlighted the fact that only one public demand fell squarely on the shoulders of the police, as seen in the key point box below.

KEY POINT—POLICE RESPONSIBILITY

'Only one demand—a visible police presence to reassure and deter anti-social behaviour—is solely a police responsibility. The others fall squarely within the remit of the local authority and other agencies—education on drug and alcohol abuse, improved street lighting, safer play areas, more leisure facilities, road safety measures and attention to environmental concerns such as dogs fouling pavements and parks.'

Audit Commission (1996:48–49)

Bright continues by focusing on the fact that the public's demands on the police broadly fall into three categories, namely more uniformed officers on the street, offenders arrested immediately, and the expectation that the police will deal with organized crime and serious crime, child abuse, and drug trafficking. Because the police cannot meet these demands, Bright argues, the refocusing of police resources has been at the expense of community reassurance and prevention work. It is therefore clear, he says, that the criminal justice system agencies' main functions are to process crime after the event and punish the very small proportion of offenders who are convicted. The deterrent, preventative effects of the system are very limited and poor value for money.

(3) 'Communities alone prevent crime.' Attacking the communitarian movement belief in empowering the community and thereby reducing crime, Bright contends that, whilst communities have a vital role to play, their capacity to resolve crime and disorder patterns is often overstated.

Anti-crime-and-disorder community strategies, he argues, are least common and least successful in the areas where they are most needed, namely poor, high-crime neighbourhoods. Whilst acknowledging the growth in voluntary crime prevention schemes, typified by Neighbourhood Watch schemes, Bright argues that there is little support for Neighbourhood Watch in areas where the risk of crime is high and there is little sense of community. Generally, it is argued, too much has been expected both of policing and community organizations to resolve crime, with communities expected to address problems they have neither the resources nor the authority to resolve.

(4) 'Crime is a single solution problem.' Highlighting this area, Bright quotes the recent suggestions to solving crime, such as more police, tougher sentences, more jails, etc. Bright's argument here is that these are not efficient ways to combat the crime problem. For him, there are only two ways to prevent crime. These are: (a) to make crime more difficult to commit, more risky, and less rewarding, whilst making better use of security and surveillance; and (b) to prevent criminal behaviour by reducing the risk factors long associated with offending, such as poor parenting and school failure.

The consequence of believing the myths for so long has been the creation of an expensive, inefficient, and self-perpetuating criminal justice system, a high crime rate, and large numbers of young people drifting into crime, which appears hard to refute. Consequently, it is argued, only a comprehensive partnership approach to tackling crime and its associated problems involving all agencies can be seen as the way forward. However, Bright (1997:113) tinges this approach with some degree of realism, appreciating that the problems of such an approach can be immense: 'To bring about this shift in policy will require the vision to see what can be achieved, and political leadership of a high order to bring it about.'

1.5 What Are Crime and Disorder Reduction Partnerships?

The Crime and Disorder Act 1998 (Home Office 1999a), as amended by the Police Reform Act 2002 (Home Office 2002a), sets out statutory requirements for responsible authorities to work with other local agencies and organizations, to develop and implement strategies to tackle crime and disorder and misuse of drugs in their area. These statutory partnerships were known as Crime and Disorder Reduction Partnerships (CDRPs), or now more commonly Community Safety Partnerships. The responsible authorities are:

• the police
• local authorities
• fire authorities

- police authorities
- local health boards in Wales
- primary care trusts in England (became responsible authorities on 30 April 2004).

Working together, these responsible authorities are required to carry out an audit to identify crime and disorder and problems of drugs misuse in their area, and to develop strategies that deal effectively with them. Partner organizations are required to work in cooperation with local education and probation authorities, and to invite the cooperation of a range of local private, voluntary, and other public and community groups, including the community itself.

Crime and disorder reduction partnerships are expected to work closely with Drug Action Teams in two-tier local authority areas and should have integrated their work in unitary authority areas by April 2004. Integration/closer working brings many benefits including simplifying local working relationships, giving greater recognition to common interests, and providing the right framework to enable more effective delivery of the crime and disorder reduction and drugs agendas. Effective partnership working is the key to lasting crime and disorder reduction.

There are several important official documents that will help the police practitioner to understand what the previous government wanted to achieve in this particular area. These include *Building Communities, Beating Crime* (Home Office 2004a), *National Policing Plan 2005–2008: Safer, Stronger Communities* (Home Office 2004b), *Confident Communities in a Secure Britain: The Home Office Strategic Plan 2004–2008* (Home Office 2004c), and the Home Office publication entitled *Neighbourhood Policing: Your Police, Your Community, Our Commitment* (Home Office 2005a). Much of these documents have been archived on the Home Office website but are still available. Many of the current practices of partnership working stem from these documents and a further influential document was the review of the Crime and Disorder Act which was published in 2006.

1.6 Review of the Partnership Provisions of the Crime and Disorder Act 1998

The review was launched as a result of an announcement in the police reform white paper in November 2004. It was published in 2006 as a result of the changing landscape within society and the criminal justice system as whole. The review considered the following main areas, namely:

- structures
- delivery
- governance and accountability
- mainstreaming and national standards.

Each of these will be briefly examined and the main recommendations high-lighted below.

Structures

- Two-tier authorities did not aid successful partnership working.
- Strategic and operational decision-making was split with the former sitting at county level.
- The list of responsible authorities was extended.

Delivery

- Intelligence-led decision-making is considered to be at the heart of effective delivery.
- CSPs were to undertake an intelligence-led, problem-solving approach to community safety.
- The National Intelligence Model was to be the framework for this practice.
- Six-monthly strategic assessments are undertaken by those responsible for strategic and operational functions.
- The six-monthly strategic assessments will inform the new requirements to produce annual rolling three-year community safety plans.
- Section 115 of the Crime and Disorder act 1998 was strengthened and a duty was placed upon responsible authorities to share depersonalized data for community safety purposes.

Governance and accountability

- Community safety partnerships will engage more with their communities.
- They will produce regular reports to their communities rather than annual reports to the Home Secretary on the implementation of their three-year strategies.
- Local people should inform decisions over local community safety issues.
- Local councillors will act as the conduit at neighbourhood level for relaying local concerns to the CSP.

Mainstreaming and national standards

- Section 17 of the Crime and Disorder Act 1998 to be strengthened in order that further agencies can be added to the list of responsible authorities.
- The introduction of a set of national standards for community safety partnership working.

This review it was hoped would have a positive impact upon the effectiveness of partnership working across England and Wales and has certainly influenced current policy and procedures in partnership working.

1.7 **Partnerships in the Big Society**

In times of economic unrest, societal change and political uncertainty, challenges facing crime and disorder partnerships are significant (Gravelle and Rogers 2009a). High on the new government's political agenda is social reform and the concept of 'big society', frequently being referred to by the current Prime Minister throughout his election campaign, this ideology remains a major plank for the Coalition Government as it sets out its vision for Britain (Cameron 2010, Piggot 2010).

1.7.1 **The 'Big Society'**

The idea of promoting community agencies, groups and individuals in an attempt to encourage social interaction and thus produce a more cohesive society is not particularly new. Previous official documents such as Wedlock's document on social cohesion (Home Office 2006) which promoted social cohesion and crime resistant communities, have urged crime and disorder partnerships to engage in these types of activities. Further, the importance of social capital has been explored in the work of Robert Putnam who considers the rise of criminal activity against a backcloth of social disengagement in the USA (Putnam 2000). Recent and current governmental ideas which extend this approach have been and are still being promoted by Halpern (2007; 2010) who served as an aide to the previous Labour Government and now advises the new Conservative–Liberal Democrat Coalition Government.

In essence, the 'big society' refers to a tripartite partnership between the citizen, community and local government (Eaton 2010). This vision requires families, networks and neighbourhoods in a postmodern society to formalize a working partnership that is effective and sustainable in its approach to solving problems, building social cohesion and setting priorities for Britain (BBC 2010). In doing so, the government along with involvement of communities is set on building a 'big society' that is bigger, stronger and accountable to all. How this equates to the practicalities of living in the UK is worthy of examination. The Prime Minister David Cameron refers to the ideology of 'big society' as liberalism, empowerment, freedom and responsibly where the top-down approach to government is abandoned and replaced by local innovation and civic action. Interestingly, critics of the government, including the general secretary of Unison refer to the 'big society' as the 'big cop-out' only concerned with cutting investment and saving money (ITN 2010). This laissez faire approach to government could spell the end for new public management and centralized performance indicators as it will be for society and communities to assess performance. However, government insists that for the 'big society' to work, it will require significant involvement, encouragement and support from communities. Fundamentally, there are five key strands to understanding the 'big society' identified by the Cabinet Office (2010):-

Empowering communities

The government aims to reform the planning and procedural systems to give local people the ability to determine how their communities will develop and be shaped in the future. Specifically, the 'big society' requires local people to have a greater say in the 'construction' of their surroundings. Accompanying these new powers, local people will also have ways of saving local facilities and services that are threatened by closure if they are deemed to be fundamental to the fabric of society. Communities will have the right to take over state-run services and facilities. Bringing about this change, the government will recruit and train 'community organizers' to support the creation of neighbourhood ground all over the UK.

Action-orientated communities

Community involvement, philanthropy and a spirit of volunteerism are an integral component of the 'big society'. The introduction of a 'big society' day and a focus on civic service will aim to increase and stimulate involvement from members of the communities all socio-economic backgrounds. A 'National Citizen Service' will be established to encourage young people to develop the skills needed in a modern society aimed to break-down negative perceptions and stimulate cohesion.

Decentralized power

A drive for decentralization and 'rolling back the frontiers of the state' are all perhaps a synonymous style of governance set by the Conservative Party in previous administrations. Reducing the size and influence of the state by stimulating local initiatives is perceived as key drivers in a move to establish a 'big society'. Greater autonomy, both financially and procedurally, is likely to be seen as government moves away from micro-management or 'nano level' management and moves to a more macro-management approach. This cultural change in governance will see local authorities and local officials having greater discretion and influence of the direction of local policy. Decisions on housing and planning are also likely to return to local councils in an effort to make the procedure of allocation and urban design more accountable to local people.

Greater social enterprises

As pluralization is to be encouraged, it is envisaged that there will be an expansion in social enterprises. Those sectors, companies, industries and organizations that have previously been operating under a monopoly or oligopoly are likely to see an increase in competition as state-run functions may be shared with other social enterprises. Public sector workers will be encouraged to set up employee-owned cooperatives encouraging innovation and quality of service for the end-user whilst being a more economically viable option for the state. Funding the 'big society' will come from dormant bank accounts which are believed will provide the necessary funding for stimulating neighbourhood groups, charities and social enterprise. As previously indicated, it is however unlikely that the 'big society' ideology drive will be funded by an unlimited supply of capital and financial constraints will play a large part in their introduction and use.

Information ability

Finally, confidence in official data and statistics has been eroded in recent years with possibly unfounded, incorrect statistics being published resulting in several official apologies being made in parliament by senior ministers. Underpinning the 'big society', the government aims to create a new culture where the public have a 'right to data' that will be published regularly in an attempt to improve accountability.

1.8 **Implications for Partnerships**

Working within the 'big society' will unquestionably have implications for the partnership approach. It is likely that with community engagement taking precedence, the community partnership working paradigm that has been adopted by partnerships over recent years with the roll-out of neighbourhood partnership working teams will continue if not be strengthened (Rogers and Lewis 2007). Partnerships may need to engage with an ever empowered community as they work together in setting short-, medium- and long-term objectives for partnership working within their local community (Independent 2010). Becoming more focused at a local level while operating in smaller geographical areas will possibly be of greater importance to partnerships and its constituent agencies such as the police if they are to facilitate the needs of the community rather than simply prescribe narrative, often enforcement-led solutions to crime and disorder problems. The transfer of power to the local level is likely to be difficult for both partnerships and community. For example, Garland (2001) points out that apart from any cultural resistance on the part of governmental agencies to engage with others, community agencies and individuals may not be sufficiently organized to enable the process to come to fruition. However, to create value, mobilize wealth in terms of reciprocity and social capital and to operate efficiently, it will be for both partnerships and community to agree and operate under a cooperative productive mutual partnership. As local communities are likely to be involved in setting of objectives, there will be a need for greater involvement from other agencies, particularly local groups, charities and local cooperatives in order to address issues which the public identify as priorities. The use of unpaid volunteers is also likely to be increased dramatically as the partnerships attempt to offer a wide range of services in times of austerity. The concept of volunteering within partnerships is not a new one. Special Constables, to use a police example, who are recruited from members of local communities, are unpaid, fully warranted partnerships officers and are the archetypical volunteer in the partnerships. However, the police service has begun to utilize volunteers that are unpaid 'civilians', to work within partnerships organizations (Gravelle and Rogers 2009b). These 'neighbourhood volunteers' assist when they can, as many volunteers enjoy the flexibility of supporting the service and their local community. Dependent on the role, whether administrative or involving some sort of community engagement, some volunteers work from different partnerships stations, and others work on the street engaging with members of the public directly, engaging in Partnerships and Communities Together (PACT) meetings, letter dropping and other operations often working alongside neighbourhood partnership teams and partner agencies. Although such schemes are utilized extensively throughout some police forces, there will need to be an expansion of this programme if partnerships are to continue to offer a wide range of services considered necessary by communities (Flanagan 2008). In the mid- to long-term, volunteer schemes may have a positive influence on communities in times of austerity. For a police force such as Lancashire, which currently has 644 volunteers, the value of volunteer time could be significant (Flanagan 2008). It has been estimated for example, that the use of just one volunteer, as a PACT Coordinator, could save for that force alone the initial sum of £43,512 year (Gravelle and Rogers 2009a). However, whilst this approach appears attractive in terms of economic savings, wider implementation of such schemes could be used to provide services previously delivered by paid professionals and this may have implications for both the volunteers and the agencies involved.

However, it is suggested that all of these will be achieved in part because of the extended partnership approach, improving confidence and cooperation. The improved relationship as well as the developed sense of ownership and inclusion may result in any targets, either quantitative or qualitative, on community safety being met. As a direct consequence, this may lead to a reduction in overall crime and fear of crime leading to a reduction in the so called 'reassurance gap' (McLaughlin et al 2006).

In terms of structure, the 'big society' will result in the devolvement of power to more local levels. The 2020 Commission (2010) conclude that directly elected crime commissions will facilitate this change in structure as power and autonomy is transferred away from partnerships and back to local communities (Home Office 2010). It is likely that the previous new public management mandate where the primary focus was on centralized targets will change, moving instead to more locally published statistics where the elected crime commissioner can be held to account. No longer, for example, will sanction detection rates or league tables be considered the sole measurement of successful partnership working. Instead, it will be public perceptions that will have more influence and these measurements are likely to increase as the number of partnership working providers in the future also increases (Jones et al 2006). It is entirely possible that funding for partnership working may be dependent on results of these types of measurements. Private contractors and a move to a more European approach to partnership working where a significant amount of partnership working tasks are contracted out to private companies and industries may also be a visible change following the implantation of the 'big society'. Of course, the assumption inherent in this idea is that private contractors are able and willing to carry out the necessary partnership function. The results of this approach may ultimately lead to partnerships becoming smaller, leaner and more focused and specialized in its approach to working, but may also increase tensions within partnerships regarding the use of expensive resources. Further, there is likely to be expansion of other types of agencies through the creation of more charities, groups and enterprise as a result of the change in philosophy regarding tackling crime and disorder. All of these factors increase the importance of better partnership working with other agencies as the need to share knowledge and intelligence becomes even more important (Rogers 2006, Williamson 2008).

1.8.1 Conclusion

Taking account of all the changes, the shift in power and finance will make for an interesting combination. As these forces play out, change will be inevitable for all public services including community safety partnerships. Accountability, accountability and more accountability appears to be paramount to the successful implementation of the 'big society' ideology as communities are empowered to change their outlook and engage in partnership working. Of course this throws open the debate concerning just how accountable volunteer groups, private organizations and others will be under any new arrangements. There is every chance that the 'big society' will be successful, especially if the perceived benefits for partnerships such as greater public engagement, more use of volunteer groups to help provide services in times of austerity and greater input from private organizations actually materializes. This, coupled with a drive for cohesion, efficacy and improving social trust in communities, will create a productive and stimulating environment, drawing on creativity and experience to solve goals identified in a changing environment. In all probability, public services such as partnerships may suffer drastic cutbacks as a result of the economic downturn. However, there is a possibility that the ideological change to utilizing the 'big society' approach, whilst not being a panacea, may go some way to help bridge any perceived gap in the provision of partnership working in England and Wales.

1.9 About This Book

Each chapter of this book considers a main theme of crime and disorder reduction activity, and includes definitions, explanations, flow charts, and diagrams, where appropriate. Scenario boxes used to indicate interesting or best practice are included where relevant and important facts and information are shown in

'Key points' boxes throughout the text. At the conclusion of each chapter there is a section entitled 'Local application', where the reader is encouraged to find out about their local crime and disorder reduction partnership and apply the knowledge in the chapter to the practicalities of multi-agency partnership activity. This is followed by a section of useful website addresses that the student may care to visit to explore further the information included in the chapter. Finally, a separate section is provided for students to write notes, etc., thereby adding to the knowledge and awareness provided by this work.

1.9.1 The chapters

Chapter 2 sets the political context of the rise of partnerships, and considers some of the problems that can still be seen within current crime and disorder reduction partnerships today. It examines how the new approach to managerialism affects partnership efforts, in particular how the impact of initiatives such as the 'Best Value' initiative, influences multi-agency working, along with national and local priorities. This chapter also examines the problems that organizational culture can have when agencies that normally work alongside each other, but not in collaboration within the criminal justice system, strive to achieve common goals. In particular the historical problem of a strong police subculture is probed, in the context of change. The chapter discusses why change is resisted and methods of how to overcome such resistance in a more sensitive and successful manner. The main problems of partnership management are then considered, such as the problem of continual staff turnover; information exchange, including the Bichard Inquiry and the implications of that report, is considered in terms of partnerships.

Chapter 3 examines the major problems that crime and disorder reduction partnerships have to contend with under the broad heading of anti-social behaviour. The problems of defining anti-social behaviour are considered and a working definition is provided. Along with a complete examination of the Anti-Social Behaviour Order process, the chapter examines and explains such ideas as Acceptable Behaviour Contracts, Parenting Contracts, and Parenting Orders. At the time of writing, the topic of anti social behaviour is being revisited and the current government's proposed changes to the Anti-Social Behaviour Order (ASBO) legislation are discussed.

Chapter 4 expands on the problems faced by communities from the general theme of anti-social behaviour and considers specific activities that tend to blight our communities. It discusses the particular legislation applied to these incidents in an effort to deal with them. For example, the chapter considers alcohol-related disorder and some of the provisions of the Licensing Act 2003 (Home Office 2003b). Alcohol disorder zones, sale of alcohol to under-age persons, confiscation of alcohol, and dispersal of groups are covered within this section as well as proposed changes introduced as a result of the Police Reform and Social Responsibility Act 2010. Drugs are a constant source of problems across and within communities, and this chapter examines the powers to close certain properties being used for dealing illegal drugs as well as exploring how to deal with noisy neighbours, animal noise, abandoned vehicles, and racially aggravated behaviour. Finally the chapter turns to crime within communities. What does the term 'crime' mean to individuals? The questions of why people don't report crime and the use of criminal statistics are considered here, along with the very important problem for crime and disorder reduction partnerships: that of fear of crime.

Chapter 5 discusses the application of crime prevention theory to everyday practice, as carried out by crime and disorder reduction partnerships. The reason why we carry out a function is as important as completing the task itself. If we know clearly why locks and bolts are fitted, the overall performance can be improved through suggestions and application of knowledge. Best practice in crime prevention could and should be disseminated throughout the country, and this chapter promotes this idea. It discusses the three main levels of interaction applied to crime and disorder reduction techniques, namely the primary, secondary, and tertiary approaches. It clearly explains the fundamental approach of situational crime prevention, including an introduction to three supporting strands of this approach, namely routine activity theory, rational choice theory, and crime prevention through environmental design. The chapter also explains, by way of example, the current Secured by Design initiative that is sponsored by the Association of Chief Police Officers. The concept of displacement of crime is considered in its many forms and also that of crime deflection and diffusion of benefits. The important idea of repeat victims of crime and how this idea can be used to reduce certain types of offences is discussed, as well as the use of the media in reducing crime and disorder and strategies for reduction of fear of crime.

Chapter 6 examines the different approaches and types of policing that appear to be prevalent throughout England and Wales within the partnership approach. It examines the idea of community-oriented policing (COP), zero tolerance approaches, and problem-oriented partnerships involving the SARA (scanning, analysis, response, assessment) approach to problem-solving. These styles are compared, and their strengths and weakness as suitable policing responses are discussed. The concept of policing signal crimes is also considered and a definition of signal crimes (along with the way they can affect communities) is explored. Police responses, including examples used in this area, are provided. Finally, the government's ideas about reassurance and high visibility are discussed, with definitions provided for this important area. This forms good contextual information for the following chapter.

Chapter 7 considers the new directions that the police service appears to be taking in policing crime and disorder reduction, and which may become more and more widespread over the next few years. The government's Police Reform Programme is examined, including a consideration of the Annual Policing Plan which forms a vital part of strategic policing today. The chapter continues this theme by considering the work of the Police Support Unit and the introduction of police community support officers, and the accreditation of others authorized by the Police Reform Act 2002 (Home Office 2002a). Citizen-focused policing, allowing for more involvement by the community and linked to the policing plan, is also discussed. Perhaps the main operational change will be seen within the introduction of neighbourhood policing teams linked to greater use of the National Intelligence Model. Both these important introductions are considered at length in this chapter.

Chapter 8 deals with one of the foundation stones of crime and disorder reduction partnerships, namely the production of local crime and disorder audits. It examines the main partnership membership, including the roles and responsibilities of Responsible Authorities, Cooperating Bodies, and Invitees to Participate. The construction of an audit is discussed in detail, as well as an explanation of the audit cycle. The construction of the strategy document that follows the crime audit is explored and a section on the construction of targets using the SMART process is included. Evaluation and monitoring methods are also considered in this chapter, along with the development of performance indicators. This chapter also includes a specific glossary of terminology to assist the student.

Chapter 9 considers the important points of information collection and consultation in light of the need for the production of a crime and disorder reduction audit and strategy. It examines the impact of sections 17 and 115 of the Crime and Disorder Act 1998 and how these sections influence the important issues of information exchange between partnerships. The chapter then examines the different types of information available to partnerships through primary and secondary data sources. The issue of consultation is also considered, in particular the reasons why consultation is so important, along with attempting to define 'hard-to-reach' groups and minority ethnic communities. This section includes a discussion of different methods of consultation, including public meetings, focus groups, and panels. Finally the chapter introduces methods of design of questionnaires, particularly as used by many partnerships when conducting crime and disorder audits, concluding with a discussion about appropriate sampling methods.

The final chapter, Chapter 10, brings together the primary legislation that historically has been used to underpin the process of crime and disorder reduction. It contains a brief contextual discussion regarding Acts of Parliament such as the Environmental Protection Act 1990 (Home Office 1990b), the Housing Act 1996 (Home Office 1996b), and the Protection from Harassment Act 1997 (Home Office 1997c), through to more recent statutes such as the Police Reform Act 2002 (Home Office 2002a) and the Anti-Social Behaviour Act 2003 (Home Office 2003a). Many of the quality-of-life issues that are fairly common in the drive for crime and disorder reduction are also covered here, such as domestic violence and disputes, harassment, truancy, public nuisances, and offences contrary to the Fireworks Act 2003 (Home Office 2003c). In addition, several major and far-reaching recent Acts such as the Police Reform and Social Responsibility Act (2010) are discussed.

1.10 **Summing Up**

1.10.1 **The term 'community safety'**

The term 'crime prevention' is often narrowly interpreted, and this reinforces the view that it is solely the responsibility of the police. On the other hand, the term 'community safety' is open to wider interpretation and encourages greater participation from all sections of the community.

1.10.2 **The Morgan Report**

Otherwise known as Home Office Circular 8/84: *Crime Prevention* (Home Office 1984b). This may be seen as a watershed in crime prevention policy. Its emphasis lay in the principle that crime prevention must be accepted as a significant and integral goal of public policy, both centrally and locally. In this circular, particular stress was placed on the need for a coordinated approach and joint strategies involving partnerships against crime. Although more often rhetoric than reality, around the country the idea of multi-agency 'partnerships' in crime prevention had clearly arrived in Britain.

1.10.3 **Police as agenda-setters**

The police are often enthusiastic proponents of the multi-agency approach, but they tend to prefer to set the agenda and dominate forum meetings, and there have been some allegations that they then tend to ignore the multi-agency framework when it suits their own purposes.

1.10.4 **The Big Society**

In essence, the 'big society' refers to a tripartite partnership between the citizen, community and local government (Eaton 2010). This vision requires families, networks and neighbourhoods in a post modern society to formalize a working partnership that is effective and sustainable in its approach to solving problems, building social cohesion and setting priorities for Britain.

1.10.5 **Local application**

Visit your local crime and disorder reduction partnership and carry out research into its formation. Find out the following information:

(1) When was it formed?
(2) What are the views of the partnership approach from members of the partnership apart from the police?

(3) Have the members of staff heard of the Morgan Report?

(4) What are their views on the Big Society?

(5) What evidence can you find of community involvement within your local crime and disorder reduction partnership?

1.10.6 Useful websites

http://www.thebigsociety.co.uk/

http://www.homeoffice.gov.uk/police/

http://www.homeoffice.gov.uk/police/pol-and-partners-comms/

http://www.homeoffice.gov.uk/crime/partnerships/

The Politics and Management of Community Safety Partnerships

2.1 **Introduction**

Being a leader, supervisor, or manager within the police organization is no longer a task that can be approached as if it were to be carried out in a mechanical fashion. It is not enough these days generally to carry out orders from a senior officer with no thought about the consequences. Officers and other police staff are expected to think, to question, and to add their views and contribute to the overall scheme of events. Nowhere should this approach be more effectively demonstrated than in the field of community safety partnerships. This is not a rank-oriented approach, as every constable and now community support officer, is expected to be a leader in his/her everyday life as a police officer. Indeed, many problem-oriented partnership approaches have been introduced as a result of input from officers and others who regularly work 'on the front line'. They are often the individuals in touch with community feelings and values.

2.1.1 **A basic understanding**

However, for the practitioner to engage fully in crime and disorder reduction and to participate in its management, there are several areas of which they need to have a basic understanding and also an appreciation of their impact. These include the rise of partnerships as a viable alternative to traditional methods of dealing with crime and disorder, some of the intricacies of management within the police organization, the structure of partnerships, change in organizations, information sharing, organizational culture, and funding considerations to name but a few. Further, there must be an understanding of the political nature of this type of approach to policing.

This chapter seeks to introduce police practitioners to these concepts and to help raise awareness and understanding, to a certain extent, of the political nature and management of community safety partnerships.

2.2 **The Political Rise of Partnerships**

The development of the partnership approach is intrinsically bound up with the growth of crime prevention. In the past two decades, agency working has become an important and growing part of the map of British government generally, and the criminal justice arena in particular. Central government initiatives, including the Urban Programme, City Challenge, and the Single Regeneration Budget, have all acted as stimuli to a 'partnership' approach across areas of social policy and urban regeneration. Consequently, there has been a proliferation of structures designed to bring together representatives of relevant statutory bodies, private corporations, and voluntary organizations, and sometimes representatives of the community. The expansion of partnerships may be seen to constitute a quiet revolution in the nature and shape of the administration of British government and has been given a new impetus by the present government's commitment to the 'big society'. However, the partnership approach and its variants are to be found not only in Britain but also across Europe and North America (Crawford 1999). It has even acquired an international status with the recognition of the resolution of the United Nations Congress on the Prevention of Crime and the Treatment of Offenders, in August 1990. This resolution reiterates the fact that crime prevention is not simply a matter for the police but must:

> bring together those with responsibility for planning and development, for family, health, employment and training, housing and social services, leisure activities, schools, the police and the justice system in order to deal with the conditions that generate crime. (United Nations 1991:14)

2.2.1 Social control and partnerships

In Britain there was a growing body of opinion that there was a greater need for multi-agency cooperation at a local level, as providing the most effective means of policy formation and service delivery. It was also argued that the need for multi-agency partnerships lay in the realities of crime and social control. Social control in modern industrial societies, it was argued, was by its nature multi-agency, with different agencies having different perspectives on a given crime problem due to their particular expertise. Different agencies interact in divergent ways in relation to specific crime problems. Criminal justice agencies therefore are both interconnected and mutually dependent. It is in the area of lack of coordination that failings can be identified in the criminal justice system.

2.2.2 Political views on partnerships

For some years, the Labour Party's official policy was to make all of us partners against crime (Labour Party 1994, 1997). Politicians were under immense pressure to be seen to be 'tackling crime', and consequently crime prevention has often been presented as the new panacea within criminal justice.

However, it was not just in the field of crime prevention that partnerships have been promoted. Lord Justice Woolf's report into the prison disturbances at Strangeways and elsewhere in the country in 1990 recommended closer cooperation between different parts of the criminal justice system (Woolf and Tumim 1991). Similarly the probation service was also encouraged to become more integrative with other agencies, as this was seen as a key means of providing that service. In other diverse fields of criminal justice, including those dealing with racial harassment and domestic violence, the importance of multi-agency work has been stressed repeatedly.

The recent growth and extensive reception of the partnership approach across policy fields in general, and in crime prevention areas more specifically, in such

25

short a period of time is quite exceptional, and in terms of crime and disorder reduction is now encapsulated in the Crime and Disorder Act 1998 (Home Office 1999a) and subsequent Acts of Parliament.

2.3 **Demands on the Police**

Historically, the police in England and Wales have been subject to much examination in terms of management accountability and this process has helped shape the police as the organization we know today. Therefore to understand the police today and the way they interact with their partners, a brief overview of the major historical performance procedures is necessary.

2.3.1 **Managerialism**

Managerialism is the implementation of a variety of techniques generally copied from the private sector within a culture of cost-efficiency service effectiveness. This idea has been a point of reference for the police service for a number of years and manifests itself within the current climate of objectives, best value, and performance indicators. Consequently there are now several major bodies involved in examining the performance of the police service and the practitioner should have at least a basic understanding of what they try to achieve. Some of these are illustrated below.

2.3.2 **How the police service was examined**

- The Home Secretary introduced targets and ministerial priorities for the police service in England and Wales. These objectives are now encapsulated within the *National Policing Plan 2005–2008* (Home Office 2004b) and are summarized below.

KEY POINT—FIVE KEY PRIORITIES FOR POLICE

The *National Policing Plan 2005–2008* lists the five key priorities for the police service. These are as follows:

(1) To reduce overall crime, including violent and drug-related crime.

(2) To provide a citizen-focused police service which responds to the needs of the communities and the individuals inside those communities, especially witnesses and victims.

(3) To take action with partners to increase detection rates, and target prolific and other priority offenders.

(4) To reduce people's concerns about crime, and anti-social behaviour and disorder.

(5) To combat serious and organized crime, within and across force boundaries.

- Local targets and objectives are set for the force through the local policing plan published every year, the performance of which must be reported and published annually.
- Her Majesty's Inspectorate of Constabulary (HMIC) and the Audit Commission also monitor, report, and publish figures on relative performance in dealing with specific matters as well as force inspections.
- The Association of Chief Police Officers (ACPO) also reports on public satisfaction under a variety of headings.
- There is a responsibility to report with the Crown Prosecution Service on Joint Performance Management, including the submission of files of evidence.

2.3.3 **The Best Value initiative**

The Local Government Act 1999 (Home Office 1999c) introduced the Best Value initiative, which attempts to ensure the provision of better quality services and value for money. This initiative applies to community safety partnerships, and is achieved by reviews of the provision of services by local authorities (including police authorities) who are instructed to: 'Make arrangements to secure continuous improvements in the way in which they exercise their functions, having regard to a combination of economy, efficiency and effectiveness.'

Local authorities and the police are accountable to local people and are required to set standards for all services for which they are responsible. They are also required to undertake performance reviews of all their services over a five-year period to demonstrate that continuous improvements are being made.

The government expects local authorities and the police to use these reviews to:

- *Challenge* why, how, and by whom a service is being provided.
- *Compare* their performance with that of others.
- *Consult* local taxpayers, service users, etc. in the setting of new performance targets.
- *Compete*, wherever practicable, as a means of securing efficient and effective services.

Consequently there is a constant review of work being carried out in order to improve performance in line with the four *C*s outlined above.

2.3.4 **National and local priorities**

National priorities alone cannot drive local partnerships—local priorities are a key concept. Local political priorities are often determined by an area's problems. For example, partnerships that cover areas of high unemployment, poverty, social deprivation, or crime may need to focus on tackling crime hot-spots, providing support to vulnerable people, or drawing in investment to regenerate run-down areas. Alternatively, in a rural district where crime is low but concern is disproportionately high, managing communications to dispel concern may be a high priority.

Irrespective of local circumstances, all partnerships need to engage and consult their local communities, gathering and sharing information that helps to determine that partnership's priorities.

2.4 Organizational Culture

Perhaps the biggest barrier to delivering better community safety is not national government or local politicians, the law, or local people; it is the difficulty of changing organizational values and the culture in local authorities, the police, and other local partnership agencies. However, this barrier is not insurmountable where there is ownership of the issue and a clear willingness to change, as exemplified by some small district councils and new unitary authorities.

The extent to which councils, the police, and other partners own the responsibility to deliver community safety is fundamental to improvement, as is the behaviour of councillors, police authority members, and senior council and police personnel.

2.4.1 A fruitful partnership

The Audit Commission's report *A Fruitful Partnership* (Audit Commission 1998) highlighted the importance of leaders' roles in partnerships, and noted that:

- leadership style should strike a balance between developing partnership working and focusing on hard-edged objectives; and
- building trust between partners is the most important ingredient of success.

Inspection and fieldwork show the critical role that effective leadership plays in achieving community safety success. Weak leadership among senior personnel is a problem identified by auditors and inspectors in a number of councils and police services, and it can be a barrier to improvement. However, overbearing leadership can also hamper performance, as it can strain relationships between local agencies. Partnership agencies need to take account of cultural differences in leadership styles when working together.

2.4.2 An improving situation in partnerships

The situation is improving, with greater trust and cooperation between partner agencies. Some local authorities and police services now actively work very well alongside each other to deliver crime and disorder reduction, building on the confidence arising from successful activity. However, in many cases senior council and police personnel need to work hard on the trust element of successful partnerships. Once these key personnel set the direction and demonstrate their commitment, partnerships can move crime and disorder reduction to the heart of basic service delivery. And by demonstrating strong ownership and a willingness to change organizational behaviour, councils and police services are more likely to gain support and commitment from other local agencies.

2.4.3 Police culture

The police force is an organization in which the lower ranks receive only limited supervision of their actions, and it would appear that on occasions this system of supervision involves turning a blind eye to their activities. This has been supported by several writers on the police, including Holdaway (1984). Holdaway was a police sergeant who engaged in an observational study of the police in action and suggested that change was needed. This study was conducted over twenty years ago, and there is evidence that a change for the better has now taken place. However, for the police practitioner involved in the management and delivery of policing initiatives the information about working practices and culture can be vital. The reason for this is quite simple: the practice of policing is considerably shaped by the lower ranks' occupational culture, and goals are developed in this setting which, even today, reflect commonly found male peer group norms. These norms are characterized by macho attitudes of glorying in violence and acting 'hard', and sexually oriented banter involving the degradation of women. Sometimes this includes derogatory attitudes towards homosexual behaviour and blacks and other ethnic groups. These attitudes are fostered by the fact that the lower ranks comprise close-knit and relatively isolated social groups who work together and socialize together. This type of attitude is also often found within groups who work in occupations where there is a shared sense of 'danger' or threat, such as the armed forces. Very often much value is placed upon the ability to control situations, to maintain order, and to engender respect rather than to lose face.

2.4.4 Evidence of change

However, there is some evidence that this type of culture has receded somewhat over the years. Practitioners serving in the police have now been assessed on their knowledge of the Race Equality scheme and their effective contribution, both as individuals and as an organization, towards the elimination of unlawful discrimination, the promotion of equality of opportunity, and the promotion of good relations between people of different racial groups. (It is worth pointing out that whilst the police are obliged to carry this out, partner agencies may not have this same obligation, and this could lead to conflict in certain areas of work.)

By involving police forces in community safety partnerships, and therefore exposing police officers to other agencies and work ethics, it is believed that this strong occupational culture will change considerably. However, there has been resistance to this approach to change within the police organization as comfort zones have had to be reconsidered. New initiatives involving partnership approaches may on occasions be undermined by a strong resistance through the practices of individuals within the police.

2.5 **The Problems of Change**

Change is necessary and inevitable in organizations. Without it no organization can hope to maintain efficiency and effectiveness, and the police service is no exception. Our society is changing all the time and the police organization must change with it. The police organization is an open system, accountable to the public and dependent upon its environment, and it needs to be aware of the changes taking place. The police service must accommodate this change which will satisfy the new environmental demand. New technology, population and economic changes, and rising public expectations are all new demands that can impact upon the delivery of police services. Another major new environmental demand for the police is working with other agencies in community safety partnerships.

The extent to which local partnership agencies work together is the critical success factor, as shown by recently published research into the effectiveness of collaboration and coordination in area-based initiatives. Working together is complex, and success is dependent both on the history, geography, and identity of the area and on the vision, skills, and behaviour of key individuals. It is through collaborative working and shared experience that partners learn to work together.

KEY POINT—AREAS OF CHANGE THAT AFFECT POLICING

(1) New technology such as the introduction of mobile phones, airwaves radio system, vehicles, equipment, etc.

(2) Population and economic changes such as immigration, job losses, relocation and change of industries, industrial relations, etc.

(3) Rising public expectations; the public, expecting more from the police than ever before, are encouraged to challenge authority and understand their rights more.

(4) New legislation which impacts upon the way the police operate such as the Crime and Disorder Act 1998, the Police Reform Act 2002, and the recent Anti-Terrorism Acts.

(5) Service restructuring which includes force amalgamations, the introduction of basic command units, flattening of management structures, greater use of unsworn officers, neighbourhood policing teams, and part-time working.

2.5.1 **Change and individuals**

Change affects not only the organization but also individuals. There must also be an understanding that not everyone welcomes change. The police service has in general tended to be a stand-alone organization for the delivery of policing services since its inception. There was a political consensus for many years that the police were the policing experts and were to be left alone to get on with it. However, now that the delivery of policing services is dependent on the multi-agency or partnership approach, certain organizational changes have to be made.

2.5.2 **Why is change resisted?**

The unknown causes fear and induces resistance. Restructuring within an organization can leave people uncertain about their future prospects, and even about their current job. People want to feel secure and have some control over the changes that are taking place. Further, not knowing the reasons for change also causes resistance. It is very often unclear to those involved why change is taking place or necessary at all. For police staff engaging in the partnership approach to crime and disorder reduction, involving other agencies may be seen as a loss of power and status.

Figure 2.1 illustrates the different forces that drive change and some of those that fuel resistance to the change. The diagram clearly shows some of the major influences that compete when change is taking place. On the right of the diagram we see some of the driving forces that may institute change in the police organization, such as the introduction of new key objectives, policing plans, etc. On the left are some of the forces that can cause resistance to changes such as fear of losing a job or status, or just a general lack of knowledge through poor communication and consultation.

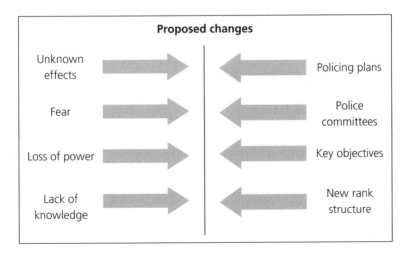

Figure 2.1 Diagram illustrating driving and resisting forces for change

2.5.3 **Overcoming resistance to change**

Having identified the fact that change is inevitable and discussed some of the reasons why change is resisted, there are strategies that the police supervisor and managers can use to assist in implementing change. People need to feel they have a degree of participation in what is taking place. The more participation, the more comfortable people feel. Change also induces anxiety and stress in people, and there needs to be a programme of support and communication if this is to be reduced. By doing so, opposition to the changes proposed will be reduced, and this makes the move forward that much easier.

KEY POINT—STRATEGIES TO ASSIST IN OVERCOMING RESISTANCE TO CHANGE

Participation—People feel valued and involved when asked to participate in the process of change.

Support—People may be anxious and stressed in times of change. Support will help reduce this.

Communication—Fear of the unknown produces resistance to change. Where there is a good communications strategy, knowledge of events will reduce wild speculation and increase understanding.

People feel comfortable with the situation they know and are unhappy about the unknown and the effect it may have on them personally—the so-called 'comfort zone'. Cultural resistance to change is based upon a system of beliefs and values that have been established over a number of years, and to change these needs an explicit communications strategy aimed at establishing new patterns of belief and values. It may involve the unlearning of the old techniques and values and the adoption of a new comfort zone which embraces the reality of the new changes to the individual's responsibility and role.

2.6 **Managing Partnerships**

2.6.1 **Managing expectations**

Community safety partnerships stimulate a variety of expectations within the community regarding the quality and quantity of policing, as well as the anticipated impact on crime, disorder, and the quality of life in the community. Some of these expectations are unrealistic and extend beyond the specific aims and objectives of the partnership. Expectations can also be raised by a lack of clarity over how the partnership resources are to be used, and this can lead to a number of misunderstandings about the partnership which only serve to undermine perceptions of success. Those in charge of managing and implementing tasks designed to carry out the partnership aims and objectives must seek to manage the community's expectations effectively. If this is not achieved then the crime and disorder reduction partnership will struggle to win over public support. Whenever this important task is left to the discretion of front-line officers, there is always the danger that personal traits and characteristics may influence the nature of delivery, which may also affect expectations.

2.6.2 Staff turnover

A separate yet important area in partnerships is the problem of staff turnover. Within a rank-oriented organization such as the police, there is a regular and constant movement of staff within and between posts and ranks. Officers may be promoted or transferred from one department to another as their career progresses and they gain experience of the police service as a large organization. This may be inevitable, but it does result in a lack of consistency on occasions, which can influence relationships between partners. Informal methods of negotiation very often achieve the desired result more efficiently than formal requests to and from bureaucratic organizations, and this level of relationship is built up over time during which members of the different agencies get to know and trust each other. However, if staff are subject to frequent turnover this can have a negative effect on the efficiency of the partnership. Of course this may also apply to local authority staff and other partnership members.

2.6.3 The role of councillors

Local councillors: Background

Local councillors must be over 21 years of age. They also need to be on the electoral register for the council area for which they wish to stand, or have worked in the area for the preceding twelve months. Individuals cannot stand for election if they are bankrupt or have a criminal record. They are also ineligible if they work for the council they want to represent.

There are around 500 principal local authorities in the UK. Each council is responsible for providing its own local services. These range from education, transport, and street cleaning to social services and housing, as well as involvement in crime and disorder reduction. To do this, they employ more than two million people and are directed by 22,000 councillors. Councillors are elected to represent an individual geographical unit on the council, known as a ward or division. They are elected by the public every four years. Some councils elect all councillors in one go, others choose to elect one-third at a time. This is because most wards have three councillors.

Councillors' duties

In general, councillors have three main components to their work. These briefly are:

(1) Decision-making. The local council has a duty to make sure that certain services are provided. Councillors make the decisions which are carried out by paid council officers.
(2) Monitoring. Councillors make sure that their decisions lead to efficient and effective services by keeping an eye on how well things are working.
(3) Getting involved locally. As local representatives, councillors have responsibilities towards their constituents and local organizations. Much of a councillor's work is done in formal council meetings, but councillors also tend to take on other duties. These often depend on what the councillor wants to achieve and how much time is available. These duties may include:
  • going to meetings of local organizations such as tenants' associations
  • going to meetings of bodies affecting the wider community such as police liaison committees
  • taking up issues on behalf of members of the public and then visiting, ringing up, or writing to council officials (the local equivalent of civil servants, i.e., permanent employees of the council)
  • running a regular surgery for residents to bring up issues
  • meeting with individual residents in their own homes.

Councillors may feel disengaged from crime and disorder reduction, despite activity to reduce crime and anti-social behaviour occurring in the wards that they are elected to represent. However, councillors see community safety partnerships as a key cabinet role under the new democratic arrangements currently being implemented. A recent Local Government Association survey of councils showed that over one-half now manage community safety in this way. County and district councils were the least likely to do so, with London and metropolitan councils most likely. Fieldwork identified the delivery of crime and disorder reduction as a key electoral commitment among mayoral candidates.

2.6.4 The role of senior council and police personnel

Commitment from, and action by, senior council and police personnel is key to delivering community safety. In particular, they are responsible for bringing leadership, coordination, and commitment to the partnerships, as well as for supporting councillors and police authority members. However, it must also be remembered that the demands of community safety partnerships for many senior council personnel, like the police, have to compete with other demands placed upon local authorities. It must also be remembered that chief executives in local authorities do not have anything like the same executive authority as chief constables. Whilst it is common practice in the police service for senior officers to delegate, the lack of power impedes this process within local authorities. This is becoming more prevalent as more and more resources are being devolved to commanders of Basic Command Units (BCUs).

This means that the police in general can act as soon as a decision is made. However, in local authorities there is a very different set of working practices. For example, if resources are required, very often local authority staff will have to take a recommendation for action back to their locally elected representatives so that the issue can be debated and a decision reached. Consequently, a decision that can be made by the police within days can often take months because of the decision-making process of partners.

2.6.5 The role of community safety officers

Crime and disorder reduction officers or coordinators are usually employed by local authorities and play a significant role in the activities of partnerships, assisted by the police local authority liaison officers when these are in post. Police and local authorities often delegate the management of the audit, consultation, and strategy formulation process to community safety officers. These individuals ideally require organizational skills, a knowledge of policies and procedures of different agencies, and political knowledge. Criticisms of this role indicate that there are gaps in the knowledge and training of some community safety officers. In some local authorities, indeed community safety officers have no specific qualifications in this area and no training, which can lead to a problem over credibility and lack of influence. Consequently, in these circumstances the community safety officer can actually impede the progress of the community safety partnerships.

2.6.6 The role of other local agencies

Delivering community safety partnerships is seen as an additional responsibility by many local agencies. This means that many local authorities and police have committed scarce resources to the process of applying for additional government grants to cover the perceived extra costs. Strong perceptions of tradition have allowed many councils and police to avoid changing their organizational culture and avoid reshaping existing spending to reflect a community safety perspective.

A few partnerships involve only the local authority and police at a strategic level. Auditors have judged these to be at risk of becoming too inwardly focused. At the other end of the spectrum, some partnerships have over twenty representatives from business, voluntary organizations, and universities. However, partnerships of this size risk confusing roles and responsibilities and being difficult to manage. Partnerships must fit local needs, and so there needs to be a balance between keeping the partnership to a manageable size and having sufficient partners to be outward looking. Coordinating and directing action between everyone involved is complex, but it is essential. The delivery of crime and disorder reduction cannot be achieved by any one local agency in isolation.

Working together requires all local agencies to share information and to collaborate in planning basic service delivery in the interests of the community. It does not require local agencies to be 'in a partnership' in a quasi-legal sense, although coordination and collaboration are essential. Many partnerships have small executive groups, and these could usefully focus on maximizing coordination and monitoring partners' performance.

Given the wide range of agencies that could be involved in any partnership, each agency's role needs to be defined clearly. For example, health services, social services, probation, and education services deliver significant benefits when fully involved in local partnerships, yet they are often not full participants.

Fire services have become increasingly involved following a slow start. Arson is a growing problem and it adds to concerns about crime. The social cost of arson is estimated by the government to have reached over £1.3 billion a year and, in an average week, 3500 fires are deliberately started, resulting in fifty injuries and two deaths.

Victim support representation on partnerships is rightly quite high. However, criminal justice system representation by local courts is perhaps not as high as it should be, neither is representation from the Crown Prosecution Service. It has been suggested that in one partnership the local criminal justice agencies excluded themselves from the partnership at its first meeting due to concerns about a conflict of interest! The exclusion of the group unhelpfully separated the two key components of the local criminal justice system and aggravated weaknesses in performance. To avoid conflicting objectives and targets, and to maximize emphasis on the needs of victims, witnesses, and offenders, it is essential that the two groups work together closely.

Representation of vulnerable groups on community safety partnerships is increasing, including representation from black and minority ethnic communities, older people, women's and domestic violence groups, and anti-homophobia groups. However, youth offending team and drug action team involvement seems to be patchy, particularly in district council areas. Involvement of these teams in specific, localized projects has been generally good. By contrast, district councils need the tactical support of county councils (which organize the teams in non-unitary areas) to ensure these teams' involvement. This is particularly important in light of the proposed merger of drug action teams with community safety partnerships.

The engagement of health services is also improving. Chief executives of primary care trusts are joining partnerships, especially where boundaries coincide.

The range of local agencies needed to implement community safety partnerships locally makes organizing delivery a complex issue. The mix of assessment agencies further aggravates the situation. By acting as community advocates under the Local Government Act 2000 (Home Office 2000c), local authorities are well placed to lead and coordinate delivery. Effective delivery of crime and disorder reduction depends upon how well local authorities and the police ensure that relevant local agencies are engaged, share a responsibility to deliver, and work together with a high degree of coordination.

2.6.7 General comments regarding police management

Strategic planning

In any organization management skills can reflect the culture of that organization. The police service appears to be no exception to this idea. When crisis occurs, police officers are very good at managing and controlling situations, quickly restoring order and displaying a large range of skills such as decision-making, communication, motivation, and short-term planning. They are 'can doers' in the absolute sense of the phrase when faced with this type of problem.

However, at the strategic level there are sometimes opportunities for improvement. Strategic planning at the tactical level seems to be fairly well organized. This is probably because at a tactical level, the majority of officers can relate to that degree of operational contact with the public. It is at the strategic planning level, the ability to see what is needed in the medium to long term, and to make the necessary provision in terms of budgets, personnel, and skills, where police officers sometimes appear to have difficulty. This is more apparent lower down the ranks. Whilst acknowledging that there are competing demands upon the time of these important officers, the inability to plan other than on a day-to-day basis, or at best a week-to-week basis, can cause problems for community safety partnerships. By failing to plan over the longer term, police managers are continually struggling with having to deal with shortages in resources.

Problem-solving

Perhaps the cornerstone of the work carried out by community safety partnerships is that of problem solving. Nowhere is this more visible than in the Annual Tilley Award for Problem Oriented Partnerships. The Tilley Award was set up by the Home Office Policing and Reducing Crime Unit (now the Crime and Policing Group) in 1999 to encourage and recognize good practice in implementing problem-oriented policing (POP). The award, funded by the Home Office, pays for winners to attend the Annual International Problem-Oriented Policing Conference in the USA. This usually provides the opportunity for winners to present their project at the conference. Although originally open only to the police, eligibility has recently been extended to include entries from any community safety partnerships.

KEY POINT—TILLEY AWARD WINNER 2010: OPERATION UNCANNY

Operation Uncanny, a project that utilized partnership working, dramatically reducing prostitution in the Spring Boroughs and Semilong residential areas of Northampton, was announced as the overall winner of the 2010 Tilley awards.

The area was identified as eligible for funding as a CASPAR project. The county and borough council members, senior officers from the statutory agencies, police authority and local Housing Association and representatives from Spring Boroughs residents association and Semilong community forum were all involved.

The Sex workers around Northampton (SWAN) partnership provided advice and support on health, housing, drug addiction and education to help the women leave prostitution. Through numerous surveillance operations, an intelligence profile was established linking pimps and drug dealers to the sex trade. This enabled partners to proactively target those providing protection and drugs to women.

In 2002, over 200 prostitutes were known to work in the area 24 hours a day. With all partners actively working together, this has been reduced to nil. There has been no evidence of displacement. Twenty-five premises that were used for prostitution and as crack houses were also shut down.

O'Byrne (2001) points out some of the problems managers and supervisors have when attempting to engage in problem-solving. Reflection upon 'what works' and 'what doesn't work' is a necessary component of this type of approach by managers. Officers who are constantly busy find it difficult to give up time to learn new skills such as statistical analysis or reflection upon performance, even if these skills are essential to being more effective in handling workloads. A separate and yet important point to acknowledge is that new skills and abilities take time to learn, implement, and apply successfully. In an organization such as the police, where the organizational culture is one of immediate action, this delay is frequently considered unacceptable. Yet staff need time to learn new skills if the police organization is to be effective in the arena of community safety partnerships.

2.7 Structure of Partnerships

The Crime and Disorder Act 1998 (Home Office 1999a) and subsequent legislation has resulted in the establishment, currently, of 310 community safety partnerships in England and 22 in Wales. In many cases, the legislation essentially formalized existing multi-agency groups, whereas in other areas the Act necessitated significant institutional change. However, even those areas which had well-established multi-agency structures needed to adapt significantly to comply with the new provisions. The review of the Crime and Disorder Act of 2006 established working protocols for partnership working in two-tier local authority areas which did not formally assist in the delivery of partnership working.

2.7.1 Model structure

Because of the significant variations in the make-up of partnership bodies throughout the country, it is difficult to promote a best-practice model of partnership structure. However, it is clear that there needs to be good links between strategic bodies such as the police, local authorities, the probation service, community safety officers, legal services, etc. A theoretical model of a crime and disorder reduction partnership structure is illustrated in Figure 2.2.

The figure clearly illustrates the strategic level of the crime and disorder approach in the responsible authorities group. This may contain the chief officer of police, the chief executive of the local authority, and other high-ranking officials from other agencies. This group also interacts with other major partners, in this case the local Youth Offending Strategy Group and the local drugs and alcohol partnership, to ensure continuity of objectives.

At a more operational level, the crime and disorder reduction partnership tasking group oversees the implementation of the strategic vision, making the

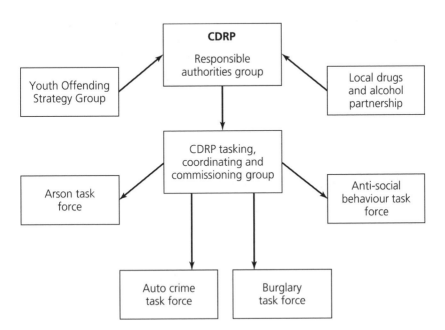

Figure 2.2 Hypothetical model of a structure of a crime and disorder reduction partnership (CDRP)

aims and objectives a reality by liaising with the different task groups to ensure that the partnership's targets are attained.

2.7.2 Two-tier authorities

In England there still exist some two-tier local authorities. These structures present particular problems for community safety partnerships. These include political antagonisms and perceptions that county councils are often far removed from local issues, and that central funds are not as available as they should be. However, the review of the provisions of the Crime and Disorder Act 1998 (2006) identified some of these problems and has put in place a revised structure splitting the strategic and operational decision-making responsibilities with the former sitting at the county level.

2.8 Control and Accountability

Accountability of the decision-making process and the delivery of services by both police and partners is paramount. Transparency and a willingness to be open, coupled with good consultation methods are important if partnership work is to be supported fully by the communities they serve.

One of the major changes invoked by the review of the Crime and Disorder Act 1998 revolved around the governance and accountability of partnerships. Partnerships are expected now to be more visible to the communities they serve and more accountable to them than hitherto. The requirement of partnerships to consult with a range of local agencies and people on the findings of their three-year audits continues. However, it is no longer a requirement for partnerships to provide the Home Secretary with annual reports on the implementation of their three-year strategies, but instead to produce regular reports to their communities.

2.9 Funding Considerations

Many reduction initiatives or projects are funded by external sources of revenue. Community safety partnerships will not be successful in obtaining external funding without effective leadership from an agency that will coordinate a bid for funding (see Figure 2.3). This is sometimes the local authority or the police. Grant funding is one of the main sources of funding for partnerships engaging on projects, and is usually provided as money for capital and/or revenue items.

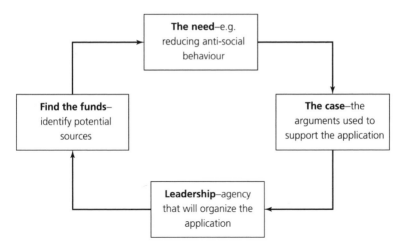

Figure 2.3 The funding cycle

KEY POINT—GRANT FUNDING

This is a reserve of money set aside for a specific purpose, usually to deliver funders' objectives, and does not have to be repaid. It usually involves an agency assessing the proposal to carry out a programme of work against a set of criteria they have created. Bids that do not meet the criteria are normally rejected.

KEY POINT—CAPITAL AND REVENUE FUNDING

Capital—Cost of physical items, e.g., buildings, furniture, equipment, etc.
Revenue—Running costs, e.g., salaries, rent, rates, telephones, etc.

Whilst there are a number of functions a police force must carry out, these are in the main funded from central government. In addition, especially when it comes to crime and disorder reduction, there are many other activities or projects that would enhance the quality of life for communities but cannot be achieved due to restrictions on the budget.

2.10 **Inter-Agency Information Sharing and Bichard**

Most community safety partnerships suggest the police to be the least problematic information source. It is encouraging that the police are able to provide this information, but at the same time it is worrying that partnerships' action may be being driven by information from just one source. There is a statutory obligation on the police to share information with bodies other than police forces in England and Wales, and the management of this information is vital if partnerships are to be effective. Equally, there is an obligation upon those agencies in receipt of this information to ensure that it is used only for the purpose for which the request was made, or, if the information they receive is incomplete or inaccurate, to inform the police at the earliest possible moment.

However, the idea of information exchange may be best seen in the theory rather than in the application. The Bichard Inquiry (HMSO 2004) into child protection procedures in Humberside and Cambridgeshire police forces examined the effectiveness of intelligence-based record-keeping and information-sharing between other agencies. This report had far-reaching effects on record-keeping and the sharing of information between agencies throughout the country.

2.10.1 Background to the Bichard Inquiry

The Bichard Inquiry was commissioned as a result of the murder of two ten-year-old girls, Jessica Chapman and Holly Wells, who went missing in the town of Soham, Cambridgeshire. On Saturday 17 August 2002, the girls' bodies were found in Suffolk. That same day, Ian Huntley and Maxine Carr were arrested in connection with their murder.

Following Huntley's conviction there was widespread public disquiet when it emerged that Huntley had been known to the authorities over a period of years. He had come to the attention of the police in relation to allegations of eight separate sexual offences from 1995 to 1999. This information had not emerged during the vetting check carried out by the Cambridgeshire Constabulary at the time of his appointment as caretaker to Soham Village College late in 2001. Consequently, an inquiry was set up by the Home Secretary to assess the effectiveness of relevant intelligence-based record-keeping, vetting practices in forces, and information sharing with other agencies. The inquiry was led by Sir Michael Bichard, hence the name of the report.

The Bichard Inquiry Report and its recommendations were published on 22 June 2004. The then Home Secretary, David Blunkett, welcomed the Report and accepted all of Sir Michael's thirty-one recommendations, on behalf of the government, in his oral statement to Parliament made on 22 June 2004. A comprehensive implementation programme has since been put in place, which is wide-ranging across the public services and involves a number of government departments and many other bodies.

KEY POINT—TERMS OF REFERENCE FOR BICHARD INQUIRY

Urgently to enquire into child protection procedures in Humberside Police and Cambridgeshire Constabulary in the light of the recent trial and conviction of Ian Huntley for the murder of Jessica Chapman and Holly Wells. In particular to assess the effectiveness of the relevant intelligence-based record-keeping, the vetting practices in those forces since 1995 and information sharing with other agencies, and to report to the Home Secretary on matters of local and national relevance and make recommendations as appropriate.

2.10.2 Recommendations

The Bichard Inquiry Report contained many important recommendations for the police service and other agencies. These were mandatory for the police service but advisory for others. However, for the purposes of this work, one of the most important recommendations lay in the area of information exchange. Bichard pointed to the fact that in terms of information exchange guidance was unclear, particularly about the retention of information and intelligence, which led to inconsistent decisions about the retention of criminal intelligence. Consequently, the possibility of information and intelligence being lost was significant. The need for a new code of practice to be introduced was made clear, with a further recommendation that it be applied under the auspices of the Police Reform Act 2002 (Home Office 2002a) to ensure application across the country. This code also covers the sharing of information by the police with partner agencies.

2.10.3 VISOR

As a result of the concerns highlighted by the Bichard Inquiry, the Violent and Sexual Offenders Register (VISOR) was rolled out to all forces during May 2005 This system allows forces to share information (not just convictions) on violent and sexual offenders. However, only officers from public protection units have been given permission to use the detailed database, which also contains information on people who have not been convicted but who are still considered a public danger. VISOR provides an online system that for the first time provides complete and up-to-date information on the country's most dangerous offenders, and will help reduce reoffending, protect the public, and save valuable time. The VISOR website is currently located at <http://www.npia.police.uk/en/10510.htm>.

2.10.4 Protocols

Information-sharing is an essential part of performance management; however, in some community safety partnerships, data gathering and analysis have become an end in themselves, rather than a means to an end. Many partnerships still have to agree an information-sharing protocol.

2.11 **Conclusion**

Crime reduction initiatives are seen as an opportunity for local partnerships to develop innovative approaches, energizing the community and agencies concerned to bring about real change as well as short-term amelioration of crime. This depends largely on the inputs promised by the agencies, coupled with a vigorous media campaign, which should also encourage the community to act to stop crime and disorder.

A lack of understanding of roles and expectations, not only between individual agencies but particularly within the police organization, and unwillingness to accept changing working practices, which are deemed to be a threat to the local police structure, can be obstacles to effective implementation of crime and disorder reduction work.

For crime reduction and multi-agency partnerships the lessons to be learnt include the fact that it is not enough to agree a goal for achievement. Success lies in achieving that goal through true inter-agency work, avoiding petty jealousies and local politics whilst attempting to understand the differing cultures and working practices of partnership members. However, this is not as easy as it seems. Once this is recognized, then perhaps common goals in crime reduction strategies will be realized.

Resource needs will be clearly shaped by a focus on priorities and challenging targets. Where resources are scarce, partnerships need to share resources (funds, staff, information, and experience) to boost delivery of community safety. For local authorities and the police, subject to a duty of best value, the effectiveness of resource management remains a key aspect of audit and inspection.

Appropriately skilled and experienced staff are vital if community safety partnerships are to deliver their objectives. The provision of staff should be on a scale proportionate to local priorities and available capacity. Some community safety partnerships have yet to appoint a crime and disorder reduction coordinator. The tendency is to appoint half-time posts in some local authorities, although some have two staff, one each from the police and the council. It would appear that district councils are the least likely to have dedicated, corporate support teams, whereas London, metropolitan, and county councils are the most likely.

There are a number of key competencies that local partnership agencies need to acquire. Secondment of staff between police, councils, and other local agencies can help to develop these competencies, as can training involving all partnership agencies.

As can been seen, leadership and management, coupled with good organizational understanding and a clear focus, support the effective delivery of crime and disorder reduction. It is further enhanced by avoiding standard, 'one size fits all' approaches to problem-solving. The closer a solution is tailored to fit the problem, the greater the chance of success. Moving towards a tailored solution service means changing the management of basic services—devolving greater freedom to managers, but also setting clear operational frameworks. Unfortunately, at this moment in time examples of good practice tend to be fragmented, as they are not systematically collected and valued by all partnerships.

2.12 Summing Up

2.12.1 The partnership approach

The development of the partnership approach is intrinsically bound up with the growth of crime prevention. Politicians were under immense pressure to be seen to be 'tackling crime' and, consequently, crime prevention has often been presented as the new panacea within criminal justice. The recent growth and extensive reception of the partnership approach across policy fields in general and in crime prevention areas more specifically, in such a short period of time, is quite exceptional and, in terms of crime and disorder reduction, is now encapsulated in the Crime and Disorder Act 1998 (Home Office 1999a).

2.12.2 Managerialism

Managerialism is the implementation of a variety of techniques generally copied from the private sector within a culture of cost-efficient service effectiveness. This idea has been a point of reference for the police service for a number of years and manifests itself within the current climate of objectives, best value, and performance indicators.

2.12.3 Best Value initiative

The Local Government Act 1999 (Home Office 1999c) introduced the Best Value initiative, which attempts to ensure the provision of better quality of services and value for money through regular reviews of services provided to the public.

The government expects these reviews to be used to:

- challenge why, how, and by whom a service is being provided
- secure comparison with the performance of others
- consult local taxpayers, service users, etc. in the setting of new performance targets

45

- ensure fair and open competition, wherever practicable, as a means of securing efficient and effective services.

2.12.4 Change

Change is necessary and inevitable in organizations. Without it, no organization can hope to maintain efficiency and effectiveness, and the police service is no exception. Our society is changing all the time and the police organization must change with it.

2.12.5 Areas of change that affect policing

- New technology such as the introduction of mobile phones, airwaves radio system, vehicles, equipment, etc.
- Population and economic changes such as immigration, job losses, relocation and change of industries, industrial relations, etc.
- Rising expectations: the public, expecting more from the police than ever before, are encouraged to challenge authority and understand their rights more.
- New legislation which impacts upon the way the police operate such as the Crime and Disorder Act 1998, the Police Reform Act 2002, and the recent Terrorism Acts.
- Service restructuring which includes force amalgamations, the introduction of basic commands units, flattening of management structures, greater use of unsworn officers, neighbourhood policing teams, and part-time working.

2.12.6 Overcoming resistance to change

- Participation—people feel valued and involved when asked to participate in the process of change.
- Support—people may be anxious and stressed in times of change; support will help reduce this.
- Communication—fear of the unknown produces resistance to change; where there is a good communications strategy it may reduce wild speculation and increase understanding.

2.12.7 Capital and revenue funding

- Capital—cost of physical items, e.g., buildings, furniture, equipment, etc.
- Revenue—running costs, e.g., salaries, rent, rates, telephones, etc.

2.12.8 **The Bichard Inquiry**

The Bichard Inquiry was commissioned as a result of the murder of two ten-year-old girls, Jessica Chapman and Holly Wells, who went missing in the town of Soham, Cambridgeshire. On Saturday 17 August 2002, the girls' bodies were found in Suffolk. The Bichard Inquiry Report and its recommendations were published on 22 June 2004. The then Home Secretary, David Blunkett, welcomed the publication of Sir Michael's report and accepted all of his 31 recommendations, on behalf of the government, in his oral statement to Parliament made on 22 June 2004.

2.12.9 **Local application**

Visit your local crime and disorder reduction partnership's administration office and obtain a copy of their annual plan. Find out the following information:

(1) What is the structure of the crime and disorder reduction partnership strategic team?
(2) Who are the members of the strategic board and the tasking group?
(3) Where does the funding come from to sustain the partnership?
(4) What local agencies are part of the partnership management?
(5) What reviews have been carried out under the Best Value initiative?
(6) By talking to members of the partnership, establish what kind of relationship they have.
(7) Speak to your work colleagues and find out what they think of the partnership approach to crime and disorder reduction. Can you establish any cultural resistance to this change in policing?
(8) What protocols exist for the exchange of information between the police and other partnership members?

2.12.10 **Useful websites**

http://www.acpo.police.uk/
http://www.homeoffice.gov.uk/hmic/hmic.htm
http://www.audit-commission.gov.uk/
http://www.apa.police.uk/apa
http://www.lga.gov.uk/
http://www.bichardinquiry.org.uk/
http://www.homeoffice.gov.uk/
http://www.cfoa.org.uk/cfoa_public/
http://www.dh.gov.uk/Home/fs/en

3

Anti-Social Behaviour

3.1 **Introduction**

The legislation regarding anti-social behaviour is currently under review at the time of writing, and the present government is undertaking a further review of the provisions of the Crime and Disorder Act and attendant legislation that deals with such matters. Consequently this chapter will consider the current legislation whilst also outlining the proposed changes that may or may not come into being in the future.

Anti-social behaviour is a problem. It can affect any community regardless of location or the people who live in it. Every person in this country has the right to live their life in a manner that allows them to do so without fear and upset. Whilst the majority of individuals generally live their lives in good order, there are some who do not sign up to this social agreement. This minority, which undermines communities and causes problems for community safety partnerships, is responsible for the majority of calls for help from law-abiding citizens in communities across the country. This disproportionate effect also means individuals are often afraid to go out of their homes, suffer from continual noise, and live in areas that are covered by litter, graffiti, and domestic rubbish.

A further problem when tackling the problems of anti-social behaviour is that because it encompasses so many activities, there is no one single agency that is responsible for dealing with all the complaints and therefore no single agency responsible for collecting data and information on these incidents. This means it is sometimes difficult to establish the level of the anti-social behaviour problem until, for example, the individual or individuals have appeared before the courts.

Government statistics suggest that some 3.6 million reports of anti-social behaviour were made in 2008–9 alone. By comparison there were 6 million crimes reported in the same period.

Tackling anti-social behaviour can help create a decent civil society in which individuals can help regenerate their communities. This means that public and private spaces should be respected by people, as well as the rights of individuals.

3.2 **Impact of Anti-Social Behaviour**

Anti-social behaviour appears to be a widespread problem that is more prevalent in deprived communities and neighbourhoods, although it can occur anywhere. Its impact is more severe in areas that suffer from a lack of community cohesiveness and where local authority services struggle to keep up with demand. In reality, it seems that much of the anti-social behaviour reported to crime and disorder reduction partnership members is committed by a small number of individuals.

Anti-social behaviour can destroy people's lives if left unchecked. It can lead to the decline of a community, with people moving away and housing being left abandoned. It can contribute to a high level of fear of crime which affects an individual's quality of life, in particular those who may be considered vulnerable such as elderly or disabled people. Further, anti-social behaviour can mean economic loss for local authorities, schools, shops, and social landlords.

3.3 **Definitions and Causes of Anti-Social Behaviour**

The first thing to note about anti-social behaviour is that there is no one, single definition encompassing everything that makes it up. It covers a wide spectrum of behaviour, from harassment to loud noise, or even depositing litter and rubbish. Also, the causes of anti-social behaviour are, in many cases, connected to some wider exclusion problems such as family breakdown, mental illness, drug and alcohol abuse, and community disorganization. Whilst young people are associated mainly with anti-social behaviour, they are not exclusively responsible for all of the reported incidents. Further, they are also at risk of being victims.

Although the term 'anti-social behaviour' is one that has been used in recent years to define a set of behaviours, this type of conduct has been around for a long time. So 'anti-social behaviour' is a generic term for a number of types of behaviour which have been fairly common in society.

Consider the following scenarios:

Scenario 1

A couple move into a house in a quiet part of a local community. Soon they are drinking in their garden area late at night, using foul language and shouting abuse at their neighbours. They become increasingly abusive and start holding parties for their friends in their garden, which go on well into the early hours of the morning. As well as the music, there is shouting, swearing, and banging of doors. Requests from neighbours to moderate the parties are ignored and met with threats. Rubbish is building up in the garden; bottles and cans litter the street. Gangs of youths are starting to congregate outside the house, hoping to join the drinks parties.

Scenario 2

In the centre of a small shopping area is a small grass patch with a few trees growing in the middle. There are a number of wooden seats provided for the comfort of people who go shopping, particularly the elderly. Increasingly, a large number of youths have begun to congregate there, drinking alcohol from cans. They are loud and swear at passers-by, and it has been noticed that damage is being caused to the trees and to the benches. There is evidence that a small fire has been started and the grass has been burnt. Shopkeepers complain of lack of customers, shoppers tell of being intimidated and abused by youths, whilst the elderly no longer visit the area as the seats are damaged.

Both scenarios depict circumstances that people would define as involving anti-social behaviour. Finding a definition of anti-social behaviour that does not fall within a criminal definition is more difficult. Behaviour regarded by some as being acceptable may not be so to another group of individuals, and sometimes tolerance and understanding of behaviour can vary within differing communities.

Some definitions are quite wide in their scope and thinking. The Chartered Institute of Housing *Good Practice Briefing* (CIH 1995) suggests that a reasonable definition would be: 'Behaviour that unreasonably interferes with other people's rights to the use and enjoyment of their home and community.' However, the Crime and Disorder Act 1998 (Home Office 1999a) states that anti-social behaviour is committed by a person acting 'in a manner that caused or was likely to cause harassment, alarm, or distress to one or more persons not of the same household as [the defendant]'.

The point about definition is quite important for community safety partnerships. How it is defined influences how anti-social behaviour is recorded and measured by the differing agencies that constitute partnerships. How it is defined also has an effect upon how strategies and initiatives are put together to combat these perceived problems. However, there are some common elements of behaviour that can be identified clearly as anti-social behaviour. These include:

- noise
- litter and rubbish dumping
- graffiti and vandalism
- problem pets
- drug abuse
- nuisance from vehicles.

3.3.1 Local definitions of anti-social behaviour

Consequently, there are some community safety partnerships that have used the official definition in the Crime and Disorder Act 1998 within a local framework, adding their own particular ideas as to what constitutes anti-social behaviour in their communities. There are benefits to this type of approach, including:

- The definition is tailored to local ideas so that it is particularly relevant to that area.
- The agencies and the community that helped to make the definition will have a certain ownership in it and ensure that it is applied.
- If a standard definition is used by all the agencies that make up the crime and disorder reduction partnership then it will not only reduce any confusion but also ensure that the monitoring and recording of such events is standardized.

3.3.2 **Why does it happen?**

Research into why individuals undertake anti-social activities has been carried out (Bright 1997). This will help the police practitioner when considering initiatives and strategies to deal with this type of behaviour.

KEY POINT—SOME CAUSES FOR ANTI-SOCIAL ACTIVITY

Group	Risk factors
Family	Parental criminality, poor parental supervision/discipline, low family income, social isolation, family conflict
School	Truancy and general lack of commitment, disruptive behaviour including bullying, low achievement, school disorganization
Individual/peer	Alienation/lack of social commitment, early involvement in problem behaviour, peer involvement in problem behaviour, high proportion of unsupervised time spent with peers
Early adulthood	Lack of skills or qualifications, unemployment or low income, homelessness
Community	Community disorganization, availability of drugs, opportunity for crime, high percentage of children in the community

---

Whilst accepting that not all these factors can be causal factors of anti-social behaviour (homelessness could be the effect of anti-social behaviour, for example), they do illustrate the wide-ranging issues involved.

3.4 **What Can be Done About Anti-Social Behaviour?**

Currently there are three types of intervention when dealing with anti-social behaviour: prevention, education, and enforcement. Prevention and education are discussed further at **3.4.1** to **3.4.4** below; enforcement in the form of ASBOs is covered at **3.5**.

3.4.1 **Acceptable Behaviour Contracts**

A study of Anti-Social Behaviour Orders (ASBOs) has revealed that in many cases there were some mitigating circumstances that contributed to the behaviour leading to the imposition of the order. These could be such factors as drug or alcohol addiction, learning disorders, school exclusion orders, or health reasons for certain behaviour (e.g., deafness). If individuals have specific needs, is an ASBO the appropriate method of dealing with them? The answer is probably 'No'. To help deal with this type of individual a less formal method of controlling them may be appropriate. This could be the use of an Acceptable Behaviour Contract.

Acceptable Behaviour Contracts (ABCs) are voluntary agreements made between people involved in anti-social behaviour and the local police, the housing department, the registered social landlord, or the perpetrator's school. They are flexible in terms of content and format. Initially introduced in the London Borough of Islington to deal with problems on estates being caused by young people aged between ten and seventeen, they are now used with adults as well as young people, and in a wide variety of circumstances. They have proved effective as a means of encouraging young adults, children, and, importantly, parents to take responsibility for unacceptable behaviour. They are being used to improve the quality of life for local people by tackling behaviour such as harassment, graffiti, criminal damage, and verbal abuse.

3.4.2 **Parental control agreements**

Inadequate parental supervision is strongly associated with offending (Graham and Bowling 1995). Research has shown that 42 per cent of juveniles who had low or medium levels of parental supervision had offended, whilst for those juveniles considered to have had high levels of parental supervision the figure was only 20 per cent. Further, it is realized that the quality of the relationship between the child and parents is crucial.

Parenting programmes have proved successful in turning children and young people away from crime and anti-social behaviour. It is crucial to work with young people in the context of the whole family approach. Alongside Acceptable Behaviour Contracts or other interventions with young people, it is important to engage with parents in enforcing the change in behaviour. It may be necessary to support the parent in building their skills so that they can respond more effectively.

Parenting programmes play a particularly important role in working with young offenders who are parents. Young parents who are constructively engaged in parenting may be less likely to reoffend. When this outlook is combined with new parenting skills they have acquired, these young parents are likely to exercise a positive impact on their children, which may prevent them from becoming offenders or committing anti-social behaviour.

There are three ways in which parents of children can work with youth offending teams (YOTs). These are:

- Voluntarily: many parents want and ask for support in maintaining control over an unruly child. This may be done either with or without a contract or order.
- Voluntarily with a parenting contract: this is a more formal approach when parents are unwilling to cooperate. Refusing to enter into a contract can be used as evidence to support an application for an order and may persuade a reluctant parent to cooperate.
- Parenting Order: if a parent is unwilling to cooperate at all, then an application can be made to the courts directly for a parenting order.

Sections 19 and 25 of the Anti-Social Behaviour Act 2003 (Home Office 2003a) give certain agencies (for example, YOTs) the power to enter into parenting contracts, offering a structured and balanced way for these agencies to work with parents on a voluntary basis.

Parenting contract

A parenting contract is a voluntary written agreement negotiated between a YOT member and the parents of a child involved, or likely to be involved, in criminal or anti-social behaviour. It consists of two main elements:

- An agreement by the parents or guardians of the child or young person that they will comply with the specific requirements for a specified period of time.
- A statement by the YOT whereby they agree to provide support for the parent or guardian for the purposes of ensuring that the contract is complied with.

A YOT worker may negotiate a parenting contract when a child or young person has been referred to him or her and there is reason to believe that the child or young person is likely to engage in criminal conduct or anti-social behaviour. This allows for early support work with parents who have consented and agree that their child has been identified as being at risk of engaging in these activities. Where the child has not been identified as being at risk of engaging in criminal conduct or anti-social behaviour, any intervention through a parenting contract must be on a voluntary basis.

Who can be referred for a parenting contract?

The following children can be referred to a YOT for consideration of a parenting contract:

- A child convicted of an offence.
- A child who has been referred to the YOT following a reprimand or a final warning.
- A child under ten who a member of the YOT has reason to believe has committed an act which, if the child had been older, would have constituted an offence.
- A child identified as being at risk of offending by a Youth Inclusion Support Panel.

Parenting contracts can include a number of specific requirements for the parents and to prevent criminal conduct or anti-social behaviour. Some examples include:

- non-attendance at certain locations unless supervised
- non-contact with certain individuals
- ensuring attendance at school
- non-contact with an individual whom the child has been harassing.

Non-compliance with the parenting contract

There is no penalty for failing to comply with a parenting contract. However, failure to comply may influence a decision by the YOT as to whether to apply for, and also a court considering whether to make, a parenting order. All failures to comply must therefore be recorded and acted upon. Sometimes, however, the terms of the original contract may need adjusting in order to ensure compliance. In this case the reasons for readjustment should also be recorded for possible future reference. In reality, where a contract has been breached, several warnings may be issued to parents before the YOT worker applies for a parenting order. However, before an application is made for a parenting order, efforts should have been made to engage with parents on a voluntary basis, whether through a contract or not.

Parenting orders

A parenting order is made in similar circumstances to a parenting contract by a criminal court, family court, or magistrates' court acting under civil jurisdiction. The relevant legislation that deals with parenting orders is sections 8 to 10 of the Crime and Disorder Act 1998, and sections 25 to 29 of the Anti-Social Behaviour Act 2003. There are two main types of parenting orders, namely the free-standing parenting order and parenting orders linked to conviction or other orders.

Free-standing parenting order

Following an assessment of the case in question, YOTs can apply to the magistrates' court for a free-standing parenting order in respect of a parent or guardian of a child or young person who has been referred to them. The idea is that the child is steered away from criminal conduct or anti-social behaviour, and parents are required to cooperate in this objective. This is quite an important point. A free-standing order should be applied for only after a parent has failed to cooperate in a parental contract.

There are two main areas for a magistrates' court to take into account when issuing a free-standing parenting order. These are:

- the child or young person has engaged in criminal conduct or anti-social behaviour, and
- the order is necessary to prevent further criminal conduct or anti-social behaviour.

Evidence required for granting a free-standing parental order could include witness statements of police officers who attended incidents or of people who were affected by the behaviour, evidence of complaints recorded by the police, professional witness statements, closed-circuit television (CCTV) footage, previous convictions, reprimands or final warnings, and copies of custody records of previous arrests relevant to the application. Evidence should also be provided of any experience of trying to engage parents through a parenting contract which has failed. Magistrates are obliged to take into account any refusal by a parent or guardian to enter into, or failure to comply with, a parenting contract.

Under section 127 of the Magistrates' Court Act 1980 (Home Office 1980a), applications made by complaints must be made within six months of the criminal or anti-social behaviour concerned.

Parenting orders linked to conviction or other orders

A court can make a parenting order in any proceedings where:

- a child safety order has been made
- an anti-social behaviour order or sex offender order has been made in respect of a child or young person
- a child or young person has been convicted of an offence
- a referral order has been made, or when a parent is referred back to court by a Youth Offending Panel (YOP) after failing to attend meetings.

Whilst the consent of the parent or guardian is not required for the issue of this kind of parenting order, there are certain conditions which must apply before the court can make the order. These are that the order would be desirable in the interest of preventing:

- a repetition of the type of behaviour which led to one of the various orders being made in the first place; or
- the commission of further offences where the child or young person has been convicted of an offence or issued with a referral order.

However, there is an additional condition when a YOP refers a parent back to court. The court would only be able to make a parenting order if it is proved to its satisfaction that the parent has failed without reasonable excuse to attend panel meetings and that the order would be desirable in the interests of preventing the commission of further offences.

Parenting order requirements

Within a framework that avoids any conflict with the parents' religious beliefs and any interference with the parents' normal working hours or attendance at any educational courses, the core requirement of the parenting order is that the parents attend a parenting programme.

This programme can last for up to three months and must be as flexible as possible. It is normally provided by the local authority social services department or a local voluntary sector organization working with parents, and the progress of the parents is monitored at suitable intervals.

The court may also make specific requirements as part of this order. These are normally tailored to address the problems that led to the parenting order and will be linked to the requirements of any order imposed on the child or young person. These specific requirements could include:

- ensuring the child attends school or mentoring sessions
- ensuring the child attends programmes which deal with such issues as anger management or drug/alcohol abuse
- ensuring the child refrains from contact with other children who are disruptive
- ensuring the child avoids particular locations or premises and is at home at certain times of the day or night.

Breach of a parenting order

There may be occasions where a parenting order issued by the courts has been breached. This may involve a particular breach, such as non-attendance at school. Following investigation into the matter to establish the extent to which parents or guardians have tried to meet the requirements of the order and how far they were able to control their child's behaviour, a decision will be taken as to how to proceed with the breach. It may be appropriate to draw up a new plan with the parents which will better meet their needs and circumstances.

If it is decided to deal with the breach formally through the courts, practitioners should remember that failing to comply with a parenting order is not an arrestable offence for the purposes of the Police and Criminal Evidence Act 1984 (Home Office 1984a). If it is reported to them, the police should pass the results of any investigation to the Crown Prosecution Service which will decide whether or not to prosecute.

If a parent or guardian is convicted he or she will be liable to a fine not exceeding level 3 on the standard scale (up to £1000). The offence is not a recordable offence for the purposes of the Police and Criminal Evidence Act 1984. Courts cannot reissue parenting orders in breach proceedings, but could impose any sentence available for a non-imprisonable offence, that is a fine, absolute or conditional discharge, community order, or curfew order. This process can be seen in Figure 3.1.

There are other ways of tackling anti-social behaviour through prevention. These include such initiatives as mentoring and diversionary activities.

3.4.3 Mentoring

A mentor may be defined as someone who helps others to achieve their potential. Mentoring may involve coaching and encouraging, constructively criticizing, explaining, listening, and guiding. One feature of mentoring is a one-to-one relationship between an adult mentor and a young mentee, established to help the young person to achieve his or her goals. However, group mentoring schemes (i.e., one mentor to a number of mentees) are also producing results.

For young people at risk, a volunteer mentor from their own community is someone they can rely on, who is not associated with other adults in authority

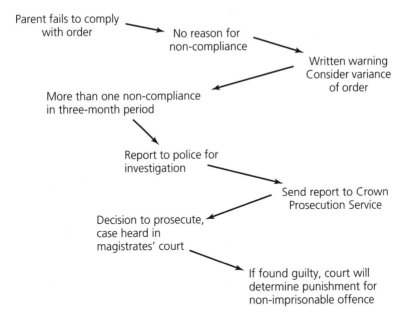

Figure 3.1 Process when a parent or guardian fails to comply with a parenting order

in their lives (police, teachers, social workers, probation officers, even parents) with whom they may have had difficult relationships. Mentors can provide mentees with extra support and a positive adult role model.

Mentoring schemes have become extremely popular in the UK. Mentoring usually consists of one volunteer who guides, advises, or supports another, less experienced person (mentee). Mentoring can be an effective tool to help raise the confidence and levels of achievement (academic, personal, or job-related) of the mentee. There are now mentoring schemes in businesses, in primary and secondary schools, in colleges and universities, and in a range of other settings.

3.4.4 Diversionary activities

One of the most effective ways to reduce crime and disorder is to prevent young people from getting into trouble in the first place.

The Youth Justice Board has helped to develop a range of early intervention and diversionary programmes, which contribute to giving young people the best chances of leading a crime-free life. The programmes aim to engage young people's interests, increase their knowledge, and consequently divert them from offending. They can often effectively address the problems that lie behind a young person's troublesome behaviour, such as family problems, substance misuse, and poor educational attainment.

Education

Half of all male prisoners in our jails were excluded from school (Home Office Strategy for Reducing Crime 2004). If children remain at school and obtain good qualifications then the risk of criminal and anti-social behaviour can be reduced. The government has introduced the Behaviour Improvement Programme, which includes measures for those who have been temporarily excluded and seeks to reduce truancy. Schools now deliver courses on citizenship and personal development which highlight the effects of anti-social behaviour on others within the community.

It has been acknowledged that bullying very often accompanies anti-social behaviour and crime outside of school hours, and every school now has a policy and strategy in place to help prevent and deal with this problem.

3.5 Anti-Social Behaviour Orders

Whilst ABCs and parenting agreements are informal procedures designed to prevent illegal activity through agreement without recourse to the legal system, the police practitioner also has access to statutory powers. Apart from the more obvious powers relating to criminal damage, harassment, and public order offences, etc., perhaps the legal power most associated with tackling anti-social behaviour is the Anti-Social Behaviour Order (ASBO).

3.5.1 An overview of ASBOs

Section 1 of the Crime and Disorder Act 1998 introduced ASBOs in England and Wales, and they have been available since April 1999. The power to impose ASBOs was greatly extended by the Police Reform Act 2002 (Home Office 2002a), which provided that orders could be made on conviction in criminal proceedings, orders in county court proceedings, and interim orders.

ASBOs are civil orders that exist to protect the public from behaviour and actions that can cause them harassment, alarm, or distress. They contain conditions that stop the offender from carrying out specific acts, or prevent an offender from entering defined geographical locations. The orders are not criminal penalties, not intended to be seen as a way to punish an offender, and can last for a minimum of two years.

ASBOs are community-based orders that involve local people not only in the collection of evidence but also in enforcement in the event of breaches of the order. They encourage local communities to become actively involved in reporting crime and disorder, and to help regenerate community spirit.

3.5.2 The civil nature of ASBOs

When a magistrates' court deals with a stand-alone application for an ASBO it does so acting in its civil capacity. Similarly, in a county court the order can be applied for during related proceedings and can also be requested (without a formal application) if an individual is convicted in a criminal court of an offence. However, an important point for the police practitioner to remember is that the ASBO remains a civil order irrespective of the issuing court. This has an effect when one considers court proceedings. The civil nature of the order means that hearsay and professional witness evidence can be heard, which also means that individuals who have been subjected to harassment or anti-social behaviour can be protected.

3.5.3 Legal definition of anti-social behaviour

Whilst there are many different definitions for anti-social behaviour, for the purposes of applying for an ASBO the definition under the terms of the Crime and Disorder Act 1998 (Home Office 1999a) is quite clear. The agency applying for the order must show that:

- the defendant behaved in an anti-social manner, and
- an order is necessary for the protection of persons from further anti-social behaviour by the defendant.

This is sometimes referred to as the 'two-stages' test.

Further, acting in an anti-social manner is defined by section 1(1) of the Act as acting in 'a manner that caused or was likely to cause harassment, alarm or distress to one or more persons not of the same household as the perpetrator'. The wide definition allows for the order to be available in a number of differing circumstances.

The use of the term 'likely to cause' is of most interest to the police practitioner. This means that someone other than the victim of the behaviour can give evidence of its occurrence. This means that professional witnesses such as the police can provide the evidence required to prove the application for the order. Those victims who feel unable to come forward for fear of reprisals or intimidation are therefore protected by the use of professional witnesses.

3.5.4 Standard of proof required

It should be noted by police practitioners that the burden of proof required revolves around the phrase 'the effect or likely effect of the behaviour on other people' that determines whether the behaviour is anti-social (Home Office 1999a). The agency applying for the order does not have to prove an intention on the part of the person appearing in court to cause harassment, alarm, or distress.

3.5.5 What type of behaviour attracts ASBOs?

The most common behaviour dealt with by ASBOs is unruly conduct, verbal abuse, harassment, assault, graffiti, and excessive noise. An ASBO can also be issued to help deal with racial abuse, throwing of stones and other missiles, and drunken behaviour. The wide range of anti-social behaviour that can be tackled by ASBOs, and the way they can be tailored to fit specific problems, means that they should be regarded as a useful and flexible tool in the armoury for dealing with community problems.

Scenario—Dealing with anti-social behaviour

A group of youths regularly congregate in a built-up area, engaging in drinking alcohol and taking illegal drugs. They harass passers-by and threaten them. They are led by three distinct individuals who encourage the behaviour of others.

Following a period of observation by the police, and in collaboration with the community, evidence was obtained and the three individuals who were seen as the ringleaders were the subject of ASBOs. The orders prohibited them from:

(1) loitering in particular areas;
(2) entering named shops and other premises;
(3) using threatening, abusive, or racist language.

The ASBOs formed part of a broader strategy which included targeting shopkeepers selling alcohol to under eighteen-year-olds and proactively targeting drug dealers in the area, following up on the behaviour after the ASBOs had been made, and prosecuting for breaches of the ASBOs. The problem of the youths congregating and behaving in an anti-social manner has now cleared up.

3.5.6 Who can apply for an ASBO?

Section 1 of the Crime and Disorder Act 1998 refer to agencies that are able to apply. These are defined as 'relevant authorities'. They are:

- local authorities
- police forces (including British Transport Police)
- registered social landlords as defined by section 1 of the Housing Act 1996 (Home Office 1996b).

Local authorities and the police may apply for an order where it is necessary to protect persons in their area, regardless of where the anti-social behaviour took place. The British Transport Police and registered social landlords can now apply for orders due to changes introduced by the Police Reform Act 2002 (Home Office 2002a). Registered social landlords can apply for orders against nonresidents as well as residents, thus attempting to deal with quality-of-life issues.

3.5.7 **Where does an ASBO apply?**

Before the changes brought into being by the Police Reform Act 2002, ASBOs and the conditions attached to them applied only in the local authority area in which the behaviour occurred and in adjoining areas. However, an order can now extend across any defined area within, or across the whole of, England and Wales.

This power is particularly useful as it deals with the problem of offenders moving address and continuing to behave in an anti-social manner. Further, an extended ASBO can be used for particular problems such as anti-social behaviour on trains, or where the offender commits offences over a wide geographical area. The more serious the behaviour, the more likely that the court will grant a geographically wide order.

3.5.8 **Interim orders**

Section 1D of the Crime and Disorder Act 1998 (as amended by section 65 of the Police Reform Act 2002) allows for the issue of interim orders by the magistrates' court and the county court. An interim order is an order made at an initial hearing held in advance of the full hearing. This order can impose the same conditions and prohibitions, and has the same penalties for breaches as a full ASBO. The application for a full order by the relevant agency should include a request for an interim order at the same time. The court will determine whether to grant an interim order on the basis of whether the application for the full order has been properly made, and there is evidence that there is an urgent need to protect the community and individuals within it.

The benefit of an interim order is that it means an order can be made that will stop anti-social behaviour quickly and protect individuals more quickly. Further, it may reduce witness intimidation by ordering the individual named in the application to cease the behaviour while the ASBO application is being processed. It also gives the courts an opportunity to send a clear message that anti-social behaviour will not be tolerated.

When an interim order is issued there are certain conditions that are attached to it. These are:

- It will be for a fixed period.
- It can be varied or discharged on application by the defendant.
- It will cease to have effect if the application for the full ASBO is withdrawn or refused.
- It may extend over any defined area in England and Wales.
- It is to be regarded as a full order for the purposes of any breach that may occur.

3.5.9 **Breach of an ASBO**

Any breach of an ASBO is a criminal offence, and criminal procedures and penalties apply. Therefore, in any proceedings for a breach of an order, the standard of proof is the criminal standard and guilt must be established beyond reasonable doubt. Breach of order proceedings are heard in magistrates' courts and may be referred to Crown Court. However, these proceedings are the same whether the order is for a full ASBO or an interim order.

The maximum penalty for breach of an order for an adult offender is five years' imprisonment, whilst for a breach by a juvenile offender the maximum sentence is a detention and training order which has a maximum term of twenty-four months. The detention and training order is available for twelve- to seventeen-year-olds; whilst a ten- to eleven-year-old can be given a community order for breach of an ASBO.

3.5.10 Collection of evidence

For the police practitioner, the collection of evidence to support a criminal prosecution is quite a normal event. However, as we have seen, the collection of evidence to support an application for an ASBO differs from a criminal event such as theft. Here the evidence that can be produced by the lead agency in the courts, whilst attempting to prove its case beyond reasonable doubt, may include hearsay evidence. The evidence in support of an application for an ASBO should prove:

- that at a specific place on specific dates the defendant acted in a specific manner; and
- these acts caused or were likely to cause harassment, alarm, or distress to one or more persons not in the same household as the defendant.

For the court the decision to grant an order is in a sense a risk assessment. It has to decide whether or not there is a likelihood of future anti-social behaviour by the defendant.

Witnesses need not prove that they were alarmed or distressed themselves, but only that the behaviour they witnessed was likely to produce an effect on others. As hearsay evidence is allowed, it may be given by professional witnesses—officers of public agencies such as the police or local authority employees, whose job it is to prevent anti-social behaviour.

KEY POINT—EVIDENCE USED TO SUPPORT PROCEEDINGS FOR ISSUE OF AN ASBO

Evidence that can be used in court proceedings may include:

- breach of an Acceptable Behaviour Contract
- witness statements of officers who attended courts
- witness statements of people who have been adversely affected by anti-social behaviour
- records of complaints kept by the police, housing, and local authorities
- statements from professional witnesses
- video or CCTV evidence
- information from diaries or logs kept by witnesses
- copies of custody records of previous arrests relevant to the application.

A complaint must be made within six months from the time when the subject of the complaint occurred. One serious incident of anti-social behaviour may be enough for an order to be made, although earlier incidents of a more minor nature could be used to support a case and show a pattern of behaviour.

Professional witnesses can give evidence of opinion regarding matters within their expertise and can also give evidence on their assessments. Examples include council officials, health visitors, station staff, teachers, doctors, and police officers.

The obtaining of the ASBO is not the end of the process. To ensure its effectiveness it has to be monitored and enforced.

3.5.11 Monitoring and enforcing the order

One of the major strengths of partnership working should be the process of information exchange. This ensures early warning of problems and, of course, clarification of who should do what to safeguard witnesses and to decide what other action needs to be taken to deal with an offender in these types of cases.

It is vitally important that the agency responsible for the management of any ASBO case be informed of breaches, appeals, and any other action relating to it. Recording of orders on the Police National Computer (PNC) will enable the police to deal with any breaches. For the police practitioner it is important to be able to establish the conditions of a particular order so that the required action, possibly an arrest, can be taken.

3.6 Proposed Changes to the Anti-Social Behaviour Legislation

Reducing anti-social behaviour is still a government priority, and it is expected to be a priority for the police and other agencies as well, particularly where it is criminal or targeted at vulnerable victims. Unchecked, anti-social behaviour can be linked to increased disorder, low-level crime and fear of crime in a neighbourhood—the so-called 'broken windows' effect discussed elsewhere in this book.

The police and their local partners, such as local councils, utilize a range of tools to deal with anti-social behaviour. Where the behaviour is criminal, it should be dealt with as such. But informal measures can nip problems in the bud before they get that far. Further, preventative civil orders can stop long-running campaigns of intimidation or harassment that are causing real harm to victims, where prosecution of a single offence could not.

The current legislation currently in use is as we have seen extensive, and runs from warning letters all the way up to court orders like the Anti-Social Behaviour Order (ASBO). However, there have been concerns that there are simply too many tools available for use, with practitioners tending to stick to the ones they are most familiar with. Some of the formal tools (particularly the ASBO) are considered to be bureaucratic, slow and expensive, which puts people off using them. The growing number of people who breach their ASBO suggests the potential consequences are not deterring a persistent minority from continuing their anti-social or criminal behaviour and the tools that were designed to help perpetrators deal with underlying causes of their anti-social behaviour are rarely used.

Consequently, at the time of writing the government is proposing a radical streamlining of the toolkit. Their ambition is to move away from having a tool for every different problem to ensuring that the police and partners have faster, more flexible tools. These, plus more effective sanctions, will help professionals and, where necessary, the courts stop anti-social behaviour earlier, and better protect victims and communities.

At this moment in time it would appear that there are plans to repeal the ASBO and other court orders for anti-social individuals, and replace them with two new tools that bring together restrictions on future behaviour and support to address underlying problems—a Criminal Behaviour Order that can be attached to a criminal conviction, and a Crime Prevention Injunction that can quickly stop anti-social behaviour before it escalates.

Further, it is proposed that these tools will ensure there are powerful incentives on perpetrators to stop behaving anti-socially—for example, by making breach of the new orders grounds for eviction from social housing. The new legislation it is suggested, will bring together many of the existing tools for dealing with place-specific anti-social behaviour, from persistent litter or noisy neighbours, to street drinking and crack houses, into a *Community Protection Order*.

By introducing this idea it is believed that it will bring together existing police dispersal powers into a single police power to direct people away from an area for anti-social behaviour and make the informal and out-of-court tools for dealing with anti-social behaviour more rehabilitative and restorative, whilst introducing a *Community Trigger* that gives victims and communities the right to require agencies to deal with persistent anti-social behaviour.

Specifically, the new legislation will introduce a new range of sanctions such as:

- Criminal Behaviour Orders
- Crime Prevention Injunctions
- Community Protection Orders.

These are briefly discussed below.

Criminal Behaviour Order

This order will be a civil order attached to a criminal conviction. It will protect people from behaviour that causes harassment, alarm or distress and could include individuals being banned from certain places, activities and may also require certain positive activities to be undertaken such as drug treatments.

Crime Prevention Injunction

This injunction will be designed to stop anti-social behaviour before it escalates. It will rely on the civil burden of proof, on the balance of probability, which is much quicker to apply than the previous ASBO and its sanctions will include curfews, supervision, activity requirements and detention.

Community Protection Order

This order will consist of two tiers. The first tier, level 1, will consist of a notice issued by practitioners to stop environmental anti-social behaviour (graffiti, noise, etc). The second tier, level 2, provides the power for police and local authorities to restrict the use of places or to close properties associated with persistent anti-social behaviour. This order will also include a simplified power for police to direct people away from an area on grounds of anti-social behaviour.

The following table compares the existing legislation with the proposed changes.

Existing legislation	Proposed changes
ASBO on Conviction/ASBO/Interim ASBO	Criminal Behaviour Order
ASB Injunction Individual Support Order	Crime Prevention Injunction
Various Closure Orders including crack house, brothels etc. Gating Orders, Dog Control Orders	Community Protection Order, level 2
Litter clearance notice, noise abatement notices, graffiti removal	Community Protection Order, level 1
Direction to leave, dispersal order	Police Direction Power

Conclusion

Whichever government is in power, clearly dealing effectively with anti social behaviour remains a priority for them. The present government has argued that previous sanctions such as ASBOs have not worked and are in the process of changing them, although they are still currently in existence. When one examines the changes however, there does not on the surface at least, appear to be much in the way of radical reform.

3.7 **Summing Up**

3.7.1 **Anti-social behaviour**

Anti-social behaviour affects communities regardless of location or the people who live in them. People have a right to live without fear and upset. Anti-social behaviour is a major source of calls to community safety partnerships, and it is estimated that it costs the public services over £3.4 billion per year. Tackling these problems helps to create a decent society and regenerate communities.

3.7.2 **Definition of anti-social behaviour**

There appears to be no single definition of anti-social behaviour used by all. However, the Crime and Disorder Act 1998 states that anti-social behaviour is committed by a person acting in a manner that caused, or was likely to cause, harassment, alarm, or distress to one or more persons not of the same household as the defendant. Local definitions that focus on local issues have been used by some community safety partnerships.

3.7.3 **Acceptable Behaviour Contract**

This is a voluntary agreement between a person involved in anti-social behaviour, the local police, the housing department, the registered landlord, or the perpetrator's school. A breach of an Acceptable Behaviour Contract (ABC) can be used as evidence when applying for an Anti-Social Behaviour Order (ASBO).

3.7.4 **Anti-social behaviour orders**

Introduced by the Crime and Disorder Act 1998, and extended by the Police Reform Act 2002, these are civil orders that protect the public from behaviour and actions that cause harassment, alarm, or distress. They contain conditions tailored to the individual concerned, and a breach of the ASBO is a criminal offence.

3.7.5 **Parental control agreements**

Inadequate parental supervision is associated with offending. These agreements are either (a) completely voluntary, (b) voluntary with a parenting contract, or (c) compulsory by a parenting order made through the courts. A parenting order may contain certain requirements, such as ensuring a child attends school or mentoring sessions, and a breach of an order can mean a parent or guardian being sentenced by the courts.

3.7.6 **Local application**

(1) What types of anti-social behaviour can you identify within your locality?
(2) How many ASBOs have been issued by your local courts so far?
(3) Why is a parenting order so important?
(4) What types of diversionary activities for young people does your local police force engage in?
(5) What ways can you think of to collect evidence for an ASBO?

3.7.7 **Useful websites**

http://www.homeoffice.gov.uk/crime/anti-social-behaviour/
http://www.direct.gov.uk/en/CrimeJusticeAndTheLaw/Reportingcrimeand
    antisocialbehaviour/DG_181715

Community Problems
and Crime

4.1 **Introduction**

Having discussed the idea of anti-social behaviour, the problems of definition, exploring what can be done, including the use of Acceptable Behaviour Contracts, Anti-Social Behaviour Orders, and parental control agreements, as well as the new government's proposlas for changing this legislation, this chapter discusses in more detail anti-social behaviour that appears to be typical and more prevalent within communities. It considers common complaints that the police practitioner will receive and be expected to deal with within the context of crime and disorder reduction, as well as considering crime in the community. In particular, the reasons why people don't or won't report crime will be examined, as well as the corrosive effect of fear of crime.

4.2 **Begging and Street Drinking**

4.2.1 **Begging**

Many large towns and cities attract individuals who, for a variety of personal and domestic reasons, seek to earn their living through the process of begging. These individuals can often be found in shopping malls and in city centres. However tragic their personal circumstances may be, this type of activity can intimidate and threaten people who visit the areas for the purposes of leisure activities or shopping. Parents, in particular, may be very wary of visiting areas with their children should this type of activity be taking place.

Very often, people involved in begging will frequent locations near to points where money is exchanged or cash withdrawn, such as shops or cashpoint machines. Sometimes people involved in begging also engage in other activities such as illegal drug-taking or other criminal activity. Very often they will be persistent in their attempts to obtain money, and end up engaging in an aggressive style of begging, almost threatening an individual until money is handed over.

Whilst an immediate answer to these problems may be one of enforcement, the police practitioner should also consider a problem-solving partnership approach to dealing with begging.

KEY POINT—TACKLING THE PROBLEM OF BEGGING

One approach to tackling begging considers the following three methods:

Support—This provides advice on accommodation and routes into drug rehabilitation and health provision.

Enforcement—Proactive stance taken by the police to arrest any person found committing the offence.

Publicity—Raising awareness of the link between drug abuse, criminal activity, and begging.

However, if beggars do not accept help and advice then action must be taken. Begging is a criminal offence and there are several important powers available to the police practitioner.

The Vagrancy Act 1824, section 3

This section creates an old offence which prohibits the act of begging or the gathering of alms in streets and public places. It is a summary offence and normally requires evidence that more than one person has been accosted for money. This Act and section would not apply to the situation where the person asking for money is performing some act such as singing or playing a musical instrument. The general power of arrest under section 25 of the Police and Criminal Evidence Act 1984 would apply to arresting for an offence under the Vagrancy Act 1824.

The Highways Act 1980, section 137

This provision states that if a person, without lawful authority or excuse, in any way wilfully obstructs free passage along a highway, he or she is guilty of an offence.

If a person is in the highway for the purposes of, say, handing out leaflets or collecting for charity, then this Act and section would not apply. However, one of the tests for the commission of this offence involves the unnecessary obstruction of the highway by unreasonably impeding the right of way of the public to pass. In the case of an aggressive beggar this may certainly be the case. Again consideration should be given to the general power to arrest under section 25 of the Police and Criminal Evidence Act 1984.

4.2.2 **Street drinking**

Another aspect of street behaviour that communities and individuals feel intimidated by is street drinking or 'drinking schools/clubs'. On occasions these are linked to the activity of street begging, and in particular may support an aggressive style of begging. Very often people are reluctant to attend shopping areas or public places because of this activity, and it can influence an individual's perception about fear of crime.

4.3 **Alcohol-related Disorder**

Whilst most people drink alcohol in a responsible manner, there appears to be a minority of individuals who cause a great many problems for the community and partnerships by engaging in crime and disorder after consuming large quantities of alcohol.

Alcohol-related disorder is a problem in most towns and cities throughout the country. People who have been drinking heavily may cause disorder or nuisances, and even commit criminal offences. This appears evident when they are spilling out onto streets at closing times for pubs and clubs throughout the country, with great concern being expressed in particular about the idea of 'binge drinking'.

4.3.1 Some definitions

Before examining some of the common problems associated with alcohol-related disorder, it is as well to understand what the different terminology used in this area means. For the purposes of this section, 'alcohol-related crime and disorder' means:

> Instances of crime and disorder that occur and/or occurred at that level of seriousness because alcohol consumption was a contributing factor.
>
> (Home Office 2003d)

The government's definition of binge drinkers is:

> Those individuals who get very drunk at least once a month.

Whilst the National Health Service, who see the end results of such activity, define it as:

> Drinking heavily in a short space of time to get drunk or feel the effects of alcohol.

(See http://www.drinkaware.co.uk for more information on this matter.)

4.3.2 Statistics relating to alcohol-related disorder

Recent research by the government into the lifestyles of young people has revealed the following information:

- 39 per cent of eighteen- to twenty-four-year-olds classified themselves as 'binge drinkers'.
- Binge drinkers were more likely to offend than other young adults; further, young male binge drinkers were more likely to offend than others.
- 60 per cent of binge drinkers admitted committing offences.
- The link between drinking alcohol and the offender was very strong for violent crimes.
- It has been estimated that 30 per cent of all sexual offences, 33 per cent of all burglaries and 50 per cent of all street crimes are influenced by the use of alcohol.

Further, although binge drinkers are more likely to be men, there is evidence to suggest that women's drinking has been rising fast over the past ten years. Whilst men are more likely to be victims of violence, women may be at greater risk of sexual assault. Whatever the results for individuals, the impact upon society is most visible from high attendance figures at the Accident and Emergency departments of hospitals. Perhaps the most controversial area of alcohol consumption revolves around the night-time economy.

4.3.3. **The night-time economy**

Whilst the night-time economy generates much in the way of economic resources for towns and cities across England and Wales, it also provides many alcohol-related problems for the police and community safety partnerships. More can be found regarding the night-time economy at the website http://www.ias.org.uk/resources/nighttime/index.html.

A Department of Culture and Sports report of 2007 found that one in five of all violent assaults now occur in and around pubs and clubs. The clustering of such incidents, with high numbers of people present, places enormous strain on policing and other emergency services. Consequently, the Police Reform and Social Responsibility Act 2011 contains two important new pieces of legislation, namely the Early Morning Alcohol Restriction Order and the late night levy when implemented will, it is hoped, have a positive effect upon the problems associated with the late night economy.

Early Morning Alcohol Restriction Orders (EMROs)

In general, the aims of section 119 of the Police Reform and Social Responsibility Act 2011 set out to deal with EMROs. The brief details and procedures for implementation are shown below:

- If the licensing authority considers it appropriate for the promotion of the licensing objectives it can make such an order.
- The period specified in the order must begin no earlier than midnight and no later than 6am.
- It contains specific premises times and dates when the order shall apply.
- There is a right for a hearing to listen to any representations to be made before an order is made.

The night-time levy

This levy provides a power to the licensing authority to charge for premises that have a late alcohol licence and can restrict hours of sale between midnight and 6am. In particular:

- It places a charge upon those businesses that benefit from trading alcohol in a safe night-time economy for the extra costs that this activity generates for the police, and their partners.
- It will apply in areas where the licensing authority decides to apply it.
- Premises are divided into 'bands' according to their ratable value and this will help determine the levy to be paid.

- The funds generated will, subject to any administration costs, be payable to the new Police and Crime Commissioner, with at least 70 per cent of the levy paid thus.

4.3.4 **Government response**

Having identified the significant impact alcohol has on individuals who commit crime and disorder, the government has stated that it will seek to tackle excessive drinking and related crime and disorder activity in several ways. These include:

(1) Education, including alcohol-reducing programmes in schools and better information for consumers. This will include renewing the code of practice for television advertising, and more support and advice for employers.
(2) Ensuring that the alcohol industry makes a significant contribution to reducing harms by informing the public of the dangers of excessive drinking, contributing to the cost of tackling local problems, and not engaging in irresponsible promotions such as 'happy hours' where strong alcoholic drinks are available cheaply.
(3) Working with local authorities to ensure that they avoid high densities of licensed premises and use new powers to clamp down on crime and disorder.

KEY POINT—THE LICENSING ACT 2003 (AS AMENDED BY THE POLICE REFORM AND SOCIAL RESPONSIBILITY ACT 2011)

When this Act is fully implemented it will strengthen existing powers to clamp down on crime and disorder. The new powers, some of which are already in force, include:

- expanded powers to close down disorderly venues instantly for up to twenty-four hours
- powers to review licences when problems arise, instead of waiting for renewals
- powers to reduce trading hours temporarily or permanently
- powers to suspend or revoke licences
- extended powers to confiscate alcohol in public places
- Early Morning Alcohol Restriction Orders
- late-night levy.

4.3.5 **Sale of alcohol to under-age persons**

The scale of the problem of sale of alcohol to under-age persons has been identified by the Alcohol Misuse Enforcement Campaign, which was carried out during the summer of 2004. It was discovered that:

- 45 per cent of the on-licences and 31 per cent of the off-licences targeted were selling unlawfully to young people under the age of eighteen.

- Over one-third of more than 12,000 alcohol confiscations during the campaign were from people under age.
- 57 per cent of those people asked about problem drinking in their area identified drinking by under-eighteen-year-olds as a key ingredient in the problem.
- 15 per cent of twelve- to seventeen-year-olds stated they had committed a disorderly or criminal act during or after drinking.

Therefore, under-age drinking appears to be a major contribution to instances of crime and disorder.

4.3.6 Confiscation of alcohol

Apart from any other power available to the police to deal with drinking in a public place, there is a specific power to confiscate alcohol from persons under the age of eighteen years. This is a discretionary power in that the police officer can apply it as he sees fit, taking into account the circumstances of the incident and, of course, human rights principles.

KEY POINT—CONFISCATION OF ALCOHOL

Section 1 of the Confiscation of Alcohol (Young Persons) Act 1997 (Home Office 1997b) states:

Where a constable reasonably suspects that a person in a relevant place is in possession of intoxicating liquor and that either—

1. he is under the age of eighteen years or
2. he intends that any of the liquor should be consumed by a person under the age of eighteen years in that or other relevant place or
3. a person under the age of eighteen who is or has recently been with him has recently consumed intoxicating liquor in that or any other relevant place, the constable may require him:
   (a) to surrender anything which is or reasonably believed to be intoxicating liquor or a container for such liquor and
   (b) to state his name and address.

Police Officers and Police Community Support Officers (PCSOs) and accredited persons (see below) have the power to confiscate alcohol from young persons under 18 and cigarettes and tobacco products from under 16s.

In addition to the above, PCSOs and accredited persons can be given the powers under the Police Reform Act 2002 to confiscate alcohol and tobacco.

1. Section 12 (2)(b) of the Criminal Justice and Police Act 2001 gives the police, PCSOs and accredited persons powers to confiscate alcohol from people who are consuming or intend to consume alcohol in a public place to which drinking restrictions apply like a Designated Public Place Order.

> 2. Consuming alcohol in a designated public place, contrary to requirement by a constable not to do so, is an offence. If the person refuses to surrender their alcohol they can be prosecuted or the officer can issue a penalty notice for disorder (PND) of £50.
> 3. Penalty notices for this offence can be given to young people aged 16–17 as part of the penalty notice for disorder scheme.

There is no requirement for the officer to be in uniform for this power to be exercised, and a relevant place is defined under section 1(6) of the 1997 Act as any public place, other than licensed premises, or any place, other than a public place, to which that person has unlawfully gained access.

Failure to comply with a requirement without reasonable excuse under this section is an offence, and a constable may arrest without warrant a person who fails to comply with a requirement imposed on him/her under section 1 of this Act.

Scenario—Confiscation of alcohol

A group of three youngsters aged between fourteen and sixteen have obtained cans of lager from the local off-licence. They have decided to sit on the bench in the local bus station drinking their ill-gotten gains. They become noisy and their behaviour attracts the attention of the police. A police constable speaks to the youths, and forms the opinion that they are under eighteen years of age. He then asks them to hand over their cans of lager. Two of the youngsters do so immediately; but the third refuses, stating he paid for them and refusing to give his name and address or to cooperate any further. Consequently the police officer arrests this person under section 1(5) of the Confiscation of Alcohol (Young Persons) Act 1997 (Home Office 1997b).

4.3.7 Dispersal of groups

Very often groups of young people will congregate within local communities and this can cause annoyance for people. In some circumstances these groups can intimidate, alarm, and distress others not only by their presence, but by their anti-social behaviour such as swearing, spitting, or shouting at passers-by. Occasionally alcohol use by under-age drinkers is a part of this problem.

Section 30 of the Anti-Social Behaviour Act 2003 empowers the police to disperse groups of two or more and return to their homes young people under sixteen who are unsupervised in public places after 9 p.m. These powers are only available where an authorization has been made by an officer of at least the rank of superintendent regarding a designated area. Before giving this authorization, however, the officer must be satisfied that significant and persistent anti-social behaviour has occurred in the locality and that intimidation, harassment, alarm, or distress has been caused to members of the public by the presence or behaviour of groups in that locality.

4.4 **Drugs**

Drugs are a very serious problem in the UK. No one has any illusions about that. Illegal drugs are now more widely available than ever before and children are increasingly exposed to them. Drugs are a threat to health, a threat on the streets, and a serious threat to communities because of drug-related crime.

The drugs problem remains formidable. For example, estimates from the 2010/2011 British Crime Survey (Smith and Flately 2011) suggest:

- Almost 3 million people aged 16 to 59 years had used illicit drugs.
- Around 1 million people used Class A drugs during the previous 12 months.
- A general increase in the use of powder cocaine since 1996.
- Cannabis remains the most commonly used drug with around 2.2 million users.

Drug problems do not occur in isolation. They are often tied in with other social problems. Partnership is the key to the approach, building on the good work that has already been done in many areas. The government's strategy has four elements:

(1) Young people—to help young people resist drug misuse in order to achieve their full potential in society.
(2) Communities—to protect our communities from drug-related anti-social and criminal behaviour.
(3) Treatment—to enable people with drug problems to overcome them and live healthy and crime-free lives.
(4) Availability—to stifle the availability of illegal drugs on our streets; this is a framework for designing and implementing policies to tackle drugs, and is just the beginning of a long-term strategy.

4.4.1 **Closure of property**

Section 118 of the Criminal Justice and Immigration Act 2008 introduced new powers for the courts to close, on a temporary basis, premises associated with significant and persistent disorder or persistent serious nuisance. Schedule 20 inserts a new Part 1A into the Anti-Social Behaviour Act 2003 (c.38) that makes provision about the issue of Closure Notices and the making of Closure Orders in respect of premises associated with persistent disorder or nuisance. This tool is similar in nature to the pre-existing crack house closure power. The intention of this provision is to empower police officers and local authorities to take action against premises that cause significant and persistent disorder or persistent serious nuisance to a community. It is up to the courts to define these terms as there is no formal legal definition. In all cases of the use of these powers, it is necessary to demonstrate that persistent and significant disorder or persistent serious nuisance is associated with the premises. When a superintendent ('authorising officer') or the local authority assesses the need for the issue of a Closure Notice, he or she has to have reasonable grounds for believing that:

- at any time in the preceding three months a person has engaged in anti-social behaviour on the premises; and
- that the use of the premises is associated with significant and persistent disorder or persistent serious nuisance to members of the public.

The type of problems that may constitute significant and persistent disorder or persistent serious nuisance to members of the public in relation to the premises are outlined below.

- Intimidating and threatening behaviour towards residents.
- A significant increase in crime in the immediate area surrounding the premises.
- The discharge of a firearm in, or adjacent to, the premises.
- Significant problems with prostitution or sexual acts being committed in the vicinity of the premises.
- Violent offences and crime being committed on or in the vicinity of the premises.
- Serious disorder associated with alcohol abuse, for example in and around drinking dens.
- High numbers of people entering and leaving the premises at all times of the day or night and the resultant disruption they cause to residents.
- Noise (constant/intrusive)—excessive noise at all hours associated with visitors to the property.

The Closure Order can last for up to three months and can be extended to six months. During the period of closure it will be an offence to enter or remain in the property and the premises will be sealed.

Noisy and disorderly premises can cause misery to people who live in the vicinity, make other people feel unsafe, and hold back the economic and social life of a community. Closure notices are designed to be a swift and effective form of enforcement, encouraging residents, licensee landlords, and club owners to take responsibility for the effect the activity surrounding the premises is having on the community.

In certain circumstances, premises that are associated with anti-social behaviour such as noise nuisance, drug dealing, or disorder can be closed temporarily. These Closure Orders are backed by criminal penalties if they are breached by the owner, tenant, or licensee landlord of the premises.

New and updated powers are provided by recent legislation to the police and local authorities to close down premises that are associated with noise, disorder, or drug taking and dealing:

- Part 6, section 40 of the Anti-Social Behaviour Act 2003 gives local authorities and authorized Environmental Health Officers the power to close noisy licensed premises for a period of twenty-four hours.
- Sections 161 to 170 of the Licensing Act 2003 extend the existing powers of the police to instantly close, for up to twenty-four hours, licensed premises that are associated with disorder or causing noise nuisance; or to apply to the magistrates' court to close all licensed premises within a geographical area in anticipation of disorder. These extended powers are now available as the Licensing Act 2003 superseded sections 179a to 179k of the Licensing Act 1964.

Scenario—Closure of premises

A flat situated above takeaway premises was being used for the supply of Class A drugs. It was the centre for serious nuisance and disorder, and was putting people off entering the area. Traders in the town were complaining of reduced trade, and in general it was affecting the image of the locality badly. Using the partnership approach, the local police, the borough council, the social landlord who owned the flat, and the local press planned a response. A test purchase took place at the premises to secure evidence that the illegal supply of Class A drugs was taking place. Subsequently, a warrant was executed at the premises, which resulted in the seizure of illegal drugs and several arrests. A Closure Order was served on the tenant, who was evicted and referred for treatment for use of illegal drugs.

4.5 **Nuisance Neighbours**

The behaviour of nuisance neighbours can have a dramatic effect upon individuals within communities as well as blighting communities themselves. There have been many examples cited in the media, highlighting how just a few families can intimidate and harass people. The police practitioner, when he or she comes into contact with this type of problem, should understand the trauma that this type of behaviour can cause to victims and act swiftly to prevent an escalation of events. Consequently, victims who are witnesses should be regarded as vulnerable individuals, and should be protected and dealt with as such.

4.5.1 **What constitutes nuisance?**

Nuisance neighbours can be extremely detrimental to the well-being of local residents and can attract increased levels of crime in the immediate area. Members of the local community can feel intimidated and threatened, and be disturbed by persistent noise and serious disorder. Nuisance neighbours may also dump litter and waste into neighbouring gardens, and leave evidence of drug misuse and other dangerous items lying around.

For example, a person living in a flat may argue that loud music is a particular nuisance for them, whilst for the elderly it may be the noise of children. However, the Environmental Protection Act 1990 (Home Office 1990b) classes several types of behaviour as statutory nuisances. These include:

- noise or vibration
- smoke, fumes, or gases from any premises
- dust, steam, or smells from business premises
- accumulation or deposits of rubbish
- animals kept in unhygienic or unsafe conditions.

However, for these to constitute a statutory nuisance there must be present a health risk or a public nuisance, for example, a neighbour regularly burning rubbish or leaving rubbish in the garden which encourages vermin. Some of these nuisances are examined in more detail below.

4.5.2 **Noise nuisance**

Daytime domestic noise

There is no particular guidance on acceptable levels for domestic daytime noise; each case should be considered on its own merits.

Section 79(1) states that, for the purposes of the Environmental Protection Act 1990, a statutory nuisance includes:

- noise emitted from premises so as to be prejudicial to health or a nuisance
- noise that is prejudicial to health or a nuisance and which is emitted from or caused by a vehicle, machinery, or equipment in a street [or in Scotland, road].

Section 79 places a duty on local authorities to carry out inspections from time to time in order to detect cases of statutory nuisance. Furthermore, where the local authority receives a complaint in relation to statutory nuisance, there is a duty to take such steps as are reasonably practicable to investigate the complaint. Such matters are dealt with under section 80 of this Act.

Animal noise

Individuals concerned about noise or other nuisance caused by animals should at first be encouraged to talk to the person responsible and explain the problem.

They may find that they can resolve the problem amicably. If the direct approach does not succeed, mediation can be effective.

The Royal Society for the Prevention of Cruelty to Animals (RSPCA) is a useful partner in dealing with animal-related problems. Its staff can advise on the animal's well-being and whether the accommodation is suitable. The local authority may also have an animal welfare officer.

An environmental health officer can use Fixed Penalty Notices (FPNs) and noise abatement notices to stop a noise that is causing a statutory nuisance.

All landlords, whether social or private, have powers to take action against tenants who are breaching their tenancy agreement by causing nuisance to neighbours, including by dogs that are not kept under proper control. This may include injunctions, which can be highly effective preventive measures to reduce the nuisance caused.

Pet owners have a responsibility to ensure that they clean up after their animals. A combination of education about the harm that dog fouling can cause to the community, and enforcement, including penalty notices, that makes it clear that certain behaviour is unacceptable, is essential in tackling the problem.

Dealing with Noise

Individuals concerned about noise or other nuisance should at first be encouraged to talk to the person responsible and explain the problem. They may find that they can resolve the problem amicably. If the direct approach does not succeed, mediation, where an independent third party will listen to the views of both parties and help them reach agreement, can be effective. Environmental improvements, such as carpets or slow-closing doors, can also be useful to resolve a dispute. Resolving problems in this way can avoid the escalation of situations.

When informal action is not possible or fails, formal action should be taken to end the disruption caused to the individual and his or her family. There is a package of measures which local authorities, both in their strategic role as crime and disorder partners, and in their role as landlords, can use to tackle neighbour nuisance problems, including noise nuisance.

Local authorities have a duty to deal with any noise which they consider to be a 'statutory nuisance'. Fixed Penalty Notices (FPNs) and noise abatement notices can be used to stop a noise that is causing a statutory nuisance. Where noise does not stop, the local authority may itself put a stop to the nuisance and recover the costs. This includes the power to seize and remove any equipment that is being or has been used in the emission of the noise in question.

All landlords, whether social or private, have powers to take action against tenants who are breaching their tenancy agreement, including taking injunction or possession proceedings. Acceptable behaviour agreements or contracts can also be effective in setting out the standards of behaviour that an individual causing nuisance should maintain.

Whilst ASBOs would not normally be the first recourse in cases where noise nuisance is the main problem, they are an effective way of tackling more serious anti-social behaviour, which may include noise nuisance. Circumstances where their use may be appropriate would include dealing with, for example, families whose anti-social behaviour, when challenged, leads to verbal abuse, threats, or graffiti, or where noise nuisance is part of a pattern of unruly behaviour by tenants or owner-occupiers which intimidates others.

4.5.3 **Vehicles**

Inappropriate use of vehicles can be intimidating and dangerous so it is important that the community is protected from such activity. Driving a vehicle off-road without authority is an offence under section 34 of the Road Traffic Act 1988 (Home Office 1988) (as amended by Schedule 7 to the Countryside and Rights of Way Act 2000 (Home Office 2000a)) and there is a range of penalties available, including the power to confiscate off-road bikes in the Police Reform Act 2002.

The courts have the power to disqualify from driving anyone convicted of any offence. This is a very appropriate penalty in cases of vehicle-related nuisance. The police, Crown Prosecution Service, and other agencies have a role in recommending this penalty to the court.

Agreements and warnings can also be used to ensure that those engaged in vehicle-related nuisance appreciate the impact on local residents. Where the perpetrators are young people it may be possible to construct appropriate diversionary or training activities such as vehicle maintenance. Environmental improvements such as bollards, gates, and CCTV can also stop inappropriate use of vehicles within a residential area. All such schemes should be supported with a clear message that the anti-social behaviour must be stopped and will be subject to further enforcement action if it continues.

Anti-social behaviour orders or injunctions can also be used to stop inappropriate use of vehicles and protect the community. These have been successfully used against perpetrators engaged in joyriding, alongside criminal prosecution, and to prohibit persistent car thieves from entering car parks.

In addition the power to disperse groups can be used in an area where there has been persistent anti-social behaviour, to prevent gangs from meeting to engage in anti-social driving.

4.5.4 **Power to seize vehicles**

In addition to any other existing powers the police practitioner has to deal with inappropriate use of a vehicle on the road, there is a specific power available that can be utilized to deal with anti-social use of vehicles. Section 59 of the Police Reform Act 2002 states that where a constable has reasonable grounds for believing that a motor vehicle is being used on any occasion in a manner which

(a) contravenes section 3 or 34 of the Road Traffic Act 1988 (careless and incon-
    siderate driving and prohibition of off-road driving), and
(b) is causing, or is likely to cause, alarm, distress or annoyance to members of
    the public,

he shall have the powers set out in subsection (3).

KEY POINT—POWERS LISTED IN SECTION 59(3)

(1) Power to order the person driving the vehicle to stop if it is moving.
(2) Power to seize and remove the vehicle.
(3) Power to enter any premises on which he has reasonable grounds for
    believing the vehicle to be for the purposes of exercising a power outlined in
    (a) and (b) above.
(4) Power to use reasonable force if necessary.

However, a vehicle cannot be seized under section 59 unless the officer has
warned the person that if the use continues or if it is repeated the vehicle will
be seized, and it appears to the officer that this has been the case. Whilst a warning would normally be issued, there are occasions when a warning is not
required.

**KEY POINT—SEIZURE WHERE A WARNING IS NOT
REQUIRED**

(1) Where the circumstances make it impractical to give a warning.
(2) Where a warning has already been given on that occasion in respect of that
    vehicle, or of another vehicle used by that person or any other persons.
(3) The officer has reasonable grounds for believing that such a warning has
    been given on that occasion otherwise than by him/her.
(4) There are reasonable grounds for believing that the person who is using the
    vehicle on that occasion is a person to whom a warning has been given
    (whether or not by that officer or in respect the same vehicle or the same or
    similar use) on a previous occasion in the previous twelve months.

4.5.5 Abandoned vehicles

Local authorities have a statutory duty to remove abandoned vehicles from the
streets and the police practitioner should always regard them as their first point
of contact. Abandoned vehicles which the local authority considers to have some
value can be removed immediately and the registered owner is given seven days
to respond before their car may be destroyed. For vehicles which the local authority considers to have no value, there has to be a twenty-four-hour notice period
before the car can be removed. Vehicles abandoned on private land are served

with a fifteen-day notice. Local authorities also have the power to recover the costs of removal, storage, and disposal from the person responsible for abandoning the vehicle. The full offence which gives rise to the power to remove the abandoned vehicle can be seen in the box below.

KEY POINT—POWER FOR LOCAL AUTHORITIES TO REMOVE VEHICLES

Section 2 of the Refuse Disposal (Amenity) Act 1978 (Home Office 1978) states:

Any person who without lawful authority—

(a) abandons on any land in the open air, or on any land forming part of a highway, a motor vehicle or anything which formed part of a motor vehicle and was removed from it in the course of dismantling the vehicle on the land; or

(b) abandons on any such land anything other than a motor vehicle, being a thing which he has brought to the land for the purpose of abandoning it there, shall be guilty of an offence.

4.6 Racially Aggravated Behaviour

Racist violence and harassment do more than just injure the victim or damage property. They affect the whole family and can generate a climate of fear across the community that has suffered attacks. They also undermine the standards of decency that underpin the wider community. For the purposes of this work a racist incident is 'any incident which is perceived to be racist by the victim or any other person'.

The Crime and Disorder Act 1998 revisited the issue of racially aggravated crime and behaviour, and tried to address some of the issues raised by the Stephen Lawrence inquiry. Consequently sections 28 to 32 of the Crime and Disorder Act 1998 did not create new offences but took existing offences and indicated circumstances in which those offences would be considered to be aggravated offences. The relevant offences are listed in the box below.

KEY POINT—OFFENCES AFFECTED BY SECTIONS 28 AND 32 OF THE CRIME AND DISORDER ACT 1998

Offence	Legislation
Wounding or grievous bodily harm	s 20, Offences Against the Person Act 1861
Causing actual bodily harm	s 47, Offences Against the Person Act 1861

Common assault	s 39, Criminal Justice Act 1988
Criminal damage	s 1(1), Criminal Damage Act 1971
Causing fear or provocation of violence	s 4, Public Order Act 1986
Intentional harassment or alarm/distress	s 4A, Public Order Act 1986
Causing harassment, alarm, or distress	s 5, Public Order Act 1986
Harassment	s 2, Protection from Harassment Act 1997
Putting in fear of violence	s 4, Protection from Harassment Act 1997

However, the Anti-Terrorism, Crime and Security Act 2001 (Home Office 2001b) amended the Crime and Disorder Act 1998, extending the definition of what are considered 'racially aggravated' offences to cover 'racially or religiously aggravated offences'.

In order for the police practitioner to prove these offences there has to be proof of the relevant offence, for example criminal damage, as well as further proof of the aggravating circumstances.

KEY POINT—DEFINITION OF RACIAL GROUP

A racial group is a group of persons defined by reference to race, colour, nationality (including citizenship), or ethnic or national origin.

Scenario—Tackling racially motivated offences

An all-purpose shop was situated in the middle of a socially deprived housing estate which had a predominantly white population. It was the only shop on the estate and was owned by an Asian family. Customers who attended the shop were abused by a gang of local youths who eventually forced them to shop elsewhere. The Asian shopkeeper, who did not speak English very well, was a repeat victim of theft and was constantly abused and assaulted. He was in fear of the offenders but was afraid to report all the instances to the police.

The local crime and disorder reduction partnership addressed the problem. Working together they decided upon the following approach:

(1) Targeting of known offenders, with a zero tolerance approach to racially aggravated offences.
(2) High visibility patrols in the area by police officers and wardens.

(3) Anti-Social Behaviour Orders for known offenders.

(4) Targeting the owners of vulnerable property with a view to improving their methods of crime prevention.

(5) Diversionary tactics for youth in the area in consultation with the local youth club.

(6) Use of interpreters to ensure that complainants could really be understood.

(7) Use of the media to highlight the problem and to publish the success of prosecutions and Anti-Social Behaviour Orders.

The consequences of this action were the regeneration of the shop at the heart of the community, with customers not afraid to visit the shop, and a decrease in crimes reported.

4.6.1 Hate crimes

We have seen how communities within England and Wales consist of many diverse groups and nationalities. This includes not just race, but also different sexual orientations. Hate crimes are directed against people because of some aspect of who they are, most typically because they are from an ethnic minority or visible religious minority, or because of their sexuality. Hate crime covers a wide range of behaviour, for example verbal abuse, racist or homophobic graffiti or physical assault. A crime can be classed as a hate crime if the victim or witness see it as being so.

The ACPO Guide to 'Identifying and Combating Hate Crime' was published in 2000. It defines hate crime as 'any crime where the perpetrator's prejudice against any identifiable group of people is a factor in determining who is victimised'. Therefore, a victim of hate crime does not have to be a member of a minority or someone who is generally considered to be 'vulnerable'. Effectively anyone can be the victim of a hate crime incident.

The McPherson Report defined a racist incident is 'any incident which is perceived to be racist by the victim or any other person'. The recording of racist incidents is therefore now based on the perception by any person that the incident is racist. 'Racist' does not simply relate to colour, but also to race, nationality, ethnic, religious or national origins.

Similarly, a homophobic incident is 'any incident which is perceived to be homophobic by the victim or any other person'. 'Homophobic' does not only relate to lesbian women, gay men, bisexuals, transgender or transsexual people, but to any person perceived to be so by the perpetrator. As with racist incidents, the recording of homophobic incidents is based on the perception by any person that the incident is homophobic. The person making the report does not need to have any evidence to show that the incident was racist or homophobic. If any person believes that the incident was so motivated, it must be recorded as such.

National research has shown that under reporting remains a common feature of all hate crimes as victims may be reluctant to report the incident to the police. It has also been identified that many victims have suffered repeated problems before they contact the police.

The impact of a hate crime can be more traumatic on the victim due to the realization that a normally impersonal crime is actually a personal attack. As well as affecting the individual, hate crime has been described by the ACPO Guide as a 'powerful poison to society' as it 'breeds suspicion, mistrust, alienation and fear'. In this present climate of heightened tension following the recent terrorist attacks, racists frequently exploit periods of raised anxiety and therefore there needs to be a heightened state of alert for hate crime with prompt action against racial harassment and strong support and reassurance for victims.

4.7 **Crime within Communities**

All countries collect detailed crime statistics for comparison and policy-making purposes. In recent years there has been a realization that crime is distributed unequally even across small areas and amongst people inside small areas with similar levels of crime. Combining the crime statistics from a quite small area with little crime with those from a larger, busier area that has a high crime rate to produce a document that purports to represent crime statistics for the combined population, really makes little sense. The police practitioner engaged in crime and disorder reduction activities must be aware of some of these problems if he or she is to carry out his or her role effectively. However, there are some apparently basic yet important points that need to be clarified first. What do we understand by the term 'crime'? Where do the statistics we use in everyday life come from, and how reliable are they? Do all people who are victims of crime or witness a crime report it? If not, why not? By addressing these questions we can start to understand that the whole idea of crime and statistics is not as straightforward as it first seems. This is especially so if we believe that crime statistics are the bedrock of all that is done in the name of reducing crime and disorder. The question of what we mean by 'crime' is examined in **4.7.1** below; the larger questions of statistics and the reporting (or non-reporting) of crime are addressed at **4.8** to **4.10**.

4.7.1 **What do we mean by crime?**

If you are asked the above question, the chances are that you will include such things as burglary, theft, use of illegal drugs, assault, robbery, and so on. These are all crimes as defined by Acts of Parliament. Therefore one definition of what constitutes a crime is a violation of the criminal law. Breaking the criminal law makes someone a criminal; and if caught, the criminal justice system applies the available legal sanctions against that person. Most people have committed criminal acts and few individuals can truly say they have never broken any laws. Under-age drinking in designated public places causes anti-social behaviour on many occasions, but in our society, few people actually wait until they are the legal age to drink for their first taste of alcohol.

Scenario—What people may or may not consider crimes

(1) Finding money in the street and keeping it rather than handing it in.
(2) Driving faster than the legal speed limit on a motorway.
(3) Taking a pen or stationery home from work.
(4) Being given too much money in change at a shop and keeping it rather than handing it back.

The answer is that all of the above are crimes in the real sense. However, most people would not consider the activities as being remotely criminal.

4.8 Sources of Criminal Statistics

There are in general three main sources of criminal statistics that are used by the Home Office and those involved in the production of crime and disorder reduction plans and policies. These are:

- official statistics
- victimization studies
- self-report studies.

Each source has its disadvantages and advantages.

4.8.1 Official crime statistics

The key publication for crime figures for England and Wales is called *Criminal Statistics*, the annual compilation of data produced by the Home Office (2004d). This is made up of information from police and court records. In the main, the focus for these crime figures revolves around what is known as notifiable offences. This does not mean all criminal offences, as almost all the more minor, summary offences are excluded (even though the police may record them for their own investigations). The significance of the term 'notifiable' is that all these offences are notified to the Home Office, and they are collectively known as 'recorded crime'.

The crime recording process is governed by three key stages, discussed below.

Reporting a crime

Someone reports to the police that a crime has been committed, or the police observe or discover a crime. In these cases the police should register a crime-related incident, and then decide whether to record it as a crime. From April 2002, the police comply with the National Crime Recording Standard in making this decision, although generally the police would record these reports of crime if they amount to a 'notifiable' offence and there is no credible evidence to the contrary.

Recording a crime

The police decide to record the report of a crime. They now need to determine how many crimes to record and what their offence types are. The Home Office issues rules to police forces on the counting and classification of crime. These Counting Rules for Recorded Crime are mostly straightforward, as most crimes are counted as 'one crime per victim' and the offence committed is obvious (e.g., a domestic burglary). However, they also cover special situations where more than one offence has taken place, maybe on several occasions over a period of time, or there is more than one offender or victim.

Detecting a crime

Once a crime is recorded and investigated, and evidence is collected to link the crime to a suspect, it can be detected according to criteria contained in Detections Guidance within the Home Office counting rules.

In many cases, someone is charged or cautioned, or the court has taken the offence into consideration (TIC). The Detections Guidance covers these detection methods, as well as certain others where the police take no further action. The guidance covering these latter methods is stringent, relying on a sufficient amount of evidence that, if given in court, would be likely to result in a conviction, and in most cases approval by a senior officer.

4.8.2 Victimization studies

These studies operate at several different levels, including nationally and, particularly in the case of crime and disorder reduction partnerships, at a local level.

National surveys

The most famous of these types of survey is the British Crime Survey, which began in 1982. For this survey, respondents are asked to give details of crimes in which they have been a victim in the previous twelve months. The data collected provide a database on crime-related topics for policy-makers, and include information on drug abuse, racially motivated crime, and the fear of crime. One of the main problems with this type of survey is that it can tend to reduce crime and its experience to a level that glosses over some of the significant differences in risk of victimization.

Local surveys

Local surveys had been carried out for a number of years prior to the introduction of the Crime and Disorder Act 1998 in response to some of the perceived problems with national surveys. By focusing in on particular localities, these surveys attempt to pinpoint the higher levels of crime and associated fear of crime in socially deprived areas, and the disproportionate level of fear of crime experienced by some vulnerable groups.

All crime and disorder reduction partnerships now engage in local surveys in order to conduct their crime audit. This in turn informs their strategic plan for the delivery of their policies.

Self-report studies

Self-report studies were first used in the USA during the 1940s, and more recently they have been used to inform international comparisons on criminal activity. These studies involve a researcher asking ordinary members of the public to report their own criminal acts. One of the major drawbacks from the use of these types of studies is that they tend to focus on what might be considered trivial or misdemeanour incidents, not on the more serious crimes committed within a community. However, for the purposes of dealing with anti-social behaviour activities this information could be very important indeed.

Summary

Whilst all these methods tell us something individually about crime and criminal activity, even when used together they exhibit some problems. Below is a summary of their strengths and weaknesses.

KEY POINT—RESEARCH STRENGTHS AND WEAKNESS		
Source	*Strengths*	*Weaknesses*
Official statistics	(1) Easy to obtain from official sources	(1) There is the problem of the 'hidden figure' of crime
	(2) Quite detailed information about crimes	(2) Not all crimes are reported
	(3) Can be used to study trends of crime over a period of time	
Victimization studies	(1) May help us discover more about the 'dark figure' of crime	(1) People may not be supplying accurate information
	(2) Can give an insight into crimes rarely reported to the police, e.g. incest	(2) A very time-consuming and expensive method
	(3) Can help with understanding fear of crime	

| Self-report studies | (1) Directly from the person who has committed the offence | (1) Some people may exaggerate their crimes, etc. |
| | (2) Can be used to confirm other data from other sources | (2) People may not own up to really serious offences |

4.9 **Why People Don't Report Crime and Disorder**

The police become aware of crime in a number of different ways. Whilst their presence on the street is likely to deter criminal acts, the police actually detect relatively few crimes as they are being carried out by the perpetrators. Consequently, the police rely on the public not only to report offences to them but also to act as witnesses and provide information that will ultimately lead to detection.

However, many crimes will not be reported to the police. McLaughlin and Muncie (2001) suggested the following explanations as to why this should be:

- People may not be aware that a crime has occurred (e.g., fraud).
- The victim may be powerless and have no one to report it to (e.g., child abuse).
- There may appear at first glance to be no victim (e.g., prostitution).
- The victim of the crime may distrust the police and may fear the police will not take the incidents seriously (e.g., sexual violence against same-gender victim).
- The victim may not believe that the police will protect him or her against further criminal episodes (e.g., racial victimization).

Of course one of the reasons why it is important for the police to encourage people to report crime is that it gives a clearer picture of what is happening in their crime reduction partnership area. This means appropriate responses can be formulated in an effort to reduce these occurrences. Therefore it is in the interests of the police and the crime and disorder reduction partnerships to encourage, wherever possible, the reporting of all crimes. It is clear that there is a gap between official figures and the number of crimes actually committed. This gap is called the 'dark figure' of crime.

4.9.1 **The hidden figure of crime**

The 'dark figure' represents those crimes which have not been reported to or recorded by the police and therefore do not appear in the official statistics. Estimates of the amount of hidden crime vary across different offences. Shoplifting and criminal damage, for example, are likely to have a substantial dark figure, and trafficking in illegal drugs and fraud offences probably contain the highest figure. However, it appears that the police come to know about a very high proportion of murders and other homicides. The key point for the police practitioner engaged in crime and disorder reduction activities is this. Many of the policies designed to solve crime problems are solely based upon what is known about crime and the criminal. However, there is a large amount of knowledge in the same area that does not find its way into official decision-making policies. We should therefore not be surprised if sometimes these policies appear not to work.

4.9.2 Intimidation or harassment

One reason why a crime may not be reported to the police is not included in McLaughlin and Muncie's list (see above). This is intimidation or harassment of the victim(s).

Intimidation or harassment is a personalized form of anti-social behaviour, specifically aimed at particular individuals. The nature of this anti-social behaviour means that victims of intimidation and harassment are often living or working in close proximity to their tormentors. Support is essential to turn these victims into witnesses. Intimidation and harassment may also be triggered by an individual taking a stand and giving evidence; agencies must provide adequate and appropriate protection and support for all witnesses.

Enforcement action must be immediate to protect those who are being harassed or intimidated. This may be through an injunction or an interim ASBO, which may be obtained without notice to the defendant and can provide immediate relief and raise confidence in the ability of local agencies to tackle this sort of anti-social behaviour.

ASBOs and injunctions are available to protect people from behaviour causing harassment, alarm, or distress. An order on conviction may be appropriate where someone has been convicted in court for an offence related to their intimidation or harassment of another person. Where action is taken in the county court an ASBO can be made against a party to the main proceedings or another adult whose conduct is material to the proceedings.

Conditions of the order may include a ban from the area where the victims live, or a specific ban on approaching or communicating with the victims. Because these court orders are made in civil proceedings, hearsay evidence can be used to protect victims who are too scared to come to court.

Injunctions may be made under the Housing Act 1996 (Home Office 1996b) where the harassment or intimidation is housing-related, or under section 222 of the Local Government Act 1972 (Home Office 1972) which enables local authorities to take court action to promote or protect the interests of the inhabitants of their area.

Intimidation or harassment may also constitute a criminal offence under the Protection from Harassment Act 1997 (Home Office 1997c). A restraining order may be made in addition to the conviction, or an injunction obtained.

Eviction of the perpetrator is another option to move individuals away from those whom they are intimidating or harassing. However, it is important that this is accompanied by other action, such as an injunction, to ensure that the behaviour does not reoccur in a new area, or that the perpetrator does not return to the area to intimidate those who assisted the eviction action.

4.10 **Fear of Crime**

Fear of crime refers to a rational or irrational state of alarm or anxiety engendered by the belief that one is in danger of being the victim of crime (McLaughlin and Muncie 2001).

Fear of crime is something that may affect people from all walks of life (which makes it different from actual crime, which tends to be concentrated on particular areas or victims and committed by a small number of offenders) at any stage of their lives. Whether it's a female who feels nervous about walking home, parents who feel anxious about sending their child up the road to buy sweets, or a shopkeeper who tenses up every time a customer enters his shop, if we let it, fear of crime can have a devastating effect on our quality of life.

Fear of crime encourages a physical and psychological withdrawal from the community, which weakens the informal social controls necessary for a community to look after itself. Similarly, encouraging people into a town centre at night might create more opportunities for crime, so crime and disorder reduction partnerships need to think carefully when considering how to reduce fear of crime.

KEY POINT—FEAR OF CRIME AND QUALITY OF LIFE

31 per cent of respondents to British Crime Survey interviews conducted in the 2001/02 financial year said that fear of crime had a moderate impact on their quality of life; with a further 6 per cent saying that their quality of life was greatly affected by it. Yet the same survey put the statistical probability of becoming a victim of violent crime at just 4 per cent.

Fear of crime can increase for a number of reasons. These include:

- direct experience
- secondary knowledge from friends and family
- police officers and politicians who want to increase awareness of criminal activity
- private security firms looking for business
- news media over-reporting violent and sexual crimes.

However, attempts to tackle the fear of crime may lead to some unexpected results.

Scenario—Lighting and its impact upon fear of crime

People who lived in a street with very poor lighting were consulted regarding their fear of crime. The lighting system was identified as being one of the causes of fear of crime, so the local authority upgraded it. Subsequently, there was a sharp increase in the number of thefts from vehicles in the area, which again led to an increase in the fear of local residents becoming victims of crime.

One of the main problems when tackling fear of crime is the lack of good communication between partnerships and the community. Many partnerships have carried out excellent initiatives which have helped reduce crime but have failed to address people's perceptions of crime. Some suggestions for spreading good news and trying to reduce fear of crime are given below:

- Engage the local newspapers and try to get them on side by encouraging them to report good news stories in a prominent position.
- Send out leaflets to affected areas giving examples of the initiatives that the local crime and disorder reduction partnership have implemented to reduce crime and disorder and improve the local environment.
- Use every opportunity to provide the community with the names, numbers, and contact details of those officers (council, police, and others) whom members of the community can contact to discuss a particular problem.
- Arrange for a series of face-to-face talks at a variety of social and communal events, using not only community police officers but also other representatives of the partnership.
- Find out what different interest, identity, and geographical groups are already running in the area, and whom you can contact to get an invitation to address them. Parish councils, schools, and voluntary/community groups, etc. are always keen for interesting speakers to come along to their meetings.

4.11 Summing Up

4.11.1 Begging and street drinking

This activity can intimidate and threaten individuals within city and town centres. It often takes place near cashpoint machines and is sometimes linked to aggressive begging, where an individual feels threatened and gives money to the person begging in order to get away from them. There are three levels of approach that should be attempted: support, publicity, and enforcement. Enforcement can be through a number of Acts, such as the Vagrancy Act 1824 and the Highways Act 1980.

4.11.2 **Alcohol-related disorder**

Alcohol-related disorder is usually caused by individuals who have been drinking heavily and who may cause disorder, nuisance, and criminal offences. This occurs most often at closing time, when large numbers of people spill out from clubs and pubs at the same time. The Licensing Act 2003 strengthens existing powers by introducing powers to close disorderly venues for up to twenty-four hours, powers to review licences when problems arise, and also powers to introduce Alcohol Disorder Zones.

4.11.3 **Drugs**

The use of illegal drugs is a very serious problem within communities in this country, and can be a causal factor in increased levels of crime and disorder. In particular the introduction of Class A drugs into the community can be devastating. The Anti-Social Behaviour Act 2003 has introduced a new range of powers to close premises which are being used for the sale of such illegal drugs.

4.11.4 **Nuisance neighbours**

Nuisance neighbours can have a profound effect upon the quality of life of others. Nuisances can include loud music, animal noise, shouting, motor vehicles, and house and car alarms. The Environmental Protection Act 1990 classes statutory nuisances for which action can be taken, whilst local authorities have provisions to deal with many common nuisances such as animal noise.

4.11.5 **Sources of criminal statistics**

There are in general three sources of criminal statistics that are used to inform crime and disorder reduction policies. These are the official statistics produced by the Home Office, victimization studies, and self-report studies. All of these sources have strengths and weaknesses, and tell us something about what is happening regarding crime in the community. However, there is a large amount of crime that occurs that we do not know about. This is called the 'dark figure' of crime.

4.11.6 **Why people don't report crime**

Not all crime is reported to the police or other agencies engaged in crime and disorder reduction. There are thought to be several main reasons for this: people may not be aware that a crime has occurred; the victim may be powerless and cannot report it; there may appear to be no victim; or perhaps the victim does not trust the police or has no faith in the criminal justice system.

4.11.7 Fear of crime

Fear of crime is a rational or irrational state of anxiety brought about by the belief that one is in danger of being a victim of crime. It can affect people from all walks of life and can have a devastating effect on the quality of life for individuals. It comes from several sources such as direct experience, information from others about crimes committed against them, the media, and private security firms trying to obtain business. Such fear can be reduced through good communication practices between crime and disorder reduction partners and by ensuring that positive messages about partnership successes are disseminated throughout the community.

4.11.8 Local application

(1) Consider alcohol-related disorder in your area. How many ways can you think of to tackle the problem?
(2) How would you go about obtaining a closure notice for premises where you know Class A drugs are being sold?
(3) Can you identify at least three types of nuisance that the police deal with in your area?
(4) What sources of criminal statistics does your crime and disorder reduction partnership rely on?
(5) How would you try to reduce fear of crime within your local community?

4.11.9 Useful websites

http://www.homeoffice.gov.uk/publications/science-research-statistics/
research-statistics/crime-research/hosb1211/hosb1211?view=Binary
http://library.npia.police.uk/docs/homeoffice/PremisesClosureNov08-01
56.pdf

5

Theory into Practice

5.1 **Introduction**

Police practitioners perform a diverse array of functions, but these tend to be connected to each other in many respects, and many elements of police work have a preventative or reduction function built into them. Sometimes, there arises a debate between the police function of crime prevention and that of law enforcement, with supporters of the various camps putting forward reasons for more resources in one at the expense of the other. However, even criminal investigation work has elements of prevention or reduction, and these must surely lie at the heart of the partnership approach to policing in this country.

Another area where people make distinctions is between the prevention of crime and the maintenance of order. Legally, there is no sharp distinction between crime and disorderliness given the wide expanse of the law in this country. There is also quite a substantial amount of research to support the view that policing disorder can in fact have an impact in the area of crime prevention, and especially upon people's perceptions of fear of crime (see Wilson and Kelling 1982; Kelling and Cole 1996 for this point). Therefore, when considering reduction the police practitioner should realize that it influences not only crimes against people and property, but all those forms of disorder that the police have to deal with.

5.2 **What is Meant by Crime and Disorder Reduction?**

The terms crime prevention, crime reduction, and community safety are often used interchangeably to describe methods or initiatives designed to impact upon levels of crime and disorder. Whilst these interchangeable terms may seem slightly confusing to the police practitioner, a very useful definition of crime reduction has been provided by Ekblom (1992), as shown in the box below.

KEY POINT—CRIME REDUCTION

'Crime reduction is closely related to prevention and can be characterised by the same framework. But it is a wider concept, encompassing both the *future* orientation of prevention, and action in the *present* to frustrate specific crimes as they happen—for example through police operations. It involves reducing the likelihood and seriousness of criminal and disorderly events by intervention in their causes, or by intervening directly in the events themselves. The focus is thus on crime and the causes of crime.'

Ekblom (1992)

What this quote illustrates for police practitioners is the move away from short-term, reactive policies towards a more scientific approach. The new approach involves the prediction of crime and disorder, and implementing prevention of the same through the use of partnerships.

5.3 **Three Levels of Intervention**

Having explained that these interventions are aimed at frustrating future or present instances of crime and disorder, there appear to be three levels at which attempts are made to influence both the behaviour of the offender and the situation where the crime and disorder event takes place. This three-level approach drew its inspiration from medicine and the natural sciences, and was first introduced in the mid-1970s by Brantingham and Faust (1976).

The approach revolves around the nature of the relationship between the intended audience and the form of prevention on offer. So primary prevention is aimed at the general population with no preconceived assumptions about their propensity to commit crime and disorder; secondary prevention, on the other hand, assumes that the audience is at risk in some way or other; while tertiary prevention focuses on reducing the criminality of people who are already assumed to be criminals and also preventing victims of crime becoming repeat victims. This approach is illustrated in Figure 5.1.

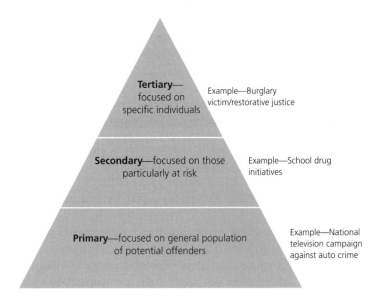

Figure 5.1 Three levels of crime and disorder reduction

5.3.1 **Primary level**

Within this approach, energies are directed towards preventing the onset of criminality, and known risk factors associated with childhood anti-social behaviour have been identified. These include poverty and poor housing, poor parenting, association with delinquent peers, and poor school attendance.

This approach tends to focus on the general population of potential offenders. Children who are exposed to multiple risks are more likely to become serious or persistent offenders. This approach is also visible in the school curriculum, which contains elements such as 'good citizenship'.

5.3.2 **Secondary level**

This approach focuses on those particularly at risk of offending or victimization. These individuals or groups have been identified because of some predispositional factor. This could be their age group, where they live, their lifestyle, their socio-economic circumstances, or some other predictor of risk. As a consequence the target audience is deemed to be more prone to criminality and therefore worthy of attention. An example of this type of approach can be seen in school education initiatives about the use of illegal drugs and other substances.

5.3.3 **Tertiary level**

This level attempts to deal with those already convicted or victimized, through crime prevention initiatives such as 'homesafe' schemes, which target burglary victims' homes to discourage repeat offences, through to restorative justice. Restorative justice techniques aim to bring together offender and victim in order to encourage the offender to make restoration of loss, either in the material or emotional sense, to the victim.

5.4 **Types of Crime Prevention Measures**

Having discussed the differing levels of intervention available to the police practitioner when attempting to influence communities in terms of crime and disorder reduction, he or she should also be aware of the two distinctive types of crime prevention currently underpinning policies and strategies in this country.

The main distinction in terms of crime prevention measures is between 'social' and 'situational' methods. It must be acknowledged at the outset that not all crime and disorder prevention initiatives fit neatly into the two main types of method, and there are occasions when both styles are in operation together.

5.4.1 **Social crime prevention approach**

This approach towards preventing or reducing crime and disorder is carried out by targeting anti-social behaviour and those at risk as well as known offenders. It also includes programmes aimed at improving the opportunities of 'at risk' groups through community involvement. This approach tends to focus on the development of schemes, such as youth clubs and activity-based projects, to deter potential or actual offenders from future offending. Jon Bright (1991:64) believes this approach also has an impact on agencies attempting it: 'It aims to strengthen social agencies and community institutions in order to influence those groups that are most at risk of offending.'

Whilst other types of crime prevention may reduce crime and disorder which occurs as a result of situational factors, for example the nature of the physical environment, they may not be effective against other types of crime such as ongoing domestic violence and homicides, which occur as a result of personal and/or social factors. Measures to address situational factors can minimize the opportunities to commit such crimes and may improve perceptions of safety in the community, but they are unlikely to stop those who are strongly motivated to commit crime.

The best way to prevent repeat offenders from committing crimes is to stop them becoming criminals in the first place. The approach discussed in this section—social crime prevention—aims for this. It is based on an understanding that there are personal and social factors that make it more likely that someone will commit crimes (see box below), and that by addressing these an individual will more likely be turned away from criminality.

KEY POINT—FACTORS THAT MAKE IT MORE LIKELY SOMEONE WILL COMMIT CRIMES

- Family background
- Schooling
- Income and employment
- Alcohol and other drug use
- Peer relations
- Moral beliefs and other cultural influences.

Creating crime-resistant communities

A neighbourhood which has strong social bonds, where people take pride in their street and 'own' their public places, where the needs of all groups in the community are met, and where people regard the area as an attractive and safe place to live and work, is likely to have a low crime rate. These neighbourhoods have a cohesion, or organization and solidity, that means they pull together and are able to resist crime and disorder.

KEY POINT—COMMUNITY COHESION

The following may be considered useful in creating neighbourhoods that have strong bonds: youth clubs, football clubs, junior theatrical societies, use of community centres for all sorts of activities, etc. In fact any neighbourhood project which gets people to meet each other, to cooperate or work together, and to play together will encourage social bonding.

> A good example of this is the playgroup. Throughout the country, young parents meet once or twice a week for their pre-school children to play together. That is the main purpose. However, the effect is to encourage friendships between parents, set up informal babysitting networks, to give children peer groups and friends before they start formal schooling, and to transfer skills and information from experienced parents to new parents. Social bonds that begin in these meetings very often last for a person's life.

Police practitioners should be aware of how important cohesive communities are, and should encourage or even assist in this process. A good example of communities working together can be seen in the following scenario, which uses an example from Australia.

Scenario—An international case study: the Good Neighbourhood Program, Victoria, Australia

The objective of the Good Neighbourhood Program (GNP) is to prevent and reduce crime through social and community development. The principle behind this approach is that the more social networks operate in a community, and the denser and more widespread these networks are, the less likely residents are to tolerate anti-social behaviour and criminal behaviour, or to engage in such behaviour. The GNP was launched in 1988 by the Victorian State Government, and provided funding to councils to set up local crime prevention committees. The state-wide framework for the GNP identified a number of crime priority areas:

- Activities for young people at risk.
- Education, training, and employment.
- Safety and security in the community.
- Tackling drug and alcohol abuse.
- Minimizing reoffending behaviour.
- Police–community relations.

The integrated development of social, recreational, and work-related skills was encouraged. Projects also encouraged contact between people of different ages, genders, and backgrounds. All projects were run within local government areas. The local council's function was to play a leadership and developmental role by managing and being accountable for the resources allocated to the projects, establishing and supporting the local GNP committee, providing opportunities for people/organizations to register interest in and participate in GNP activities, ensuring local networks, organizations, and people were made aware of the GNP, endorsing local GNP committee recommendations, and contributing to the resourcing of projects.

The neighbourhood was the focal point of the GNP, which sought to encourage development and cohesion at this level. Young people were a particular target, with their skills being used wherever possible (with pay, where this was available). The successful local committees had strong council involvement and enthusiastic coordinators. Support came from local councillors and mayors, the involvement of local police, and from the council. Further youth services coordinators and a clear focus on crime prevention were the characteristics of this type of successful local programme.

These types of programmes aim to encourage vital communities, which should include a representative mix of age, gender, and ethnicity. However, some of these groups may be more at risk of criminal behaviour than others.

5.4.2 Situational crime prevention approach

In general terms, so far as current partnerships in the community safety area are concerned, the main type of visible crime prevention strategies that are being implemented, and success claimed for, are those termed situational crime prevention. Many of these initiatives revolve around specific crimes such as burglary and car crime.

Whilst social crime prevention focuses on tackling the disposition to offend through improved welfare and educational programmes such as mentoring schemes, situational crime prevention pays attention to the opportunity to commit crime itself. It could be argued that in terms of cost, situational crime prevention is much easier to implement and can also give quicker results, making it easier to evaluate the success of the partnership.

A brief history of situational crime prevention

It is generally agreed that the situational approach to crime prevention was most fully developed by 'administrative criminologists' working at the Home Office Research Unit in the 1970s. Jock Young (1992) first coined the phrase to describe the dominant establishment approaches to understanding both crime and its control in Britain at this time. The term 'administrative' is used to capture the politically pragmatic and seemingly theory-limited perspective of such criminologists when compared with the previously dominant perspective of mainstream criminologists who were mainly concerned with the individual criminal and his/her reasons for committing crime. The latter were, according to their Home Office critics, obsessed with the search for the causes of criminality (often termed the aetiology of crime). In contrast, administrative criminology argues that the search for causes is futile, but the opportunities to commit crime can be controlled. The historical context behind the emergence of this new approach in the UK may be summarized as follows. Between the 1940s and the 1970s in the UK, as elsewhere, both criminologists and policy-makers tended to concentrate on dispositional rather than situational variables in their explanations of crime and in their strategies of prevention and control. This focus led to an emphasis on treating individual dispositions to crime rather than altering the situations that led to the crime being committed. Dispositional variables are those features associated with the character, intelligence, values, etc. of offenders that dispose them towards committing crimes. These theories imply that whether or not an individual commits a crime on a given occasion is largely determined by his or her personal characteristics or attributes—they seek to explain criminality rather than criminal acts.

Reaction to crisis

However, during the 1970s a crisis appeared to be revolving around the rising crime rate during a period of relative affluence. Crawford (1999) points to the fact that research findings began to suggest that the formal processes of criminal justice—through the detection, apprehension, prosecution, and sentencing of offenders—had only a limited effect in controlling crime. Further, the work of Hough and Mayhew (1983) revealed extensive non-reporting of crime, thus highlighting the fact that for most offenders and victims of crime, the formal criminal justice system was largely irrelevant. In response to these problems, Home Office criminologists and officials appeared broadly to agree that there was no evidence to show that deterrence through punishment would have any significant effect on the rising crime rate. Further, improvements in policing or increases in police resources would have no significant effect on the rate of crime. While crime prevention through social reform might be desirable, it was not a realistic possibility and there was little or no evidence that it had any measurable effect upon reducing crime, and treatment programmes that were geared to changing the criminal disposition of offenders were unproductive. Instead, the Home Office researchers looked to other pragmatic pieces of research for a possible answer to the problem of what was to be done to reduce or prevent crime.

In particular, inspiration was found in several areas, namely routine activity theory, rational choice theory, and crime prevention through environmental design (CPTED). It is these ideas of which the police practitioner should have a basic knowledge in order to understand and implement crime and disorder reduction initiatives effectively. They are examined in further detail at **5.4.3** to **5.4.5** below.

5.4.3 **Routine activity theory**

The idea behind routine activity theory (RAT) is that the amount and distribution of 'volume' crime, that is those direct-contact crimes in which one or more individuals attack the person or property of another, are closely related to three variables, namely motivated offenders, a suitable target, and the absence of a capable guardian. This comes about because of the routine practices of everyday life. Therefore, crimes are linked to normal behaviours such as work, school, transport, recreation, shopping, and so on. Recent changes in the routine activities of our lives have placed more people at particular places at particular times, which can increase their suitability as realistic targets of crime. Because of the increase in leisure time, for example, more people are likely to be away from their homes, reducing their activities as capable guardians of their property and thus opening up the possibility of greater opportunities for crime.

Another example is the recent increase in mobile phone use and the attendant increase in thefts of these items. Figure 5.2 illustrates the three component parts of the crime and disorder incident that RAT seeks to influence.

Routine activity theory focuses on changing day-to-day activities and practices that can frustrate potential offenders and stop victimization of easy targets. Critics of this approach argue that it tends to overlook the offender and cannot supply an answer as to why some people are more motivated to commit crime than others. However, this approach appears not to have any major criminological pretensions, and should be considered as a useful tool that produces practices to help the practitioner in reducing crime and disorder.

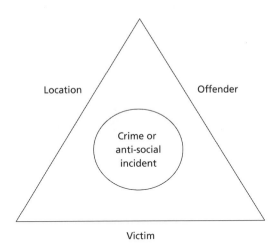

Figure 5.2 Component parts of a crime or anti-social event

VIVA

The RAT approach also considers the criminal event from the perspective of the property or person involved in the event. Suitability of target is seen as being characterized by four attributes, namely value, inertia, visibility, and accessibility (VIVA). These are factors that play a part in whether or not an offender will commit an offence. The following box illustrates this idea.

KEY POINT—VIVA

The four attributes of a suitable target:

(1) Value—calculated from the offender's perspective.
(2) Inertia—the physical aspects of the person or property that hinder or interrupt its suitability as a target.
(3) Visibility—marking out the person or property for attack.
(4) Accessibility—this increases the risk of attack.

CRAVED

Another acronym used to describe a suitable target is CRAVED. This relates to six problems the criminal has to solve. The criminal has to conceal the property, remove it from the owner, have it available, find it valuable, be able to enjoy it, and be able to dispose of it readily. Items such as money and small pieces of jewellery are very easily concealed about the person, whilst a commonly-used vehicle is easier to conceal than a unique one. Smaller items and things on wheels are the easiest types of property to steal. Further, items that are produced in great numbers and kept near a door are more likely to be stolen because they are available, whilst items have to be valued by the perpetrator. For the young, perhaps, popular music CDs would be popular and classical music perhaps not so popular. Further, items that a person may enjoy, such as tobacco, alcohol, clothes, etc., would be attractive targets, whilst the items stolen will in all probability need to be easily disposed of. The CRAVED model is useful in that it helps us to understand what types of items actually invite theft.

KEY POINT—CRAVED

C—concealable
R—removable
A—available
V—valuable
E—enjoyable
D—disposable

The above are considered by the motivated offender before committing an offence.

5.4.4 Rational choice theory

Rational choice theory is an understanding of the crime problem that is rooted in administrative criminology. This version of criminology was largely associated with work emanating from the Home Office during the early 1980s. Gilling (1997) argues that it constitutes neither a new nor a general explanation of crime since elements of attributing the ability to make choices and decisions to criminals and criminal behaviour are present in a range of criminological perspectives. Indeed this approach is linked directly to the criminological perspective of classical criminology whose central idea is that people commit crime as a result of a rational decision-making process.

KEY POINT—KEY FEATURE OF CLASSICAL CRIMINOLOGY

The key feature of classical criminology is its central presumption that individual criminals engage in a process of rational calculative decision-making in choosing how to commit crime. This view is underpinned by two further assumptions: one that individuals have free will; the other that individuals are guided by hedonism, the maximization of pleasure, and the minimization of pain.

A change in approach

These ideas were important in that they shifted attention towards punishing the offensive behaviour rather than punishing the individual's social or physical characteristics. The shift had an enormous influence on changing attitudes towards punishment and towards the purpose of the law and the legal system. However, in contrast with earlier concerns with the rationality or otherwise of the offender, the concerns of rational choice theory are framed to address the central question of crime prevention. Again, it has been argued that rational choice theory refuses to address the causes of crime but is more concerned with its management. Clarke and Mayhew (1980), the main proponents of this theory, believe that criminological theories have been little concerned with the situational determinants of crime. Instead, the main object of previous theories has been to show how some people are born with or come to acquire a disposition to behave in a consistently criminal manner. Consequently, they believe this bias has had unfortunate consequences for the issue of crime prevention.

KEY POINT—PROBLEMS WITH PREVIOUS CRIME PREVENTION APPROACH

'These difficulties are primarily practical, but they also reflect the uncertainties and inconsistencies of treating distant psychological events and social processes as the causes of crime. Given that each event is in turn caused by others, at what point in the infinitely regressive chain should one stop in the search for effective points of intervention?'

(Clarke and Mayhew 1980:44)

The criminal as economic decision-maker

Rational choice theory suggests that effective intervention can be established by understanding the criminal as an economic decision-maker. The idea of treating human beings as driven by the motive of profit maximization is one that has a long-standing tradition within the discipline of economics. Further, the work of Pyle (1995), which builds on the earlier work of Anderson (1976), points the way to intervention in the criminal cycle by focusing on the marketplace itself, and disrupting the factors affecting supply and demand. The disruption of street-level drug trading by the police appears to have met with some measure of success by disrupting the economic trading that takes place.

Scenario—Disrupting a drugs market

A local nightclub is believed to be the centre of illegal drug trading, with the problem of disorder frequently occurring outside the premises at the end of licensing hours. In order to disrupt the marketplace, with the agreement of the owners, police use an automatic drug-testing machine using swabs from customer's hands which will indicate whether or not they have been handling illegal drugs. Agreement to this procedure is a condition of entry into the nightclub. This measure results in several arrests for suspicion of possession of illegal drugs, the removal of individuals who were suspected of dealing drugs within the club, and a consequent decrease in incidents of public disorder.

The economic approach rests on the assumption that most potential criminals are normal individuals. The early work of Becker (1968) and Ehrlich (1973, 1975, 1977) argues that an individual will commit crime if the expected net benefit from committing the crime exceeds the expected benefit derived from legitimate activity. It is inherently risky because of the possibility of being caught. For Becker (1968), criminals were deterred from committing crimes by increases in the probability of being caught and punished, and by the level of punishment if caught. Both reduced the expected utility from criminal activity. Ehrlich (1973, 1975, 1977), on the other hand, used an allocation of time between criminal and legitimate activity, indicating that other economic factors, such as earnings in legitimate work, returns to criminal activity, and the probability of employment, could affect crime rates.

Capable guardians

The interventionist idea in the cycle of crime has been extended by Felson (1998) and Clarke (1997). They state that the placement of a capable guardian within the cycle of crime is an essential element to prevention.

> **KEY POINT—CAPABLE GUARDIAN**
>
> 'The most likely persons to prevent crime are not police officers (who seldom are around to discover crimes in the act), but rather neighbours, friends, relatives, bystanders, or the owner of property targeted. The absence of a suitable guardian is crucial.'
>
> Clarke and Felson (1993:3)

Capable guardians can be non-humans as well, such as the presence of a CCTV camera. The point is, the presence of a capable guardian affects an individual's decision-making process regarding committing crime and disorder.

Limits to rational choice theory

Thus the rational choice process of decision-making is used to account for not only the decision to commit crime but also the time and the place in which such a crime is committed. However, some effort is made to recognize that such decision-making may be limited by the availability of information or inaccurate information. So this theory, whilst influenced by the assumed rationality of the economic human being, contains within it an appreciation that such rationality is limited. The greatest value of this perspective lies in its crime prevention potential. Making crime riskier or harder to carry out may often deter if many offenders, and predatory offenders in particular, weigh at least some of the potential risks against gains they anticipate from lawbreaking and criminal acts. This criticism highlights the central problem of rational choice—displacement of crime. It begs the question, if target hardening deters the criminal, what happens to the motive of profit maximization once the decision not to commit a crime has been made? Is this transformed into something else? These questions will be discussed later in this chapter.

Rational choice theory is not centrally concerned to address the underlying causes of crime, so it could be argued that the question of displacement is of little consequence. However, every crime prevention policy carries with it some costs, whether quantitative (resource led) or qualitative (social fear of crime), and these need to be weighed against the potential gains of the kinds of situational measures that this theory proposes. This theory attracts its critics. It has been argued that by focusing attention on preventing the behaviour of the individual criminal, it detracts from alternative policies or initiatives that might be considered more expensive.

5.4.5 **Crime Prevention through Environmental Design**

Another component part of the situational crime prevention approach lies in the concept of crime prevention through environmental design. This idea owes its origin to work conducted into territoriality and defensible space by Newman

(1972, 1976) and carried on under the title of Crime Prevention through Environmental Design (CPTED) (Jeffery 1971; Allat 1984).

Secure environments

It was argued that poorly designed buildings such as high-rise tower blocks, containing large, low-income families, produced crime and disorder far more than adjacent lower-rise buildings with socially identical residents and with a similar population density. The problem seemed to lie in a combination of individuals, including architects, financiers, and landowners, who had contrived to build the maximum space at the cheapest cost, regardless of any social problems this might have caused. The solution was to create secure environments.

KEY POINT—SECURE ENVIRONMENTS

There are four ways to achieve this:

- Enhance territoriality by subdividing places into zones which discourage outsiders and encourage residents to defend their areas.
- Increase surveillance by positioning windows so that residents can survey the exterior and interior public areas of their environment.
- Improve the image by redesigning buildings to avoid the look of low-cost housing.
- Enhance safety by placing this type of housing in a wider area of perceived safety.

Newman's work concentrated upon an attempt to use architectural form to rescue public housing in the USA from the depredations of crime. He believed that the design of public housing developments discouraged residents from taking responsibility for public areas and from exercising their normal territorial instincts to exclude predatory offenders.

However, in his later work, Newman (1976) reported some successes in reducing crime in public housing developments in the USA through application of this procedure. A major component of CPTED involves the prime concept of natural surveillance. This enables the introduction of 'guardians' into potential areas of criminality which, it is argued, substantially reduces the risks of criminal acts being carried out.

A popular approach

As Hughes (1998) points out, rational choice theory and CPTED are popular in public policy-making circles because they appear to offer an economical answer to an array of questions.

KEY POINT—SUPPORT FOR CPTED

'It resonates with common sense, being most in accord with the everyday explanations of crime and misbehaviour. It lends itself to neat, effective and attractive action. It cuts through all complexities and qualifications of sociological theorising and substitutes simple principles in their place.'

Rock (1989:4)

Encouragement for the CPTED approach for architecture and builders in England and Wales may best be illustrated by the Secured by Design initiative.

Secured by Design

Secured by Design (SBD) is a police initiative to encourage the building industry to adopt crime prevention measures in development, to assist in reducing the opportunity for crime and fear of crime, creating a safer and more secure environment. Ownership of the project and the Secured by Design title lies with the Association of Chief Police Officers (ACPO). Secured by Design is also an award scheme, run by ACPO, which aims to encourage housing developers to 'design out' crime, with a particular emphasis on domestic burglary, at the planning stage. It aims to do this and to deter criminal and anti-social behaviour within the area or grounds of an estate; it strives to introduce appropriate design features that enable natural surveillance and create a sense of ownership and responsibility for every part of the development. These features include secure vehicle parking, adequate lighting, control of access to individual and common areas, defensible space, and landscaping that enhances natural surveillance. This basic approach combines the elements of target hardening and natural surveillance, shared ownership, and defensible space discussed previously in this chapter. An important element of SBD is the integrated approach involving all of the ideas mentioned. However, it has in the past been criticized because of the focus by police on the target hardening element, thus dismissing the other complementary approaches to crime and disorder reduction.

The developers' award

The SBD award is a certificate given to developments which, following discussions with local police architectural liaison officers, are built in a way which conforms to the ACPO guidelines and so reduces the opportunity for crime. This means that doors and windows meet minimum quality and security standards, and that the development layout makes good use of natural surveillance and defensible space.

It is claimed that residents living on SBD developments are half as likely to be burgled and two and a half times less likely to suffer vehicle crime. Secured by Design developments also suffer 25 per cent less criminal damage.

113

Architectural liaison officers

Architectural liaison officers are police officers who have been specially trained to assist the building industry in the planning stages of a building development. These officers influence architects at the planning stage and try to get them to plan a new development with the ideas of target hardening, natural surveillance, defensible space, and shared ownership inbuilt so as to reduce the opportunities for crime and anti-social activities at the outset. Each police force in the country has a specially selected and trained architectural liaison officer.

5.4.6 **Summary of approaches**

Situational crime prevention and its component parts, therefore, comprise opportunity-reducing measures that:

(1) are directed at highly specific forms of crime
(2) involve the management, design, or manipulation of the immediate environment in as systematic and permanent way as possible
(3) make crime more difficult and risky or less rewarding.

Primary emphasis is placed on the immediate features of the environment or situation in which an act might be committed. In common with classicism, this approach views crime as the actions of rational, reasoning people making psychological judgements or calculations in response to specific situations or circumstances. The two guiding techniques to this thinking are target hardening and surveillance. Target hardening is intended to make the commission of crime more difficult, often by very practical nuts-and-bolts measures of strengthening and making more secure the technology of everyday devices like doors or telephone coin boxes. Surveillance, on the other hand, refers to the controls exerted by people in everyday life. For example, attention is given to the design of the built environment and how this might either hinder or be redesigned to help people control their own environment. This concern draws on the early work of Jacobs (1962) and Newman (1972) in the USA, and can be seen in this country in the work of Coleman (1985) in redesigning the architecture of housing estates.

5.4.7 **Situational crime prevention success stories in the UK**

Much of the advice on crime prevention given to crime prevention partnerships in England and Wales comes directly from the Home Office and, therefore, given the history of its development as an approach, concentrates on situational crime prevention. It has become a favourite approach for many government-sponsored crime prevention initiatives, such as the Safer Cities programme (Tilley 1994). In particular, target hardening initiatives that look at burglary prevention and car crime (Forrester et al. 1988; Bennett and Durie 1999) are circulated as being best practice and worthy of repetition.

Scenario—Kirkholt burglary project

Whilst some years old, this project is worthy of study as it was one of the first to consider the problem of repeat victimization, as well as trying to address burglary as a particular problem. Researchers discovered that the most obvious factor in burglary profile was the taking of money from the prepayment gas and electricity meter; 49 per cent of burglaries in Kirkholt involved the loss of the meter. Therefore the reduction or elimination of prepayment meters was part of the initiative. Also included in the initiative were the following:

- Improved security through target hardening and the use of locks and bolts.
- The introduction of a community support team whose primary role was to visit victims of burglary, offer support, and direct them to other agencies; they were also involved in postcoding of valuables.
- The introduction of cocoon neighbourhood watches, which involved small groups of people watching each others' property.

The results published by the research team indicated a reduction of burglary by 75 per cent over a three-year period.

Forrester et al. (1988)

The driving force behind many of these initiatives lies in the recognition that many victims are repeat victims of the same type of crime (Anderson et al. 1995; Bridgeman and Hobbs 1997). Consequently, many initiatives revolve around the fitting of locks and alarms on the homes of burglary victims soon after the initial offence occurs. These responses appear to be based firmly in rational choice theory and revolve around a crime being examined from three perspectives, namely the location of the offence, the offender, and the victim. However, it appears that the area that receives more attention from most partnerships is the location of the offence. Felson and Clarke (1998) reinforce the belief that it is the absence of some form of capable guardian at or near the location that is a prime cause for concern.

KEY POINT—GUARDIANSHIP

Guardianship is often inadvertent, yet still has a powerful impact against crime. Most important, when guardians are absent, a target is especially subject to the risk of criminal attack.

The drive for an increase in Neighbourhood Watch and the introduction of many CCTV systems throughout the country may be seen in the light of providing capable guardians in the absence of formal policing arrangements.

By focusing on the criminal event, it is claimed, there is a much greater chance of reducing crime immediately. This aspect of situational crime prevention is very important for partnerships. The 'quick win' approach, coupled with effective use of the media to publicize good results, is seen as vital if crime prevention partnerships are to attract funding from European Community (EC) grants, as well as central and local government funding, and sponsorship from private businesses.

KEY POINT—DOMESTIC BURGLARY AND REPEAT VICTIMS

The British Crime Survey shows that security devices are effective in reducing the risk of burglary. For example, victims of burglary are less likely to have security measures in place at the time of the incident than non-victims. Furthermore, victims of burglary with entry tend to have less security than victims of attempted burglary, which suggests that security is effective in thwarting at least some offenders.

Over the past ten years, levels of home security have continued to increase, and this may partly account for the reduction in burglary over the period. For example, 26 per cent of households said they had a burglar alarm in 2000 and 75 per cent window locks. The figures in 1998 were 24 per cent and 71 percent respectively.

Scenario—Domestic burglary

A large housing estate was the subject of numerous burglaries, with many repeat victims. Vulnerable individuals were identified, i.e., victims of previous burglaries and those individuals considered at greatest risk, e.g., the elderly. The local crime reduction partnership engaged in a target-hardening programme involving the free fitting of security devices to doors, repair of fences surrounding properties, and fitting of security lighting to the outside of houses, and embarked on a media campaign to raise awareness. There was a subsequent decrease in domestic burglaries of over 40 per cent and a decrease in repeat victim burglaries of over 90 per cent.

Scenario—Burglary reduction through situational crime prevention

Many domestic burglaries are committed via rear entrances, this being particularly the case in older terraced houses that have rear lanes or alleys running behind them. One method of reducing the instances of burglary is to control exits and entrances to the lanes by the installation of 'alley gates'.

Only residents and local emergency and utility services have keys to open and close these gates. Residents sign an agreement regarding their use, and local by-laws are sometimes introduced to prevent the illegal use of the alley ways by those who do not have legal access rights. This type of initiative has been successful throughout England and Wales, and domestic burglary has reportedly decreased, whilst there appears to be an increase in regeneration and use of the alley ways by residents for legitimate reasons.

Scenario—Vehicle crime

A multi-storey car park situated in a town centre was notorious for having vehicles stolen during the daytime as well as cars being broken into. Despite some successful police observation and arrest operations, it was a continuing problem. Consequently, CCTV cameras were installed at all levels of the car park, security lighting was enhanced to ensure there were no dark areas, a system of barriers controlled by a pay-as-you-leave ticket system was introduced, and warning notices to motorists to ensure their vehicles were locked and secure with property stored out of sight were placed at all entrances and exits. The incidence of theft of and theft from motor vehicles in the car park was reduced dramatically.

KEY POINT—ALCOHOL-RELATED CRIME

- A quarter of all adults claim to have been a victim of alcohol-related violence themselves, in a pub (14 per cent), on the street (4 per cent), or in their homes (7 per cent).
- Street drinking was felt to be a problem by seven out of ten people surveyed, with the majority (57 per cent) seeing teenagers as the worst offenders.
- Whilst 80 per cent would support a ban on drinking in some public areas, almost half say they have no confidence that the police would be able to enforce the ban effectively.
- More than half those surveyed thought that alcohol-related crime was still increasing, both on the street (61 per cent) and in the pub (52 per cent).

Scenario—Alcohol-related crime

Many public houses have been in use for a long time. Consequently, very little attention has been paid to the interior of these establishments. One of the major contributory factors to assaults within the confines of public houses has been found to be the inclusion and use of a pool table. The reasons for this are as follows:

117

- Pool tables were found to have been situated in small rooms, usually near to entrances and exits for toilets, etc., thereby ensuring a steady stream of people walking past the table.
- The games require individuals to use a considerable amount of space to play, with collisions resulting between the players and people walking past the table.
- This, mixed with the liberal consumption of alcohol, the ready availability of weapons to hand, i.e., pool balls, cues, and drinking glasses, led the use of the pool table to be a major contributing factor in assaults within public houses.

Removal of the pool table to a specified room with no thoroughfare and better surveillance from the bar area, coupled with the use of plastic glasses, resulted in the pool table no longer figuring as a major contributor to assaults within public houses.

Scenario—Multi-agency approach to alcohol-related incidents

A multi-agency initiative established in Cardiff, to prevent pubs and clubs from being the centre of crime and disorder, has now been extended into the surrounding areas of South Wales.

Community Safety Partnerships adopting the 'traffic light' rating system to help identify drinking places which attract disproportionate antisocial trouble.

Every time an incident is reported to the police in connection with a club or pub, a point is added to its score on a database. Police will intervene if trouble continues, and the ultimate sanction is the removal of a pub or club's drinks licence.

The initiative in Cardiff city centre saw alcohol-related incidents linked to licensed premises drop from 2,442 in 2006 to 1,552 by 2008, saving £93,224 in policing time.

5.4.8 Opportunity reducing techniques

Clarke (1997) has conducted a large amount of research into situational crime prevention techniques and has produced a very useful matrix entitled 'Sixteen opportunity reducing techniques' (see Table 5.1). Whilst any classification is subject to review and amendment, and may include some elements of overlap, his work is useful for considering approaches to reducing crime and disorder.

Whilst there are many claims for the success of situational crime prevention techniques, it is not without its critics. One of the main complaints regarding

Table 5.1 Sixteen opportunity-reducing techniques

Increasing perceived effort	Increasing perceived risks	Reducing anticipating rewards	Removing excuses
1. Target hardening Steering locks	*5. Entry/exit screening* Automatic ticket gates Baggage screening	*9. Target removal* Removable car radios Phone cards	*13. Rule setting* Customs declaration Hotel registration
2. Access control Entry-phones Car park barriers	*6. Formal surveillance* Speed cameras Burglar alarms	*10. Identifying property* Property marking Vehicle licensing	*14. Stimulating conscience* Speed cameras and campaigns
3. Deflecting offenders Street closures Pub location	*7. Surveillance by employees* CCTV systems Park attendants	*11. Reducing temptation* Off-street parking Rapid repair	*15. Controlling disinhibitors* Under-age drinking laws
4. Controlling facilitators Credit card photo ID cards	*8. Natural surveillance* Defensible space Street lighting	*12. Denying benefits* PIN for car radios Graffiti cleaning	*16. Facilitating compliance* Easy library checkout

Source: Clarke (1997).

this type of approach lies in the concept of displacement, which is examined further at **5.5** below.

5.5 **Displacement or Diffusion?**

5.5.1 **Displacement**

Displacement theory argues that removing the opportunity for crime, or seeking to prevent a crime by changing the situation in which it occurs, does not actually prevent crime but merely moves it around. When a target of crime is blocked, it is argued, the would-be offender does something else instead. Much of what is known about displacement is based on interview data with convicted criminals and is subject to the flaws inherent in that type of data-gathering. For example, criminals may boast about their activities to impress the researcher, or may underplay their reasoning for fear of it being used to apprehend them in the future.

It is said that there are five main ways in which crime is moved around as a result of crime prevention techniques. These include geographical displacement, where crimes are moved from one location to another; temporal displacement, where crimes are moved from one time to another time; target displacement, where a perpetrator will direct attention from one target to another; tactical displacement, where one method of committing crime can be substituted for another method; and crime type displacement, where one kind of crime can be substituted for another.

> **KEY POINT—FIVE WAYS IN WHICH CRIME CAN BE DISPLACED**
>
> **Geographical**—changing location of offence, e.g., from alley way to garage area.
> **Temporal**—changing time of offence, e.g., from early evening to night time.
> **Target**—changing the target, e.g., from garden sheds to retail outlets.
> **Tactical**—changing method of committing crime, changing modus operandi.
> **Crime type**—changing the crime, e.g., from burglary to auto crime.

As can be seen, the type of displacement that can occur covers many possible courses of action. It therefore follows that the ways in which this occurs are varied indeed.

However, there tends to be an assumption that displacement is always a bad thing. There is an important distinction to be made here, between what Crawford (1998) refers to as malign and benign displacement. Malign displacement refers to a move away from the original crime to a more serious offence, or to other types of offences that will have a more serious consequence; benign displacement occurs where a less serious offence or non-criminal act is committed, or an act of similar seriousness is committed on a victim or in a place where it has fewer consequences.

Scenario—Benign displacement

The displacement of prostitutes from residential areas and into industrial zones or non-residential areas through the creation of zero tolerance, in which prostitution is not prosecuted, may be considered a form of benign displacement. The new location may be considered to have a less harmful impact on the wider society and local communities.

5.5.2 Diffusion of benefits

There appears to be some evidence that far from displacing crime automatically, crime reduction methods may also result in something called a 'diffusion of benefits'. Here the idea is that crime reduction in one area actually spills over into another. For example, CCTV on one car park will tend to reduce auto crime not only in that car park but also in others close by. This may be seen as the opposite effect of displacement and is also known as the 'halo' effect.

> **KEY POINT—DIFFUSION OF BENEFITS**
>
> The spread of the beneficial influence of an intervention beyond the places which are directly targeted. This may influence the individuals who are the subject of the intervention, the crimes, or the time periods involved.

Examples of the effect of displacement and diffusion can be seen in Table 5.2.

Table 5.2 Diffusion and displacement

Type of displacement	Definition	Diffusion effect	Displacement effect
Geographical	Change by area	Reduction in nearby area	Increase in another area
Temporal	Change by time	Reduction at times not covered by initiative	Increase when initiative not being operated
Target	Change by object	Reduction against targets not covered in initiative	Increase in those not covered by initiative
Tactical	Change by method	Reduction in crimes using different methods	Increase in tactics not covered by initiative
Crime type	Change by crime	Reduction in crimes other than targeted	Increase in crimes not covered by initiative

Source: Adapted from Smith and Tilley (2004).

5.5.3 **Anticipatory benefits**

Another idea worthy of note is that of anticipatory benefits. This occurs where reduction in crime happens in an area where a crime reduction initiative is about to be carried out. For example, a burglary reduction scheme may be planned to run for a particular period of time, commencing at a particular date. However, a substantial reduction in burglary occurs before the commencement of the initiative. It appears that this happens as a result of pre-initiative publicity, which generates a deterrent effect and discourages the would-be offender from committing crime in that area.

Table 5.3 Approaches to crime and disorder reduction

	Police	Partnership	Non-police
Enforcement approach	Routine patrol Zero tolerance Intelligence led Problem-solving	Town guards/wardens Neighbourhood wardens Security guards	Trading standards Noise legislation Licensing
Situational approach	Targeted patrol	Public CCTV Neighbourhood Watch Preventing repeat victimization	Private CCTV Improving car security Architectural design
Community/ social approach	Police oriented Youth clubs	Youth work Drug education Schools liaison Community action groups	Citizenship schemes Mediation schemes
Rehabilitation	Cautioning YOTs	Caution plus referral groups YOTs	Drug treatment Mentoring schemes

Source: Hough and Tilley (1998).

5.6 **Repeat Victims of Crime**

One of the fundamental problems in crime reduction approaches is always where and how resources should be deployed; in other words, how to utilize crime prevention resources to make them more effective. A person whose home is burgled twice is a repeat victim; but so too is a person who is robbed then later burgled, and whose car is stolen as a getaway vehicle. The study of repeat victimization was given a new impetus as a result of the Kirkholt burglary project discussed at **5.4.7** above. There, it was discovered that a considerable number of burglary victims were repeat victims, and that by targeting those individuals with crime prevention a large percentage of crime reduction was achieved. Therefore, when discussing ways of attempting to reduce crime and disorder, and the methods employed, the study of repeat victimization offers the police practitioner another way of achieving success in this area.

KEY POINT—REPEAT VICTIMIZATION

Repeat victimization is the recurrence of crime in the same places and/or against the same people. The Home Office adds, 'when the same person or place suffers from more than one incident over a specified period of time'.

Past victimization can predict future victimization, and therefore this is preventable.

5.6.1 **Effects of repeat victimization**

Victims of crime and disorder do not get used to being victims. Many suffer emotional trauma, even when the crime and disorder event is seemingly trivial. It may be compared in some instances to the loss of a loved one, where victims progress through various stages after each incident. This may involve feeling unsafe, poor health, or the introduction of lifestyle changes, including withdrawal from contact with the community. Many repeat victims may have little faith in the police, and this could lead to a failure to report future incidents to them.

5.6.2 **The extent of repeat victimization**

For a number of reasons, the extent and nature of repeat victimization remained hidden for some time. That said, at a local level, many police practitioners will have been aware of repeatedly victimized individuals and locations. Through surveys such as the British Crime Survey, the scale of repeat victimization has now been revealed. For example, the British Crime Survey (Todd et al. 2004) showed that if a person had been a victim of crime during the previous year, he or she had a much higher perception of risk of being the victim of various types of crime than if he or she had not been a victim. This is an important point, as perception equals reality for many individuals and this helps fuel the 'fear of crime' factor. Further, as regards domestic burglary, a house that had been the subject of a burglary was four times more likely to be targeted than houses which had not been burgled before. In terms of domestic violence, it has been estimated that only 10 per cent of assaults on women involve an isolated incident; the other 90 per cent involve systematic assaults, often with escalating violence.

KEY POINT—REPEAT VICTIMS

- The British Crime Survey estimates that 4 per cent of victims account for between 38 per cent and 44 per cent of all crime reported to the survey.
- Patterns of repeat victimization have been found for both property and personal crime, such as burglary and domestic violence.
- Evidence suggests that high-crime areas have such high crime levels because they have more heavily victimized victims.

KEY POINT—TARGETING REPEAT VICTIMS

Tackling repeat victimization:

- helps reduce crime and disorder
- makes better use of limited resources
- targets prolific offenders and assists with the problem-solving approach
- addresses people's fear of crime and can improve quality of service to the victim.

5.7 **Crime Prevention through the Media**

The media are a potent force in influencing the public's perception of important issues: politics, culture, the environment, and importantly their views on crime and crime reduction. An effective method of reaching the wider local community is through the news media. The media can in fact help individuals to consider changing their habits whilst also helping to inform public opinion. This can then help in addressing the important elements of crime reduction and fear of crime within communities. For crime reduction partnerships the media can also help to raise their profiles, encouraging individuals, communities, and businesses to support them. Positive images about crime reduction will increase public confidence in the way in which crime and the fear of crime is reduced.

5.7.1 **Working with the media**

Local communities need to be given the full picture so that they can see the crime reduction partnership working towards a long-term solution of what is after all a complex problem. Above all, seeing the local media as part of the solution to crime and disorder reduction rather than a problem is more likely to produce good results.

The news media include newspapers, radio, and television stations. They have the ability to reach people in their cars and homes, and as they go about their daily lives. They are usually well trusted by local people. They are also important organizations that are part of the wider community and are influential businesses. Responsible reporting, particularly of success stories in the field of crime reduction, may help to achieve crime reduction partnership goals. Of course, journalists rate newsworthiness according to a story's ability to grab the attention of their readers or viewers, and are always looking for novel approaches or surprises. They also look for examples of human interest stories, so an opportunity clearly exists for crime reduction partnerships to show how they are making a difference to the lives of local people. In particular the local media can be used to publicize a quick win or hit, such as an environmental clean-up, which will encourage wider participation, especially from residents, and will start to renew confidence in the locality.

News coverage, however, can be difficult and unpredictable. Journalists may not take too kindly to being told what to publish; and you cannot guarantee they will print your story, as space is limited and they have to manage unpredictable events within the wider community.

Scenario—Use of media for crime prevention

A local crime reduction partnership used a free local newspaper to inform people regarded as vulnerable about free locks and bolts for their doors. This was backed up by a leaflet campaign in libraries, doctors' surgeries, and other public buildings which drew a major response. The crime reduction partnership then had a further article published highlighting the success of the campaign and explaining how burglary had been reduced in the area.

Clearly there is ample scope for crime reduction partnerships to work together with local news media, ensuring that the right and appropriate message about crime and crime reduction is circulated throughout the community (see Table 5.4).

Table 5.4 Using the media for crime and disorder reduction purposes

Positive points	Negative points
Is usually free of charge and reaches a wide audience	May be unpredictable in obtaining publication
Can help publicize a quick win scenario for the crime reduction partnership to help gain support from the community	May help promote fear of crime if issues not dealt with sensitively
Good relations with the media will ensure support for the partnership if there is a crisis	You can't guarantee your message will hit the right audience
By using the media you can connect with interests and concerns of the community	Journalists may be on the lookout for bad news stories

5.8 **Summing Up**

5.8.1 **Crime and disorder reduction**

The terms crime prevention, crime reduction, and community safety are often used interchangeably to describe methods or initiatives designed to impact upon levels of crime and disorder. For the police practitioner this is the move away from short-term reactive policies towards a more scientific approach. The new approach involves the prediction of crime and disorder, and implementing prevention of the same through the partnership approach.

5.8.2 **Primary level of intervention**

This level of prevention is aimed at preventing criminality from the outset. It includes such areas as tackling poverty, poor housing, poor parenting, and also school attendance. It focuses on the general population of potential offenders. An example of this type of approach would include a national television campaign against auto crime.

5.8.3 **Secondary level of intervention**

This level of intervention focuses on groups who may be at risk of offending or victimization. The group may be targeted as a result of their age, where they live, their lifestyle, or some other predictor of risk. An example of this type of approach can be seen in drug awareness sessions held within schools as part of the good citizen curriculum.

5.8.4 **Tertiary level of intervention**

This level addresses those individuals who are already victims of crime, through crime prevention schemes such as target-hardening burglary victims' homes against repeat victimization, or through restorative justice schemes. These schemes bring together victim and offender in order to encourage restoration of loss to the victim.

5.8.5 **Social crime prevention methods**

Social crime prevention focuses chiefly on changing social environments and the motivations of offenders. Its measures often tend to focus on the development of schemes to deter potential or actual offenders from future offending. Mentoring schemes in schools are an example of this type of approach.

5.8.6 Crime-resistant communities

A crime-resistant community is a neighbourhood which has strong social bonds, where people take pride in their street and 'own' their public places, where the needs of all groups in the community are met, and where people regard the area as an attractive and safe place to live and work. As such, it is likely to have a low crime rate. Good neighbourhood programmes, including activities such as youth clubs, theatrical societies, or any project that brings people together, encourage social bonding. This in turn encourages pride within communities and assists in resisting crime and disorder.

5.8.7 Youth Inclusion Programmes

Youth Inclusion Programmes (YIPs) were established in England and Wales during 2000, and are tailor-made programmes for thirteen- to sixteen-year-olds who are engaged in crime, or who are identified as being most at risk of offending, truancy, or social exclusion. YIPs target young people in a neighbourhood who are considered to be most at risk of offending, but are also open to other young people in the local area. The programmes currently operate in most deprived/high-crime estates in England and Wales.

5.8.8 Situational crime prevention methods

Situational crime prevention chiefly concerns the reduction of opportunity to commit crime, such as the installation of surveillance technology (CCTV) in public spaces to reduce the opportunity to steal cars or crimes of violence in a night-time drinking area.

5.8.9 Routine activity theory

This approach believes that crimes, especially those where one or more individuals attack the person or property of another, are closely related to three variables, namely motivated offenders, a suitable target, and the absence of a capable guardian. This comes about because of the routine practices of everyday life. Crimes are linked to normal behaviours such as work, school, transport, recreation, shopping, and so on. Recent changes in the routine activities of our lives have placed more people at particular places at particular times, which can increase their potential as realistic targets of crime.

5.8.10 Rational choice theory

This theory believes that offenders make rational choices to commit offences within the constraints of time, ability, and the availability of information/

property. It concentrates on the criminal's behaviour rather then being concerned with the underlying reasons for a person committing crime. Effective intervention in the criminal act can be made by the introduction of capable guardians, who can be either humans (police officers, neighbours, bystanders, etc.) or non-humans (e.g., CCTV cameras). Capable guardians affect the rational decision-making process of the criminal.

5.8.11 Crime prevention through environmental design

This idea is based on research into territoriality and defensible space, carried on under the title of Crime Prevention through Environmental Design (CPTED). It is argued that poorly designed buildings such as high-rise tower blocks produce crime and disorder far more than adjacent lower-rise buildings with socially identical residents and with a similar population density. Territoriality can be enhanced by subdividing places into zones which discourage outsiders and encourage residents to defend their areas.

The general improvement in redesigning buildings to avoid the image of low-cost housing and the enhancement of safety by placing this type of housing in a wider area of perceived safety, all adds to the prevention of crime.

5.8.12 Secured by Design programme

Secured by Design (SBD) is a police initiative to encourage the building industry to adopt crime prevention measures in development, to assist in reducing the opportunity for crime and fear of crime, creating a safer and more secure environment. Secured by Design is also an award scheme, run by ACPO, which aims to encourage housing developers to 'design out' crime, with a particular emphasis on domestic burglary, at the planning stage.

5.8.13 Displacement or diffusion

Displacement theory argues that removing opportunity for crime, or seeking to prevent a crime by changing the situation in which it occurs, does not actually prevent crime but merely moves it around. There tends to be an assumption that displacement is always a bad thing. Whilst malign displacement refers to a move away from the original crime to a more serious offence, benign displacement occurs where a less serious offence or noncriminal act is committed instead. For a crime to be displaced, however, it has to be prevented first.

'Diffusion of benefits' refers to the idea that successful crime reduction methods in one area may have a similar effect in another area. It is also known as the 'halo' effect.

5.8.14 **Repeat victims of crime**

Repeat victimization is the recurrence of crime in the same places and/or against the same people. Past victimization can predict future victimization, and therefore this is preventable.

Tackling repeat victimization is important as it helps reduce crime and disorder, makes better use of limited resources, targets prolific offenders, assists with the problem-solving approach, and addresses people's fear of crime whilst improving quality of service to the victim.

5.8.15 **Crime prevention through the media**

An effective method of reaching the wider local community is through the news media, which can help individuals to consider changing their habits whilst also helping to inform public opinion. This can then assist in addressing the important elements of crime reduction and fear of crime within communities. For crime reduction partnerships the media can also help to raise their profiles, encouraging individuals, communities, and businesses to support them. Positive images about crime reduction will increase public confidence in the way in which crime and the fear of crime is reduced.

5.8.16 **Local application**

(1) Can you identify what types of crime reduction approaches are in use in your local crime and disorder reduction partnership?
(2) Consider a crime and disorder problem in your area and apply the crime and disorder triangle (see Figure 5.2 above) to it. Consider what solutions you can come up with.
(3) Identify three levels of intervention (primary, secondary, and tertiary) that are in being within your crime and disorder reduction partnership area.
(4) Ascertain whether your police force has an architectural liaison officer and discover what type of advice he or she dispenses to building companies.
(5) Identify any social crime prevention activities that are in place in your area.
(6) When walking through a street containing domestic dwellings, consider what situational crime prevention techniques may be put in place to prevent burglaries or theft from and of vehicles.
(7) Establish how many victims of crime in your area are considered 'repeat victims of crime'. How much do these figures contribute to the overall figure of crime?

(8) When reading a local newspaper, count how many stories relate to crime and disorder activities. Discover how many of the stories carry positive items about your local crime and disorder reduction partnership.

5.8.17 **Useful websites**

http://www.youth-justice-board.gov.uk/YouthJusticeBoard/
http://www.jdi.ucl.ac.uk/index.php
http://www.crimestoppers-uk.org/crime-prevention
http://www.direct.gov.uk/en/CrimeJusticeAndTheLaw/CrimePrevention/index.htm
http://www.securedbydesign.com/

6

Policing Partnerships 1: Styles of Policing

6.1 **Introduction**

No partnership crime and disorder reduction activity could possibly be a success without the cooperation of the local police. This applies not only to the supply of up-to-date information regarding crime patterns and victims, but also to the implementation of a policing style that complements the aims of a particular crime prevention/reduction programme. Policing styles vary from force to force and even from one Basic Command Unit (BCU) to another. In general, however, it appears that there are several distinct styles of policing that are either used as independent strategies, or amalgamated as the partnership requires, and each style has its strengths and weaknesses. Police practitioners need to understand these, and to place them in a local partnership context.

6.1.1 **Styles of policing**

The main policing styles currently in vogue are community-oriented policing, zero tolerance policing, and problem-oriented policing. In addition to these approaches, the government has recently announced its neighbourhood team policing initiative, which relies upon close connection to local communities and use of the extended policing family to carry out these schemes. All of these policing styles, however, rely upon considered information and intelligence in order to be an effective solution to crime and anti-social behaviour. Therefore, the introduction of the National Intelligence Model (NIM) is seen as a major step in coordinating policing efforts in producing effective crime reduction partnerships. It is important that the styles of policing, neighbourhood teams, and the National Intelligence Model are understood by practitioners in this field.

Overarching these considerations is the government's reform agenda for the police in England and Wales. The Police Reform Act 2002 (Home Office 2002a) and other aspects of the reform initiative have made, and will continue to make, a considerable impact upon policing crime and disorder for the foreseeable future.

6.2 **Community-oriented Policing**

Community-oriented policing (COP), or community policing as it is more commonly referred to in the UK, appeared in the mid 1970s as a topic of discussion among police administrators and academics. Since then it has spread worldwide as the summit of enlightened thinking. Fielding (1995) described the 1970s attempts as short-term tactics to repair police-public relations, a cosmetic exercise which masked reluctance to make major changes when entrenched patrol and investigation methods failed. More recently, COP has embraced the concepts of problem-solving within the community, attempts to reduce the fear of crime, and targeted foot patrols. The idea of community-oriented policing can be traced to the philosophy introduced by Sir Robert Peel in his famous 'Principles of Policing' which underpinned the introduction of the Metropolitan Police Act 1829, in particular Principle Number 7, which can be seen in the box below.

KEY POINT—POLICE AND THE PUBLIC

'The police shall at all times maintain a relationship with the public that gives reality to the historic tradition that the police are the public and that the public are the police.'

Peak and Glensor (1996:8)

Community safety and crime reduction partnerships often involve the use of community policing ideas. Therefore, the enormous influence of the community policing approach raises the question of what it is and also why it is claimed to be successful.

6.2.1 The problem of definition

Herein lies the first problem with community policing. It is not easy to provide a particular definition of community policing, even though it is a commonly-referred to idea. In an attempt to provide a working definition, Friedman (1992) examines community policing from three perspectives, namely the police, the community, and a combination of both. For the police it is a vehicle used to improve ties with the community for the purposes of relying on community resources to assist them, e.g., Neighbourhood Watch, to improve intelligence gathering, and to increase the acceptance of the police within the community. The community realizes that it deserves and should receive improved police services with greater accountability and an increase in the power-sharing in police decisions. When combined, both the police and the community assume that crime and disorder are produced by factors over which the police have little control, such as education and welfare issues, and that crime reduction needs to focus on these factors.

Policing in this style tends to assume a more proactive stance, with greater emphasis on quality-of-life issues, with greater understanding of human rights and civil liberties, which are essential to successful democratic policing. Different and diverse tactics used by the police are seen as a way of improving quality of life and increased community satisfaction.

6.2.2 A working definition

In summing up this view of community policing, Friedman (1992) attempts to provide a working definition, which can be seen in the box below.

> **KEY POINT—ONE DEFINITION OF COMMUNITY POLICING**
>
> 'Community policing is a policy and a strategy aimed at achieving more effective and efficient crime control, reduced fear of crime, improved quality of life, improved police services and police legitimacy, through a proactive reliance on community resources that seeks to change crime causing conditions.'
>
> Friedman (1992:4)

It can be seen that community policing is not a single idea that can be explained easily, and it is different to rapid response and enforcement-oriented policing (Reiner 2000). Police staff are closer to the community and can represent its members, a process by which crime and disorder problems are shared with the public or as a means of developing links with the community and interest groups. The term 'community policing' conjures up images of police and community relations in a stable and agreeable community, where crime is an annoyance and disorder largely consists of minor vandalism. In reality, of course, this is seldom the case.

6.2.3 **Reactions to community policing**

The use of community policing in crime and disorder reduction partnerships raises some problems that police practitioners should be aware of. One of the main influences in this area, both in this country and the USA, was Robert Trojanowicz (1983, 1986, 1990; Trojanowicz and Bucqueroux 1990). Trojanowicz based his work upon policing experiments in Michigan and provides a working framework for community policing. These include the understanding that it is an idea and a strategy in one; that it requires a new type of police officer, who can work proactively and independently of police supervision yet is able to work in partnership with many other agencies. Importantly, community policing rests on the idea that those law-abiding citizens deserve an input into the policing process, and that solutions to problems mean allowing both police and residents to explore creative options.

So far, the idea of community policing has, in the main, been greeted as a positive step. This can be seen in the box below.

> **KEY POINT—A POSITIVE VIEW OF COMMUNITY POLICING**
>
> 'A review of community policing evaluation studies in twelve locations portrayed the schemes in a favourable light with both police and local residents expressing more positive attitudes after programmes had been implemented.'
>
> Lurigo and Rosenbaum (1994)

However, despite the official support and apparent success of community policing schemes, they are not without their problems, and there have been some failures. Police practitioners can learn a great deal from the problems of the past.

6.2.4 Why has community policing failed in the past?

Scenario—Obstacles to success

A small village area was chosen for a community policing initiative which involved the local council 'paying' for more high-visibility policing and police presence. After a period of time, the initiative was evaluated and it was found that overall it had not been successful, with recorded crime and fear of crime actually increasing. The obstacles to success were:

- insufficient consideration given to exactly what community policing would comprise and how it would assist the aims of the project
- ineffective management of residents' expectations
- removal of dedicated officers from the initiative to work elsewhere
- considerable turnover of staff which ensured lack of continuity.

It has been suggested that there are three main reasons that explain why community policing schemes fail in the UK. Firstly, the level of emergency demands from the public, through 999 calls, mobile phones, etc., prevents a more proactive style of policing. Secondly, sometimes the opposition of middle management, struggling to cope with the demands and facing additional burdens and responsibilities that go hand in hand with consultation-style policing. Thirdly, there may be an organizational culture that is resistant to a community policing orientation. A slightly different explanation for failure is put forward by Sadd and Grinc (1994). They found patrol officers unwilling to implement and unenthusiastic about what they perceived as 'top down', 'flavour of the month' initiatives. Also the necessary more effective inter-agency collaboration is not always forthcoming. Finally, a major barrier to improved police community relationships can be the history of fear and suspicion by residents. This may especially be the case in minority ethnic community groups. Clearly police practitioners have to be committed to the ideals of community policing, with the understanding that crime reduction partnerships are now a permanent feature in this country. This approach also involves recognizing the differences between traditional policing methods and new approaches to policing a community.

6.2.5 Traditional versus community policing

The difference between traditional style of policing and community policing can be seen in Table 6.1.

Table 6.1 Traditional versus community policing

Question	Traditional approach	Community policing
Who are the police?	A government agency responsible for law enforcement	Police are the public and the public are the police; police officers are paid to give full attention to the duties of every citizen
What is the relationship of the police force to other public departments?	Priorities often conflict	Police are one of many responsible for improving quality of life
What is the role of the police?	Focused on solving crimes	A broader problem-solving approach
What determines the effectiveness of the police?	Response times	Public cooperation
What view do the police take of service calls?	Deal with them only if there is no real police work to do	Vital function and great opportunity
What is police professionalism?	Swift effective response to serious crime	Keeping close to the community
How do the police regard prosecutions?	As an important goal	As one tool among many

Source: Adapted from Peak and Glensor (1996:73).

In contrast to the community policing type approach, a separate style of policing that has been used in tackling crime and anti-social behaviour has become known as the zero tolerance approach.

6.3 **Zero Tolerance Policing**

That there has been substantial historical political support for a zero tolerance style of policing cannot be in doubt. Politicians of all persuasions appear to have climbed on board a political bandwagon in support of what appeared to be a revolutionary approach to tackling crime. The current government has given its full support to the concept of zero tolerance policing and is committed to promoting it (Labour Party 1997). However, the precise origins of the term 'zero tolerance policing' appear to be obscure. It has become most famously associated with New York City and other parts of North America, although it has not been universally adopted there. It has also been used to describe certain policing initiatives in the UK, in particular in the King's Cross area of London, Hartlepool, Middlesbrough, and Strathclyde.

6.3.1 **Broken windows**

The particular policing style is said to be rooted in the 'broken windows' theory developed by Wilson and Kelling (1982), based on a study of police foot patrols and community interaction in Newark, New Jersey. This idea developed when a connection was made between the neglect of an area and the criminal activity that takes place over time. In essence, if a window is broken and remains unrepaired this will be taken as a sign of neglect and other windows will soon be broken. The air of neglect will start to develop as more vandalism occurs in an ever-widening circle. This has led to the theory being called the 'broken window' theory.

6.3.2 **Policing incivilities**

It was believed that public toleration of routine, minor incivilities on the street, such as drunkenness, window-breaking, vandalism, aggressive begging, or public urination, generated fear, encouraged a spiral of community decline, and ultimately increased the risks of more crime occurring. Fear of crime appears greatest in these disorderly neighbourhoods, which prompts respectable citizens to leave, and this process undermines the community's ability to maintain order so that decline follows. For that reason it was important for the police to arrest beggars, drunks, vandals, and others committing the so-called 'quality of life' offences. The reasoning continues that it is easier to prevent a neighbourhood sliding into crime at the beginning rather than trying to rescue it once the slide has taken hold. The idea states that even the most minor misdemeanours must be pursued with the same vigour as more serious crimes to create a deterrent effect. As Palmer (1997) points out, it appears that incivilities such as these undermine the bonds of community, leading to further disorder, and a downward spiral into lawlessness occurs, creating communities of 'no-go' areas of criminality.

Perhaps the biggest influence in the implementation of zero tolerance policing throughout the world is the model introduced by the chief of police in New York City, William Bratton. It is useful for practitioners to understand the origins of this approach to policing as it still remains a potent force, and is often demanded by communities and their representatives when dealing with crime and disorder.

6.3.3 **The New York City model of zero tolerance policing**

> Crime is down in New York City; Blame the Police!!
>
> Bratton (1998)

Bratton's claims for the introduction of his policies of policing in New York City are worthy of examination as they have had a profound influence on policing in some parts of this country and stimulated much debate. During the period 1990 to 1996, the number of murders in New York City dropped from 2245 to 983—a

56 per cent decline. During this period, it is claimed, the general crime rate was reduced by 37 per cent, whilst burglary had declined by a quarter over a two-year period, with total robberies being reduced by 40 per cent (Crawford 1998). It is small wonder, then, that much attention was directed to New York City.

Much of this apparent success was attributed to more police officers on the streets, coupled with a more aggressive approach to so-called 'squeegee merchants' (individuals who engage in windscreen washing at traffic lights) and tackling aggressive begging. Consequently, New York City turned from being the crime capital of the world to being proclaimed as one of the safest big cities in the world. Much of the perceived success concentrated on the street level activity of the New York police in being visible and apparently tackling quality-of-life issues.

However, perhaps a more subtle approach introduced by Bratton, but rarely highlighted, should be examined. Whilst it was true that an extra 7000 police officers were also employed in New York City in 1990, where the existing numbers of police were already high, it seems that Bratton was also able dramatically to improve the low morale that had existed in the force at this time. By doing so a sense of purpose and self-worth was re-established (Crawford 1998).

Organizational change

The New York City scheme is the product of several important organizational changes which are rarely discussed. The first is based on the introduction of eight specific crime control strategies to address drugs, guns, youth crime, auto theft, corruption, traffic, domestic violence, and quality-of-life issues. Prior to the introduction of these specific strategies, there had been little or no direction for local police commanders. The second innovation was the introduction of a system to measure the success of the crime control objectives, called the COMPSTAT process (Comprehensive Computer Statistics). This has been described as a crime management tool that uses weekly crime statistics, computer mapping, and intensive strategy sessions to direct the implementation of crime-fighting strategies (Pearce and Harrison 1997). This entailed four basic premises, namely the availability of accurate timely intelligence data; the rapid response of resources; effective tactics; and relentless follow-ups. Silverman (1998) points out that the COMPSTAT system supports the various strategic approaches, of which zero tolerance is just one. The main measure of performance in New York, says Silverman, is the crime rate. If a precinct's arrests, search warrants, and parking tickets have increased and the crime rate is still up, local police commanders need to do something about it. Police commanders for each borough have to give periodic briefings to the senior management of the New York Police Department (NYPD). These take place weekly in the central command room of the department which is set out like a wartime operations centre. While the crime statistics are displayed on screens behind the commander, and are selected by the management team, the commander is called to account for them. There can be little doubt that these often brutal periodical interrogations by senior management have provided sufficient motivation to achieve success in fighting crime.

Criticisms of the New York model

The claims for zero tolerance policing in New York City are not without their critics. Commentators point out that crime fell in most big American cities, albeit less dramatically. The fall came about on the back of an incredibly steep rise in crime rates, particularly homicides, in the late 1980s, together with the demise of the crack cocaine epidemic. This explained the fall in crime, it is alleged, coupled with a general ageing in the population that has resulted in fewer young men in their late teens, the group disproportionately likely to be involved in crime. The decline in gang violence related to drugs, whilst acknowledged as part of a wider and more complex set of factors, is a vital point for Bowling (1996:11): 'By the time Bratton took office and unleashed the cops, much of the drug war had already been won and lost and murder was on the decline.'

In the New York City model, claims for the 'broken windows' or zero tolerance style of policing are open to different interpretations. The major influence lies in the perceived increase in the number of police officers on the street, coupled with aggressive policing aimed at quality-of-life offences. It is this aspect of the model that influenced several police forces throughout the world, including Britain.

6.3.4 Zero tolerance policing in Britain

> Police saying they can't reduce crime is like footballers saying they can't score goals.
>
> Mallon (1997a:22)

> I think the police service has forgotten it can reduce crime.
>
> Mallon (1997b:16)

The popular American image of zero tolerance policing as an enforcement-led strategy directed against quality-of-life offences committed by young males in public places has been reinforced by politicians and the media in this country. This fits in nicely with demand-led policing and the preference for action and excitement (Holdaway 1984; Choongh 1997; Reiner 2000). It has meant that zero tolerance policing has been regarded as a possible antidote to the problems of crime and disorder.

The fall in New York City's crime statistics is cited worldwide as evidence for the efficacy of zero tolerance tactics. The apparent success led the British police to reconsider their impact upon crime and disorder, as may be seen principally from the work of then Detective Superintendent Mallon in the Cleveland Constabulary (Mallon 1997a, 1997b; Dennis and Mallon 1998; Romeanes 1998), and from the work of other forces such as Strathclyde Police's Spotlight initiative

(Strathclyde Police 1996) and the Metropolitan Police's Welling Garden initiative (Griffiths 1997).

The approach adopted by the police in Strathclyde claimed to be the first of its kind in Britain and based its zero tolerance policy on four major areas. These were: addressing public concerns, exploiting a corporate approach, addressing serious crime through concentration on minor crime, and maximum presence of uniform officers on the beat. However, in none of the British examples was there any evidence of the COMPSTAT management and information approach that is so central to the New York City model (Neyroud 1998).

6.3.5 Some British problems

However, this type of approach can leave the police open to a number of allegations, including corruption. For example, allegations over the misuse of informants involved in the zero tolerance programmes have been made in the past and several officers have been suspended from duty. This in turn can lead to severe criticism of the zero tolerance tactics employed in any initiative (Wainwright 2000).

Allegation of police corruption, however, is just one major concern of zero tolerance policing. Enforcement-led policing in Britain has shown that this approach can be the spark for large-scale public disorder, as witnessed in several inner cities during the early 1980s (Benyon 1984; Waddington et al 1989; Benyon and Solomos 1993; Della Porta and Reiter 1998). Lack of consultation, heavy-handedness, and the poor relationships between the police and many minority ethnic communities can lead to rioting, as seen in Brixton, Toxteth, Bristol, and the Broadwater Farm housing estate in London during the 1980s.

6.3.6 Civil liberties

A separate and equally important problem as far as zero tolerance policing in Britain and elsewhere is concerned revolves around the issue of civil liberties. Wadham (1998) argues that the use of this type of initiative is likely to target those individuals who are marginalized sections of communities. Given that the majority of zero tolerance initiatives in this country appeared to have an emphasis on street offences and the so-called quality-of-life offences, the young and homeless could become prime targets for criminalization. Similarly, street culture engaged in by certain groups, for instance Afro-Caribbean young men 'hanging out' on the street, or the homeless and beggars literally living off the street, appears to make them a legitimate target for zero tolerance type policing on occasions.

6.3.7 Success stories

Zero tolerance policing in Britain, therefore,was limited to a number of highly publicized initiatives that all claim some success.

Scenario—Dealing with aggressive begging

A railway station in a city suffered from a large number of individuals engaged in prostitution and drug-selling. Aggressive begging was common and passengers were regularly accosted. A zero tolerance initiative was set up and, following weeks of surveillance and information gathering, a number of individuals were identified as being key players. An operation took place in which these individuals were arrested and dealt with by the courts. For a period of time following this, any individual found committing any offence in and around the railway station was also arrested or reported and dealt with by the courts. The problems previously experienced disappeared.

However, there is a move away from the use of the term 'zero tolerance' because of some negative images of the approach. Certainly, Cleveland Constabulary has softened the media hype over their zero tolerance activities: there appears an official reluctance to use the term 'zero tolerance policing', substituting instead terms such as 'here and now policing', 'confident policing', and 'positive policing'. The phrase has itself become something of a politician's media soundbite, perhaps more attractive than the rather bland term 'crime prevention'. The problem with the approach is that by holding out the belief that the police alone can solve the problem of crime, this may serve to undermine the fact that the police need the support and trust of the local public and other agencies. Zero tolerance policing is both confrontational and aggressive, and poses problems for civil liberties and the rights of certain marginalized groups of people. It trades on nostalgia, but in reality, as a policing strategy, it is misleading. It does not entail the rigorous enforcement of *all* laws, which would be impossible let alone tolerable, but rather involves highly discriminatory enforcement against specific groups of people in certain locations. This type of approach for police practitioners perhaps is one that can be used as a tactic in certain circumstances, but never as a whole strategy for crime reduction partnerships.

6.4 Problem-oriented Policing

Scenario—Problem-solving as time saving

It is late on a Friday night in a busy town. There are limited police resources available. An emergency call is received from an elderly lady, that a man has broken into her house through the chimney and is stealing the furniture. Two double-crewed cars attend the scene as well as the single-crewed supervisor. At the scene it is discovered the elderly lady suffers from delusions, and the call is a well-intentioned one but false. The officers spend a considerable amount of time at the scene, reassuring the lady and arranging for a neighbour to look after her. One of the police officers present states that it was the third time that week he had received a call from this lady. The supervisor, when he returns to the station, checks the address on the computer system and finds that in total, some sixty hours of police time in the previous month had been spent at the address dealing with unfounded complaints from the lady. A phone call, followed by an official letter to the local health authority and welfare department, meant the lady being hospitalized and treated for her complaint. The police received no more calls to the address.

Problem-oriented policing (POP) is a recent innovation that is closely associated with the concept of community policing and is inspired by the work of Herman Goldstein (1990). It tries to replace the call for a police service with the 'problem' as the basic unit of police attention. Thus, POP focuses on the crime and disorder 'event' and analyses why it should have occurred. This is a major change in the way policing has traditionally been delivered.

6.4.1 **Police business**

Tilley (1997:1) attempts to explain the philosophy behind Goldstein's work by using the following story taken from Goldstein (1990):

> Complaints from passengers wishing to use the Bagnall to Green Fields bus service that drivers were speeding past bus queues of up to 30 people with a smile and a wave of the hand, have been met by a statement pointing out that it is impossible for the drivers to keep to their timetable if they have to stop for passengers.

This is a simple example of a problem with modern-day policing. Preoccupation with the smooth running of the organization for its own ends can come to take priority over the fulfilment of the purpose for which the organization is there in the first place. Goldstein's (1990) work on problem-oriented policing is concerned with ensuring the police keep their 'eye on the ball' and that the 'ball' encompasses the concerns that the public brings to them. These concerns in general tend to be problems that affect their quality of life. Therefore, for the police, all business the public brings to the police is police business, not just crime. Problem-oriented policing is about taking seriously all the problems the police are there to deal with. This involves:

- looking out for problems systematically from police data, other agency data, and contact with the communities served
- trying to analyse the problems to find their underlying causes
- attempting imaginatively to intervene to address underlying causes that are realistically open to change

- setting up systems to learn about what works, how, for whom, and in what circumstances
- feeding lessons back into growing problem-oriented wisdom within the police service
- designing crime reduction techniques and approaches.

6.4.2 Problem-oriented policing and traditional policing

Problem-oriented policing, like community-oriented policing, is another step away from the traditional reactive and stand-alone approach to policing. The box below illustrates the main differences.

KEY POINT—FOUR WAYS IN WHICH PROBLEM-ORIENTED POLICING IS DIFFERENT FROM TRADITIONAL POLICING STRATEGIES

(1) Problem-oriented policing enables the police to be more effective. At the moment, the police spend a lot of time responding to calls for service. Rather than just attending call after call, problem-oriented policing offers the police a way of addressing the underlying conditions that create the calls in the first place.

(2) Problem-oriented policing allows police officers to utilize the experience gained over a number of years to resolve problems in a creative and effective manner.

(3) Problem-oriented policing entails the involvement of the wider community to make sure that the correct problems and concerns are addressed. These are the bedrock of long-term solutions to identified problems.

(4) Much of the information required to provide long-term solutions to problems are not just held in police records. Partnerships with other agencies play a major part in the problem-oriented approach to policing.

Adapted from Goldstein (1990)

Again, this approach can pose problems for the police culture, as it is opposes the strict law enforcement model that tends to predominate police thinking. Resistance from individuals can thwart good intentions. As Goldstein says:

> Over and over again I have seen first line supervisors whose relationship with their subordinates reinforces the notion that the police function consists of going in and getting out as fast as you can. (Goldstein, quoted in Mulraney 2000:22.)

What is also needed is a new form of supervision that makes it legitimate to take the time to get beyond simply applying emergency treatment to a problem and moving on to the next problem with the same approach.

6.4.3 **Problem-oriented policing and communities**

Problem-oriented policing is an important development for the police, especially when engaged in partnership work. In the past the police were considered the experts in policing and needed very little, if any, assistance. They were regarded as the professionals, and it was thought right that they should be left alone to get on with their job. The reality is that the police cannot get the job done by themselves. They need all the resources of various agencies that contribute to crime reduction and control of anti-social behaviour. The police need the help of the community and other agencies if problem-solving initiatives are to be successful. A good example is shown below.

Scenario—Problem-oriented policing and begging

A scheme to remove beggars involved the identification of known beggars, the identification of legitimate begging pitches that could be set aside for legitimate use, and a fast-track drug rehabilitation programme. This, coupled with a new drop-in centre and regular meetings with all agencies involved in the scheme, allegedly reduced the number of beggars by two-thirds. Interestingly enough, a very localized zero tolerance approach to begging was utilized in the vicinity of cash point machines, with offenders being arrested when found committing offences in these areas.

Under the POP approach police officers are encouraged to explore new avenues, using a bottom-up approach, not top-down, to introduce creative alternatives in their use of a wide range of methods for preventing or reducing problems. This includes altering the physical environment, mediating disputes involving the community, employing civil law, and bringing other local authority services or regulatory agencies to bear.

Several police forces in this country profess to have adopted Goldstein's philosophy of problem-oriented policing, including Surrey (Beckett 1998), Leicestershire (Tilley and Brooks 1996), and Cleveland (Romeanes 1996). All report that the initiatives are extremely successful. There also appears to be a concerted drive by the Home Office to implement POP throughout the country. Documents produced by the Home Office concentrate on the perceived benefits of POP, highlighting a better service to the public (whose concerns are attended to at source) and officers with enhanced job satisfaction from bringing the public real benefits. More importantly, perhaps, more manageable demands on the police are achieved because underlying problems are solved, reducing the large number of repeat calls to the police (Leigh et al 1996, 1998; Read and Tilley 2000). Some forces have developed the idea even further. Lancashire police, for example, stage an annual event, involving a special award, the Tilley Award, which encourages their officers to tackle specific community problems in a problem-oriented manner. This scheme involves great use of a variety of partners, including park rangers, schools, shopkeepers, youth groups, the media, etc., in solving different community problems. This force has in fact elevated problem-oriented policing even further, to the level of problem-oriented partnerships.

6.4.4 **Analysing problems**

In order to identify repeat problems and to try and solve them using the appropriate resources, scanning technology and the ability to use it must be of the highest order. This, until recently, was not readily available to most police forces in this country. The assumption was that whilst perhaps forces wanted to be involved in problem-solving, the ability to deliver it effectively was lacking. This was emphasized by Read and Tilley (2000), who highlighted the weakness in the ability to analyse information and data-sharing limitations as being major obstructions to successful problem-solving. However, most police forces now operate with specially trained staff who analyse information at BCU level and perform this valuable role in identifying crime hotspots and community problems. The 'problem' is therefore an important part to this policing approach. The box below considers just what a problem is.

KEY POINT—CONSTITUENT ELEMENTS OF PROBLEM-ORIENTED POLICING

- A problem is considered to be the basic unit of police work—rather than one crime, case, call, or incident. A problem is a group of crimes, cases, calls, or incidents.
- A problem is something that concerns or causes harm to citizens—not just the police. Things that concern only police officers are important, but they are not problems in this sense of the term.
- Addressing problems means more than just quick fixes; it means dealing with the conditions that create problems.
- Police officers must routinely and systematically investigate problems before trying to solve them—just as they routinely and systematically investigate crimes before making an arrest.
- The investigation of problems must be thorough, even though it may not need to be complicated. This principle is as true for problem investigations as it is for criminal investigations.
- Problems must be described precisely and accurately, and broken down into specific aspects of the problem. Problems often aren't what they first appear to be.
- Problems must be understood in terms of the various interests at stake. Individuals and groups of people are affected in different ways by a problem and have different ideas about what should be done about the problem.

Adapted from Goldstein (1990)

Having identified what the problem is, then steps have to be taken to solve it. One important way of achieving this is through the use of the problem analysis triangle.

6.4.5 **Using the problem analysis triangle**

Sometimes it can be difficult to see how a particular problem can be solved. The problem analysis triangle (sometimes referred to as the crime triangle or PAT) provides a way of thinking about recurring problems of crime and disorder. The problem analysis triangle was derived from the routine activity approach to explaining how and why crime occurs (see Figure 5.2 in Chapter 5). This theory argues that when a crime occurs, three things happen at the same time and in the same space:

- A suitable target is available.
- There is the lack of a suitable guardian to prevent the crime from happening.
- A motivated offender is present.

So we see that this idea assumes that crime or disorder results when (1) likely offenders and (2) suitable targets come together in (3) time and space (location). The problem analysis triangle (PAT) is illustrated in Figure 6.1.

6.4.6 **Responding to the problem**

Whilst the PAT concentrates on the analysis of the problem, we can add another outer level for each of the three original elements. This helps us consider how to respond to the problem we have identified by adding a controller for each of them:

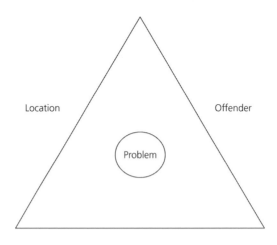

Figure 6.1 A simple problem analysis triangle

- If we consider the victim or target element of the PAT, we can add the control element of *guardian*, usually people who protect their property, etc.
- For the offender element, this control is called the *handler*, someone who perhaps knows the offender well and who can exert control over him or her. This could include parents, friends, teachers, husbands, wives, etc.
- Finally, in terms of the original element of location the controller is called the *place manager*. This is someone who has responsibility for the place, and could include janitors, teachers, bus conductors, etc.

Consequently, our simple PAT now looks like this (Figure 6.2):

Figure 6.2 Another view of a simple problem analysis triangle

Having examined the PAT and the definition of problems, consider the circumstances in the box below and apply the triangle to this incident.

Scenario—Problem-oriented policing and youth annoyance

A number of complaints have been received from residents in a neighbourhood regarding the congregation of youths at an old-fashioned bus shelter every evening between 7 p.m. and 11 p.m. Passengers at the bus stop feel intimidated, whilst residents nearby complain of noise and litter left at the bus stop. Further, there is a nearby infants' school, and it is alleged that minor damage is being caused as a result of the youths congregating. By using the PAT and applying the broad principles of POP to this information, we can consider the following responses:

(1) What do the youths have as an alternative to the shelter? (the location)

(2) Has anyone actually spoken or consulted with them? (the offenders)

(3) What facilities can the infants' school offer regarding an alternative to the bus shelter as a shelter for the youths? (the location)

(4) What can the bus company/local authority do regarding the use of the bus shelter? (the location)

(5) What consultation has taken place with the community, especially in the vicinity of the bus shelter? (the victims)

(6) Is there anyone in the community who can offer youth mentoring or youth club facilities? (the offenders)

(7) Why are the youths congregating at this location at this time? (the offenders)

Of course you should also consider what other agencies can be involved in this process. The point to note is that the triangle allows you to examine problems in a more structured manner.

As you can see, once the PAT is applied and the three elements explored, many options appear that can be assessed to provide an answer to the 'problem' highlighted above.

6.4.7 The SARA model of analysis

A commonly used problem-solving method is the SARA model (scanning, analysis, response, and assessment). It can be used to identify underlying causes of problems and to discover how they may fit into a wider a pattern of similar problems. It can also help the police practitioner and prevent him or her jumping straight to a response that may be the wrong one. The individual elements of the SARA model are discussed below.

Scanning

Problems are identified through a wide range of data and other information, including local police knowledge, intelligence, crime reports, and public information, collected for later analysis. Here, problems become grouped or clustered.

The process can be seen below.

KEY POINT—SCANNING

- Identifying recurring problems of concern to the public and the police.
- Identifying the consequences of the problem for the community and the police.
- Prioritizing those problems.
- Developing broad goals.
- Confirming that the problems exist.
- Determining how frequently the problem occurs and how long it has been taking place.
- Selecting problems for closer examination.

Analysis

Here the details of the problem are examined in more detail. Scanning might tell us that a large amount of criminal damage is taking place, but analysis will tell us the times, dates, methods, types of property damaged, witnesses, suspects, etc. It is at this stage that information from partner agencies should be incorporated, which will provide alternative perspectives and extend the possibilities for finding trends and patterns.

Analysis therefore involves the actions listed in the box below.

KEY POINT—ANALYSIS

- Identifying and understanding the events and conditions that precede and accompany the problem.
- Identifying relevant data to be collected.
- Researching what is known about the problem type.
- Taking inventory of how the problem is currently addressed and the strengths and limitations of the current response.
- Narrowing the scope of the problem as specifically as possible.
- Identifying a variety of resources that may be of assistance in developing a deeper understanding of the problem.
- Developing a working hypothesis about why the problem is occurring.

Response

This stage involves the implementation of suitable action to resolve the problem. It can involve the assistance of other agencies and partnership members where appropriate. Responses to problems may be multi-layered, involving police action against a suspect, victim support for individuals or groups of people, and changes to the geographic location where offences have occurred, e.g., the introduction of street lighting, CCTV cameras, etc. The response stage is summarized below.

KEY POINT—RESPONSE

- Group discussions for new interventions.
- Searching for what other communities with similar problems have done.
- Choosing among the alternative interventions.
- Outlining a response plan and identifying responsible parties.
- Stating the specific objectives for the response plan.
- Carrying out the planned activities.

Assessment

This is the evaluation phase where the effectiveness of the response to the problem is assessed. Here, the decision is made as to whether the objectives have been met. Assessment should consider not only the effects of the response but how it was used. For example, there may have been more than sufficient resources available for the task yet the result was not as positive as would have been expected. The assessment stage involves the following steps.

KEY POINT—ASSESSMENT

- Determining whether the plan was implemented (a process evaluation).
- Collecting pre- and post-response qualitative and quantitative data.
- Determining whether broad goals and specific objectives were attained.
- Identifying any new strategies needed to augment the original plan.
- Conducting ongoing assessment to ensure continued effectiveness.

Even initiatives that do not achieve their objectives should not be discarded, as they may well provide information that makes the next initiative more effective.

The SARA method is illustrated in Figure 6.3.

For any response to crime and disorder to be effective it must rely on a strong and systematic process of analysis of the underlying problems and their causes. The PAT (above) and SARA are two of the most commonly and successfully used techniques in problem identification and problem-solving.

There is growing evidence that crime and disorder incidents can cluster in ways that are identifiable by these methods. They are sometimes referred to as 'signal crimes', and they are intrinsically linked to policing crime and disorder as they call for particular police and other agency intervention. Signal crimes have a direct influence on community perceptions about crime and disorder and are worthy of the attention of the police practitioner.

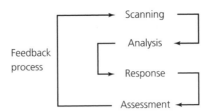

Figure 6.3 A simple schematic chart showing the SARA process

6.5 **Policing Signal Crimes**

The signal crimes perspective is an important idea that can inform reassurance-style or high-visibility policing. In summary, it states that:

- some crimes and disorders act as warning signals to people about their exposure to risk
- these signals impact on the public's sense of security
- they cause people to change their beliefs and/or behaviours to adjust to the perceived risk
- the perspective covers a whole spectrum of crimes and disorders
- the perspective gives an opportunity to target those problems that matter most to the public
- police and their partners can establish 'control signals' to neutralize signal crimes and signal disorders.

The main idea behind signal crimes is to focus upon how people react to crime and disorder, and how they attribute meaning to their experiences of these types of social problem. In essence, it is an approach that understands crime and disorder as having communicative properties, with people interpreting the various incidents that they encounter to construct judgements about the levels of risk that are present. What appears to happen is that some instances of crime and disorder matter more than others in terms of communicating a sense of risk to the public. This is because certain incidents have a higher 'signal value' than others. For most people much crime and disorder functions as little more than background 'noise' to the conduct of their routines in everyday life. However, certain incidents have far more significance for them—these are signal crimes and signal disorders.

6.5.1 **Visibility and context**

There are two factors that explain why some incidents function as signals, namely visibility and context. Context refers to the ways that the contextual conditions in which crime and disorder occur shape whether an incident will function as a signal to the public or not. Communities are more or less resilient to different types of social problems, depending upon their socio-economic and demographic make-up. Thus the social context in which a problem occurs is a significant influence in terms of whether people will view it as a signal or not. Relatedly, the social visibility of an incident will help to determine whether it functions as a signal—if people are unaware of the presence of a crime or disorder it cannot function as a signal to them. In some instances the visibility of a problem is amplified by media coverage. However, enhanced social visibility may also occur through people encountering a problem directly on a regular basis. This latter dimension helps to explain why people routinely attribute high degrees of significance to problems of incivility and anti-social behaviour occurring in their neighbourhoods. It is believed that by targeting activity to those incidents of crime and disorder that have a particularly high 'signal value', the police can achieve disproportionate impact in terms of tackling the problems that are especially generative of a sense of public insecurity.

6.5.2 **Reassurance policing**

The concept of control signals also provides an important link between the signal crimes perspective and reassurance policing. The emphasis upon control signals identifies a need for police to ensure that their activities are visible to the people they serve, if they are to reassure them about levels of safety. Thus one justification for the police engaging in highly visible foot patrol activities is that it can function as a potent control signal to members of the public. Uniformed foot patrol signifies to people the presence of an authoritative figure that can be called upon to restore social order should it be disrupted in some way. An aim of reassurance policing is to find ways of identifying and acting against risks in the local neighbourhood that have a disproportionate impact upon people's experiences and perceptions of security. Thus the signal crimes perspective provides a mechanism for thinking about how this objective can be achieved. Through a combination of targeting signal crimes and disorders, and ensuring the presence of visible control signals, the police, in partnership with other local agencies and communities, can act to improve levels of neighbourhood security.

The idea of signal crimes and the intervention process is shown in the box below.

Scenario—Signal crimes

The area around a railway station had become a dumping ground for abandoned vehicles and other rubbish. People did not like to use the railway station unless they had to, and it had become a magnet for undesirable activity during both daytime and night time.

The solution was to get the local community involved in a clean-up operation, which was later to involve the removal of over 15 tons of rubbish. Approximately fifty-five local residents, councillors, school staff, and members of the people's panel turned up to lend a hand and to turn the location around. Rail staff also participated and provided a grab lorry to remove the larger items. Local businesses were approached and kindly agreed to provide refreshments for the volunteers.

The initiative came about through an allocation of a problem-solving task that had been given to a local police community support officer. This officer produced a video showing the extent of the problem, and suggested that a community clean-up day would be the most effective and most lasting solution. Most important was the announcement that, following the cleanup day, future transgressions such as fly-tipping would be dealt with by way of enforcement.

Posters were placed at the location, following the event, advising residents and visitors that the volunteers had carried out the cleaning operation and asking that the area remain clean. So far this has worked.

As part of the assessment cycle you could use to evaluate this type of scheme, you could have considered the following, to feed back into the SARA system.

KEY POINT—CONSIDERATIONS FOR POLICING SIGNAL CRIMES

- The problem was identified jointly by partners and the community, with a real desire by the community to see improvements.
- Partners coordinated their efforts and resources on the day.
- The community support officer, vitally, adopted a strong 'can do' attitude. This emphasizes the need for a local champion who acts as a central point of reference for such schemes.
- The event was covered by the media and success was celebrated.
- The initiative was reinforced afterwards with strong statements of intent regarding future offenders.
- There was a strong community involvement; the police did not attempt to dominate or monopolize the event and gain all the credit.

Crime is not evenly distributed across time, place, or people. Increasingly, police and researchers are recognizing some of these clusters as:

- repeat offenders attacking different targets at different places
- repeat victims repeatedly attacked by different offenders at different places
- repeat places (or hotspots) involving different offenders and different targets interacting at the same place.

6.6 Neighbourhood or Local Policing

Neighbourhood policing, or local policing, is an approach that seeks to increase contact between the public and the local communities, and neighbourhood policing teams utilize many of the approaches discussed in this chapter thus far. The practical application of neighbourhood teams is fully discussed in Chapter 7. Evidence of the impact of the national Reassurance Policing Programme on public confidence, victimization and anti-social behaviour rates helped lead to the introduction of neighbourhood policing to all neighbourhoods in England

and Wales between 2005 and 2008. The approach emphasizes a local approach to policing that is accessible to the public and responsive to the needs and priorities of neighbourhoods. The main elements of the approach can be seen in the following key points box.

KEY POINTS—NEIGHBOURHOOD OR LOCAL POLICING TEAM ELEMENTS

- The presence of visible, accessible and locally known figures in neighbourhoods, in particular Police Constables and Police Community Support Officers (PCSOs).
- Community engagement in both identifying priorities and taking action to tackle them.
- The application of targeted policing and problem-solving to tackle neighbourhood concerns.

The Flanagan Reviews of Policing (2007, 2008) argued that neighbourhood policing needed to be more closely integrated with neighbourhood management and that the future of neighbourhood policing depended on it being part of a wider process of collaboration and joint working. A recent Home Office research report (2012) entitled *Delivering neighbourhood policing in partnership*, concluded that the delivery of neighbourhood policing is viewed positively by partners and local residents with one of the benefits being that of delivering services to communities far more efficiently.

6.7 Summing Up

Partnership activity needs the active cooperation of the police. Several styles of policing seem to be developing across the country in order to deliver crime reduction activities, and these vary from force to force and from BCU to BCU.

6.7.1 Community-oriented policing

This style involves the belief that the police are paid to give full attention to broader community problems, keeping in close touch with the community and requiring full public cooperation. Prosecutions are seen as just one tool among many that can be used to solve all service calls to the police. Quality-of-life issues are seen as being of high importance.

6.7.2 Zero tolerance policing

This approach has received substantial political support in the past and owes its introduction to this country to its alleged success in New York. It is an enforcement-led approach that limits the discretionary powers of the police, aiming to reduce serious crime by focusing on street level activities and antisocial behaviour. Whilst possibly effective as a short-term tactic, it can pose major problems in terms of civil liberties when strictly enforced.

6.7.3 Problem-oriented policing

Problem-oriented policing (POP) is an innovative concept introduced by the work of Herman Goldstein. It requires the police to rethink their traditional reactive approach and to work to solve problems at source, rather than treating the symptom. The police need to work with others within the community to help solve problems, and the approach relies heavily on identifying problems, analysing them using the SARA model of analysis, and producing long-term solutions.

6.7.4 Policing signal crimes

Some crimes and disorders act as warning signals to people which cause them to change their routines and activities. This can be an important factor when recognizing problems within communities, and when these are identified the police can have a great impact within the community in terms of tackling problems that increase insecurity and fear of crime.

6.7.5 Reassurance policing

This idea is linked to that of signal crimes. It can be used as an intervention when signal crimes have been identified. By targeting signal crimes and disorders and providing high-visibility policing, the police in partnerships can act to improve levels of neighbourhood security.

6.7.6 Local application

(1) What style of policing can you identify in your local police force?
(2) What good practice can you identify in terms of community policing in your local police force?
(3) Show how you would apply the PAT to a local problem.

6.7.7 **Useful websites**

http://www.homeoffice.gov.uk/rds/index.html
http://www.acpo.police.uk/
http://www.popcenter.org/
https://www.ncjrs.gov/pdffiles/commp.pdf

Policing Partnerships 2: New Directions

7.1 **Introduction**

The police service in this country is undergoing a tremendous amount of change. Not only has there been a large number of Acts of Parliament introduced during the last decade or so, but also the manner in which the police operate has also come under scrutiny. This, coupled with changes in society, the public's expectations as to what the police can and cannot do, a growing awareness of the rights of individuals, and a tremendous increase in available technology such as mobile phones, has greatly affected the way the police carry out their duties. In addition, a change in government philosophy towards policing, with the election of the Conservative–Liberal Democrat Coalition in 2010, against a backcloth of economic recession which occurred in 2008, has meant reductions in budgets for police and their partners. Further, the rise in global terrorism has also fuelled the drive for change. It is no wonder that the police service is moving swiftly in new directions, and this chapter will discuss several prominent changes that have affected partnership policing since the introduction of the Crime and Disorder Act 1998.

7.2 **The Police Reform Act 2002**

The overall intention of the Police Reform Act is highlighted in the box below:

KEY POINT—TITLE OF THE POLICE REFORM ACT 2002

'An Act to make new provision about the supervision, administration, functions and conduct of police forces, police officers and other persons serving with, or carrying out functions in relation to, the police; to amend police powers and to provide for the exercise of police powers by persons who are not police officers; to amend the law relating to anti-social behaviour orders; to amend the law relating to sex offender orders; and for connected purposes' [Long title of the Police Reform Act].

Home Office (2002a)

The Police Reform Act 2002 is one of the most important Acts of Parliament regarding the police and policing in England and Wales in modern times. It forms the backbone of the government's agenda for reforming the police service in England and Wales and received Royal Assent on 24 July 2002. The provisions of the Act are being brought about in stages by a series of Commencement Orders, thus allowing the government to implement certain parts of the Act when it sees fit. Perhaps one of the most influential aspects of this act was the introduction of Police Community Support Officers.

Police Community Support Officers

The Police Reform Act enabled chief police officers to introduce as police authority support staff community support officers, investigating officers, and detention and escort officers, in order to help police officers to deal with low-level crime and anti-social behaviour. This was initially proposed in *Policing a New Century: A Blueprint for Reform* and has three main functions:

(1) Freeing up officers' time for their core functions such as dealing with volume crime, by making more effective use of these individuals.
(2) Employing more specialist investigating officers to provide expertise in combating specialist crime such as in the areas of finance and information technology.
(3) Providing additional capacity to combat low-level disorder, and thereby help reduce the public's fear of crime. In this way, the government proposes to harness the commitment of those already engaged in crime reduction activities such as traffic wardens, neighbourhood and street wardens, and security staff.

Accreditation of others

The Act introduces the ability to accredit members of the extended policing family, for example street wardens. This means under certain circumstances, limited police powers can be granted to persons already engaged in community safety activities. It could also include individuals such as football stewards, as well as security guards within the private security industry. Even persons with official powers, such as environmental health officers, may be included. Each relevant chief officer has discretion for conferring powers on accredited individuals, and they may also attach conditions and restrictions to the powers. Schedule 5 to the Police Reform Act 2002 lists a menu of powers that may be conferred upon accredited individuals. The following box contains these powers:

> ### KEY POINT—POWERS AVAILABLE FOR ACCREDITED PERSONS
>
> - Power to issue fixed penalty notices (FPNs).
> - Power to require giving of name and address.
> - Power to require name and address of a person acting in an anti-social manner.
> - Power to prevent alcohol consumption in designated public places.
> - Power to confiscate alcohol and tobacco.
> - Power to remove abandoned vehicles.

Other areas

The Police Reform Act 2002 also establishes independence in the investigation of complaints against the police by the introduction of the Independent Police

159

Complaints Commission. It modifies and introduces police powers including adding to the list of arrestable offences, strengthening police powers when dealing with anti-social use of vehicles, and introducing interim orders for the Anti-Social Behaviour Order process.

7.3 The Big Society

The idea of promoting community agencies, groups and individuals in an attempt to encourage social interaction and thus produce a more cohesive society is not particularly new. Previous official documents such as Wedlock's document on social cohesion (Home Office 2006), which promoted social cohesion and crime resistant communities, have urged crime and disorder partnerships to engage in these types of activities. Further, the importance of social capital has been explored in the work of Robert Putnam who considers the rise of criminal activity against a backcloth of social disengagement in the USA (Putnam 2000). Recent and current governmental ideas which extend this approach have been and are still being promoted by Halpern (2007, 2010) who served as an aide to the previous labour government and now advises the new Conservative–Liberal Democrat Coalition Government.

In essence, the 'big society' refers to a tripartite partnership between the citizen, community and local government (Eaton 2010). This vision requires families, networks and neighbourhoods in a postmodern society to formalize a working partnership that is effective and sustainable in its approach to solving problems, building social cohesion and setting priorities for Britain (BBC 2010). In doing so, the government along with involvement of communities is set on building a 'big society' that is bigger, stronger and accountable to all. How this equates to the practicalities of living in the UK is worthy of examination. The Prime Minister refers to the ideology of a 'big society' as liberalism, empowerment, freedom and responsibly, where the top-down approach to government is abandoned and replaced by local innovation and civic action. Interestingly, critics of the government, including the general secretary of Unison, refer to the 'big society' as the 'big cop-out' only concerned with cutting investment and saving money (ITN 2010). This laissez faire approach to government could spell the end for new public management and centralized performance indicators as it will be for society and communities to assess performance. However, government insists that for the 'big society' to work, it will require significant involvement, encouragement and support from communities. Fundamentally, there are five key strands to understanding the 'big society' identified by the Cabinet Office (2010):

1. Empowering communities

The government aims to reform the planning and procedural systems to give local people the ability to determine how their communities will develop and be shaped in the future. Specifically, the 'big society' requires local people to have a greater say in the 'construction' of their surroundings. Accompanying these new powers, local people will also have ways of saving local facilities and services that are threatened by closure if they are deemed to be fundamental to the fabric of society. Communities will have the right to take over state-run services and facilities. Bringing about this change, the government will recruit and train 'community organizers' to support the creation of neighbourhood ground all over the UK.

2. Action-orientated communities

Community involvement, philanthropy and a spirit of volunteerism are an integral component of the 'big society'. The introduction of a 'big society' day and a focus on civic service will aim to increase and stimulate involvement from members of the communities from all socio-economic backgrounds. A 'National Citizen Service' will be established to encourage young people to develop the skills needed in a modern society aimed to break down negative perceptions and stimulate cohesion.

3. Decentralized power

A drive for decentralization and 'rolling back the frontiers of the state' are all perhaps a synonymous style of governance set by the conservative party in previous administrations. Reducing the size and influence of the state by stimulating local initiatives is perceived as key drivers in a move to establish a 'big society'. Greater autonomy, both financially and procedurally, is likely to be seen as government moves away from micro-management or 'nano level' management and moves to more of a macro-management approach. This cultural change in governance will see local authorities and local officials having greater discretion and influence of the direction of local policy. Decisions on housing and planning are also likely to return to local councils in an effort to make the procedure of allocation and urban design more accountable to local people.

4. Greater social enterprises

As pluralization is to be encouraged, it is envisaged that there will be an expansion in social enterprises. Those sectors, companies, industries and organizations that have previously been operating under a monopoly or oligopoly are likely to see an increase in competition as state-run functions may be shared with other social enterprises. Public sector workers will be encouraged to set up employee-owned cooperatives encouraging innovation and quality of service for the end-user whilst being a more economically viable option for the state. Funding the 'big society' will come from dormant bank accounts which it is believed will provide the necessary funding for stimulating neighbourhood groups, charities, and social enterprise. As previously indicated, it is however unlikely that the 'big society' ideology drive will be funded by an unlimited supply of capital and financial constraints will play a large part in their introduction and use.

161

5. Information ability

Finally, confidence in official data and statistics has been eroded in recent years with possibly unfounded, incorrect statistics being published resulting in several official apologies being made in parliament by senior ministers. Underpinning the 'big society', the government aims to create a new culture where the public have a 'right to data' that will be published regularly in an attempt to improve accountability.

Clearly there is a drive for greater involvement of communities to engage at all levels of public service delivery and community safety is a prime area for the involvement of other agencies as well as charities and volunteer services. In particular, the use of volunteers is of particular interest.

7.4 **Volunteers**

A clear theme of the current government agenda for reform and modernization of the public services is the development of new ways of involving local communities in shaping the priorities and outputs of public service delivery. This involves identifying new and less formalized methods of communication between the public services and service users to make delivery of services more responsive to the needs of local people. This has gained far more prominence of late due to the present government's commitment to a concept the 'big society'.

7.4.1 **The rise of volunteers**

The concept of volunteering within today's police service is not a new one, and indeed has been in use in different countries for a number of years. For example, Special Constables in England and Wales—unpaid, fully warranted police officers—are recruited from members of local communities, and, are the archetypical volunteer in the police in that country, whilst in the United States of America, police volunteers have been extensively utilized (see <http://www.policevolunteers.org/> for detailed information regarding these schemes). However, there now appears scope in England and Wales for the introduction of a very different type of volunteer. The police service has increased the use of volunteers that are unpaid 'civilians' to work within the police organization. These are members of the public who have expressed an interest in working with the police, undertaking various roles and responsibilities within the organization; however, they are not special constables, have no police powers and are unwarranted. These 'neighbourhood volunteers' assist when they can, as many volunteers enjoy the flexibility of supporting the service and their local community in whatever way they can. Dependent on the commitment of the volunteers and the role, whether administrative or involving some sort of community engagement, some volunteers work from different police stations, and others work on the street engaging with members of the public directly, engaging in Partnerships and Communities Talking (PACT) meetings, letter-dropping, and other operations often working alongside neighbourhood police teams and partner agencies.

Case Study -The Lancashire Constabulary volunteer scheme

The introduction of the neighbourhood volunteer scheme in the Lancashire Constabulary is worthy of further examination. Here, the service is currently recruiting volunteers from the local community, aiming to bring it closer to the communities it serves. Launched in June 2004, there are currently 644 support volunteers, encompassing different ages, ethnic groups, gender and backgrounds (Flanagan 2008). Consequently, Lancashire now has some 55 volunteers over the age of 70, a group which the police service in general finds it difficult to engage. Clearly by encouraging cooperation with these groups, new relationships can be formed, and volunteers perform different roles which include neighbourhood policing, quality of service auditing, administrative duties, and public enquiries. A volunteer scheme of this size will inevitably have major implications on the service. This would include having extra staff means extra physical resources, reducing pressure on front line services, and in many cases it is hoped that police officers can be freed up to return to front line duties, a key objective for many chief police officers to increase high-visibility policing. To employ this number of part-time staff would be economically prohibitive, and almost impossible for police forces to sustain. Whilst acknowledging that there are some costs in providing minimal training requirements for volunteers, using volunteers could potentially save hundreds of thousands of pounds a year for the police service. Taking into account the potential number of volunteers, the possible economic savings are considerable, without allowing for the other diverse advantages attached to their use.

7.4.2 The advantages of using volunteers

To ensure the volunteers are representative of the community, and fully reflect the demographic make-up of the community, most police services will attempt to recruit individuals of different backgrounds, ages, ethnic minorities, and religions. In many cases across the country this could include university or college students, those retired and others from diverse communities. Having applied, volunteers are usually vetted and receive training to better equip them for working within the police organization. In order to assist in their work, some forces have opted to dedicate specialist police officers to deal with the neighbourhood volunteer schemes, whereas others have designed a new administrative position, often referred to as a 'volunteer co-coordinator'. The role of the co-coordinator is to oversee recruitment, welfare of volunteers and operations, in essence to manage issues, concerns, training, recruitment, advertisement, and financial expenditure relating to volunteers. Involving the public in different volunteer schemes has many advantages, not least the additional human resources gained.

This is especially useful when faced with the prospect of a diminishing supply of funding and an increasing demand for service delivery. Inclusion and engaging with the community will not only make the delivery of policing more transparent, but will, given time, create a sense of ownership and pride, resulting in an improved relationship between the public and police service. In the mid- to long-term, volunteer schemes may have a positive influence on National Policing Plan targets (Home Office 2005). This will be achieved in part because of the extended partnership approach, improved confidence and cooperation. The improved relationship as well as the developed sense of ownership and inclusion may well result in targets on community safety being met. This may come about in part as the public begin to engage with initiatives, such as PACT meetings and neighbourhood watch. As a direct consequence, this may lead to a reduction in overall crime and fear of crime leading to a reduction in the reassurance gap. Fear of crime, whether it is rational or irrational, is a matter of perception, and for the public, perception is reality. As actual crime reduces, if this combined with the public's perception that crime is reducing, fear of crime then reduces, resulting in a reduction in the reassurance gap (McLaughlin et al 2006). Indeed, the overall product of effective community engagement should not be underestimated. The recent report by Her Majesty's Inspectorate for the Constabulary noted that the role of the volunteer was vital in the fight against crime (Flanagan 2008a). The report concludes that the work being carried out by the volunteers, which includes PACT coordination, reassurance call-backs, and other initiatives, is having a positive impact. Subsequently, there has been an improvement in the service provided by the public, more diverse representation of the community within the constabulary and an overall increase in public confidence shown towards the police. This further illustrates the importance of the 5 per cent target increase for community participation set out in the National Policing Plan 2005–08 (Home Office 2005). An area that we may see the greatest impact of the use of volunteers is that of neighbourhood policing.

7.5 **Neighbourhood or Local Policing Teams**

The *Home Office Strategic Plan 2004–2008* (Home Office 2004c) and the White Paper *Building Communities, Beating Crime* (Home Office 2004a) set out a vision for policing which is accessible and responsive to citizen's needs. These documents represent neighbourhood policing teams as a key component of the police reform programme. In addition, the public service agreements (PSAs) for the Home Office and for many other government departments reflect a commitment to neighbourhoods. A local approach to policing represents a more flexible approach which can link with local circumstances. This means in practice that there will be no definitive model of neighbourhood policing imposed across the country as this would not conform to flexibility for local communities. Of course, the concept of neighbourhood policing forms part of the basis for the National Intelligence Model.

7.5.1 **The purpose of neighbourhood policing**

> The idea is to go back to a time when I was very young, when you expected the police to be part of the community and the community to be part of policing and where people were joined together in partnership, making it work.
>
> David Blunkett (2004)

The concept of neighbourhood team policing appears quite straightforward. It is about dealing with crime and disorder more intelligently and building new relationships between the police and the public. This relationship should be one built on cooperation rather than mere consent. It relies upon local people being part of the solution to local problems of crime and disorder.

Neighbourhood policing has been described as delivering control in response to public priorities. This means that an organized approach to tackling public concerns is required within the mainstream of police activity, while maintaining the high standards of response and quality of service. Neighbourhood policing is therefore dependent upon evidence-based deployment of resources and tactics.

The approach should be much more than just high-visibility reassurance policing. It uses local knowledge and intelligence from local people to target crime hotspots and disorder issues causing most concern to local communities. The government has stated that the latest technology will support the initiative including the issue of mobile telephone numbers to individuals within neighbourhoods so that they can contact the local beat manager directly.

7.5.2 **The aims of neighbourhood policing teams**

Neighbourhood policing aims to achieve getting the right people at the right locations in the right numbers in order to create neighbourhoods that are safe and feel safe. In order for this to be achieved it is dependent upon three main themes, namely:

(1) A dedicated and accountable team and resources with specific geographical ownership.
(2) Intelligence-led targeting of the concerns that matter most to the public.
(3) A partnership approach to taking action by the police, partner agencies, and the public.

Some important questions arise for the police practitioner here. What does the neighbourhood team do, who will take part in it, and what is a neighbourhood anyway?

7.5.3 **The principles of neighbourhood policing teams**

There appear to be several important principles that underpin the philosophy of neighbourhood policing teams. These are:

• It is an organizational strategy that allows the police, their partners, and the public to work closely together in partnership to solve the problems of crime and disorder, improve neighbourhood conditions, and improve feelings of security.

- It is managed within mainstream policing activity, integrated with other policing services, and should not diminish policing activity that addresses volume or serious crime.
- Neighbourhood policing needs evidence-based allocation of teams against an identified need.
- There is a need to establish dedicated identifiable accessible and responsive policing teams which provide all citizens with a named point to access.
- Neighbourhood policing approaches reflect local conditions and will be flexible and able to adapt to local conditions.
- By working closely with local people in identifying problems, it will give people direct influence over local priorities.
- Because it takes a partnership approach to policing problems it establishes a way for engaging other agencies and the public in this type of approach.
- Neighbourhood policing uses the National Intelligence Model as a basis for deployment of resources: this offers the means to identify response and assess the impact of policing at neighbourhood level.
- Neighbourhood policing requires an engagement communication and feedback strategy, and a clear understanding of where accountability lies.
- Neighbourhood policing should be subject to a stringent performance management which includes performance monitoring set against the local plans and commitments made to neighbourhoods.

7.5.4 **What is a neighbourhood?**

Neighbourhoods can be described as geographic areas which are of a size that best serves the needs of the local communities. They are defined through local agreement of the police, their partners, and citizens. Communities themselves often express identification with a locality based on history and culture rather than any geographic logic. Where neighbourhoods are large, in terms of population or geography, it is likely that some more specific locations will need to be policed with dedicated teams or possibly through a sub plan.

KEY POINT—WHAT IS A NEIGHBOURHOOD

To a person living in the inner city, the idea of neighbourhood may seem different to someone living in a country village. A whole council may appear to be a neighbourhood in one instance, whilst in some areas it can mean a political ward.

The government, in pursuing this initiative, have suggested that the definition of neighbourhood should be left up to local communities, police forces and authorities and their partners rather than being told by themselves.

Home Office (2005a)

To help identify neighbourhoods, analysts will need to use data which can ensure that teams are intelligence led. The following data sets are considered suitable for this task:

- Crime statistics—burglary dwelling, criminal damage to dwelling, and racial incidents.
- Deprivation statistics—income deprivation and employment deprivation.
- Education statistics—educational attainment.
- Demographic statistics—proportion of young people between the ages of fifteen and twenty-four.
- Intelligence and local knowledge and understanding.
- Neighbourhood policing teams mean that people will:
- know who their local police officers are and how to contact them
- have a real say in local policing issues and setting local priorities
- know how well their police are doing locally in tackling crime and anti-social behaviour.

7.5.5 How it operates in practice

Figure 7.1 illustrates how the neighbourhood teams operate in reality. Neighbourhood policing appears to be a good example of effective partnership that yields visible results of benefit for the community. It is about moving policing from policing by consent to policing with cooperation, engaging with local people, and responding to their needs and concerns.

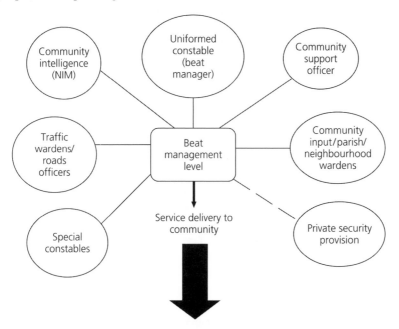

Figure 7.1 A schematic representation of a typical neighbourhood policing team

167

Scenario—Neighbourhood policing

Merseyside police have had teams in forty-three 'neighbourhoods' which equate to two or three council wards each. Teams are headed by an inspector, who has responsibility for a number of sergeants and constables, supported by community support officers, special constables, and volunteers. In consultation with the community they tackle issues that really affect people. Local surveys indicate that crime has been reduced and public satisfaction increased since their introduction.

In Leicester officers are given small areas or 'micro beats' to patrol and oversee. These can be a small number of streets, an estate, or a hotspot. Officers are considered as guardians for their area, solving problems and listening to local people. In one area alone, crime has fallen by 20 per cent as a result of this initiative.

ACPO (2005b)

Neighbourhood teams are an excellent example of delivering police services through a variety of different people, not just sworn police officers. The group of people engaged in this activity are often referred to as the extended policing family.

7.6 The Extended Policing Family

The way a police organization operates can be influenced by many factors. These could include the leftovers from previous activities such as crime operations or from influential community policing leaders such as James Alderson (1984).

We have seen from the Police Reform Act 2002 (Home Office 2002a) that substantial change is in store for the police service and it is this Act that enables us, with some accuracy, to predict the future delivery of policing. The introduction of police community support officers, coupled with the use of Neighbourhood Watch and local warden schemes, will introduce a more flexible method in dealing with community problems, even if at this stage they may lack sufficient powers to carry out their full role. The idea of the extended police family, responsible for ensuring the tackling of day-to-day policing of crime and disorder, is worthy of exploration, particularly in light of the Big Society and the increased use of volunteers as discussed previously.

7.6.1 Uniformed constable

The role of the uniformed constable is crucial in that he/she will act as the 'manager' of the coordinated service delivery. This enables the constable to perform a more proactive role in consultation, coordinating delivery through the various officers available, and where necessary using the full powers vested in a police constable. The role dramatically alters the perception of constable from one of enforcer of laws only to that of facilitator and leader. This will require a more professional approach and therefore perhaps a more highly qualified individual to perform the role. Evidence of the introduction of this role and the changing requirements of the constable can be seen in the drive for competencies and skills instituted by the police Standards and Skills Organization (now Skills for Justice), the introduction of foundation degrees, and the multitude of further and higher education institutions that offer undergraduate and postgraduate degrees in policing and in particular community safety. The constable, it is envisaged, will be directly accountable to his/her line supervisor, the sergeant, who will have responsibility for two or more of the policing teams.

7.6.2 Police specials

The powers owned by police specials, who are volunteers, are exactly the same as those of regular officers. They receive, in theory at least, the same amount and level of training as regular officers, wear the same uniforms, and provide invaluable support in many situations. However, it is questionable whether or not they will be able to fully augment the work of regular officers due to their lack of regular availability. As volunteers, they are able to offer only a certain amount of their time. Despite this fact, they should, if their availability is intelligently managed, provide useful high-visibility patrols, backed up with the lawful authority to use force if necessary, just like regular sworn police officers.

7.6.3 Police Community Support Officer

The Police Community Support Officer (PCSO), working with the other members of the delivery team, will be used not only to provide reassurance through visible patrolling at relevant times, but also through use of his/her powers to resolve order maintenance problems. Evidence now exists that tends to support the view of the usefulness of the role of PCSOs and in particular the extended use of powers available to them (Crawford and Lister 2004). They will provide the beat manager with invaluable assistance in dealing with minor instances of public disorder and anti-social problems. There appears little doubt that PCSOs figure largely in the government's plans in this area.

7.6.4 Traffic wardens

With the concept of traffic wardens not only enforcing road traffic offences but also being able to issue fixed penalty notices for certain other offences, this role becomes a vital part of the integrated policing system. They can further operate as a conduit of information for the policing model, supplying criminal and community intelligence through their visible presence on the street. They will be available to deal with local traffic problems as well as being involved in maintaining safety on the roads. However, the police practitioner must be aware that traffic wardens are generally the responsibility of local authorities or private companies acting on behalf of local authorities rather than the police service.

7.6.5 Parish or neighbourhood warden schemes

Whilst originally conceived as an eyes-and-ears approach for the police, coupled with concierge and reassurance functions, these warden schemes may well be able to issue fixed penalties for various offences such as minor criminal damage (graffiti) to the depositing of litter. The increase in surveillance and reassurance by high-visibility patrolling that these schemes provide will be an invaluable asset to the beat manager.

7.6.6 Private security provision

It is feasible that within the integrated policing model use could be made of private security officers to enhance the policing capability. Whilst the main function of the private security industry has in the past been the protection of private property, there has been an increase in their use for such roles as prisoner escort, as well as other custody duties assisting sworn officers. The Private Security Industry Act 2001 (Home Office 2001c), which regulates the industry, will have wide repercussions for the use of private security in the public domain of policing. The main areas of current activity include the roles of wheel-clamping and guarding premises, and as security consultants. However, at a more basic level, those licensed individuals who act as door supervisors for clubs and public houses should not be discounted from the model. Section 40 of the Police Reform Act 2002 (Home Office 2002a) introduces the community safety accreditation scheme which is designed to extend limited police powers to persons already engaged in community safety duties. These include local authority wardens as well as security guards within the private security industry.

7.6.7 Intelligence and partnerships

Community and criminal intelligence will be of importance if the multiple police services available to the beat manager are to be directed effectively. This would be greatly enhanced by the ability of the public to have direct access in many cases to the beat manager who can then react more quickly to the community's needs.

Consultation with the community at this level, through formal structures such as regular meetings with representatives from the community and surgeries for the public to attend and air their concerns, coupled with sophisticated community intelligence available to the police, will be effective tools in the drive to maintain order. It is envisaged (John and Maguire 2004) that the link between this model and the National Intelligence Model will be forged through the normal tasking and intelligence briefing groups held within every BCU. The review of the Crime and Disorder Act carried out in 2006 recommended that community safety partnership adopt the intelligence-led approach in conjunction with the police, utilizing the National Intelligence Model discussed below.

7.7 **The National Intelligence Model**

> The Model has real value in that it clearly outlines the component parts of the intelligence process and clarifies terminology which is all too often misunderstood. Adoption of the model throughout the UK will ensure commonality in working practices and an understanding of the intelligence requirements which will ensure greater effectiveness in the future.
>
> John Orr, OBE, QPM (NCIS 2000)

The National Intelligence Model (NIM) is a major introduction in the context of police reform. NIM is a model that ensures information is fully researched and analysed to provide intelligence that senior police managers can use to inform strategic direction, and to help them make tactical decisions about resourcing and operational policing, and in managing risk. One important point to note is that the model is not just about intelligence, it can be used for most areas of policing. For example, it sets the requirements for the contribution of patrolling, reactive, proactive, and intelligence staff.

7.7.1 **A business process**

The National Intelligence Model is a business process (see Figure 7.2). The intention behind it is to provide focus on operational policing and to achieve a disproportionately greater impact from resources applied to any problem. It is dependent upon a clear framework of analysis of information and intelligence, allowing a problem-solving approach to law enforcement and crime prevention. The expected outcomes are improved community safety, reduced crime, and the control of criminality and disorder, leading to greater public reassurance and confidence.

The National Intelligence Model is the product of work carried out by the National Criminal Intelligence Service on behalf of the Crime Committee of the Association of Chief Police Officers (ACPO). It is a method whereby more rigour can be introduced into the management decision-making process for both strategic and tactical purposes. Its introduction, it is believed, will greatly help 'joined-up' law enforcement.

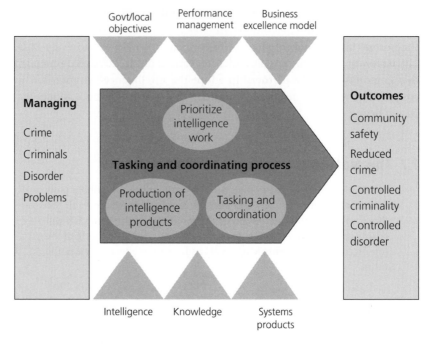

Figure 7.2 A simplified schematic model of the National Intelligence Model

The model has been designed to have an impact at three levels of police activity, namely levels 1, 2, and 3. These levels are explained in the following box.

KEY POINT—LEVELS OF ACTIVITY IN NIM

Level 1: Daily tasking—local issues which are the crimes, criminals, and other problems affecting a BCU. This area will encompass wide issues from low-level theft to murder, and it is anticipated that the handling of volume crime will be at this level.

Level 2: Force/regional level tasking—cross-border issues that affect more than one BCU. This may include problems that affect a group of BCUs or neighbouring forces, and may also involve support from the National Crime Squad, HM Customs and Excise, or the NCIS. Common problems, the exchange of data, and provision of resources for the benefit of all concerned will be key issues at this level.

Level 3: National tasking—serious and organized crime which usually operates on a national and international scale will be dealt with at this level.

7.7.2 **The National Intelligence Model and partnerships**

Whilst the National Intelligence Model is firstly a business model used to allocate police resources, there will be a strong link between it and partnership working. An integral component part of the model is information and partners should be encouraged to provide as much information as possible at the beginning of the process and to accept results following research and analysis so that they can be better informed about tactical or strategic issues.

However, much of the intelligence that is produced by NIM at the tactical level may be restricted or confidential and often will include names of targets and offenders. Users of NIM should be aware that there are a number of readily identifiable sources of information. These include victims, witnesses, offenders, and informants. It is therefore essential that police officers gather information and intelligence from all sources and that it is processed through the intelligence systems in place.

In terms of local partnerships, the tactical tasking and coordinating group (TT&CG) comprises a chairperson and a small group of senior managers who have responsibility for one BCU and who can make resourcing decisions. Part of their function is also to consider corporate intelligence products which may impact upon their area as well as being represented at force level.

7.7.3 **Community intelligence**

Community intelligence will be vital if crime and disorder reduction partnerships are to dovetail into the process of intelligence-led policing. It should never be underestimated as not only will it address policing issues from general quality-of-life perspective, but can also be used to address serious crime and of course terrorism.

Local effective arrangements to capture this vital information should be put in place as the success of neighbourhood policing will depend in part upon them.

KEY POINT—COMMUNITY INTELLIGENCE DEFINED

'Community Intelligence is local information which, when assessed, provides intelligence on issues that affect neighbourhoods and informs both the strategic and operational perspectives in the policing of local communities. Information may be direct and indirect and come from a diverse range of sources including the community and partner agencies.'

ACPO (2005b:12)

7.8 **Summing Up**

7.8.1 **Police Reform Act 2002**

The police reform programme is a series of changes currently being insti-
gated by the government. It has far-reaching effects for the policing in general and for partnerships in particular in the country, and manifests itself in
the introduction of the Police Reform Act 2002. The Act introduces the
following:

- An Annual Policing Plan which sets the government's strategy for policing
  for the next five years.
- Powers to ensure a force solves problems of inefficiency and ineffectiveness.
- Powers for the removal of a chief constable in the interest of the public.
- Provision for the introduction of police community support officers,
  investigating officers, and others who can help the police deal with low-
  level crime and anti-social behaviour.

7.8.2 **Big Society**

This term relates to the present government's idea regarding the provision
of public services through greater use of volunteers and charities as well as
other agencies. The area of crime reduction seems an appropriate area for
this type of activity.

7.8.3 **Volunteers**

A clear theme of the current government agenda for reform and modernization of the public services is the development of new ways of involving local
communities in shaping the priorities and outputs of public service delivery.

7.8.4 **The extended policing family**

This term relates to the mixed and varied delivery of policing services to the
community. It is a term that crosses over the boundaries between public and
private policing and refers to all organizations involved in policing. It
includes the following (amongst others):

(1) sworn police officers (the constable and special constable)
(2) police community support officers
(3) neighbourhood watch and warden schemes
(4) volunteers from the community
(5) private security companies
(6) the community itself.

7.8.5 **Neighbourhood or local policing teams**

Neighbourhood policing teams are made up of various roles engaged in delivering policing services. They include police constables, special constables, police community support officers, neighbourhood wardens, members of the community, volunteers, and possibly private security staff. This mode of policing focuses on local problems, and means that people will:

(1) know who their local officers are
(2) have a say in local policing issues
(3) know how well police are doing in tackling local crime and disorder.

7.8.6 **The National Intelligence Model**

The National Intelligence Model (NIM) is a business model introduced to ensure that information is fully researched and analysed to provide intelligence for strategic decision-making. The model has three levels of activity:

(1) **Level One**—which looks at issues affecting a basic command unit (BCU)
(2) **Level Two**—which considers issues such as cross-border criminality and supports national policing including HM Customs and Excise, NCIS, and National Crime Squads.
(3) **Level Three**—which considers organized crime at a national and international level.

NIM can be a vital tool in tackling crime and disorder as it contains readily identifiable sources of information such as victims, witnesses, and informants.

7.8.7 **Community intelligence**

Community intelligence is local information which, when assessed, provides intelligence on issues that affect neighbourhoods, and informs both the strategic and operational perspectives in the policing of local communities. Information may be direct and indirect, and come from a diverse range of sources including the community and partner agencies.

7.8.8 **Local application**

(1) What evidence can you see of reform in your local police force as a result of the police reform programme?
(2) What positive points can you list for the introduction of neighbourhood policing teams?
(3) In what ways can you identify the usefulness of the National Intelligence Model?
(4) What 'intelligence products' can you identify within your local BCU?

7.8.9 **Useful websites**

http://www.homeoffice.gov.uk/
http://www.policesupers.com/
http://www.polfed.org/
http://www.police-information.co.uk/policelinks.html
http://www.audit-commission.gov.uk/index.asp

8

Crime and Disorder Reduction Performance

8.1 **Introduction**

The problems of crime and disorder are not simple ones and there are in reality no quick fixes that will remove them all at one fell swoop. There is now a recognition that the police alone cannot deal with all these matters, and that all agencies that can make a contribution to reducing crime and disorder need to work in partnership. However, perhaps one of the most influential factors that affects the reduction of crime and disorder is the understanding that these issues are complex and that they need to be understood in their local contexts. This in turn means that crime and disorder strategies need to be tailored to the local community requirements. The purpose of this chapter is to explain the audit process in such a manner that the police practitioner and others will find easy to understand and helpful.

The Crime and Disorder Act 1998 (Home Office 1999a) places a statutory responsibility upon crime and disorder reduction partnerships to carry out local audits to implement evidence-based strategies and to deal with agreed priorities in the reduction of local problems of crime and disorder. This Act seeks to reinsert the community into policing, and one of the key ways in which this is achieved is through the process of the local audit of crime and disorder. The guidance in the Act specifies a wide range of organizations, agencies, and community groups or representatives who it is intended should be involved in the process. Some of the original guidance within this Act has, however, been modified as a result of the review of the partnership provisions of the Crime and Disorder Act published in 2006. The local policing plan should include objectives determined by the Home Secretary and the police authority currently, but by the Police and Crime Commissioners from November 2012, and should also include performance targets set by the authority. This is an important point for police practitioners, who may, occasionally, not realize that many of the daily functions they perform are the result of a process that involves audits, consultation, and the production of strategies that include local and national priorities. Indeed the process of auditing crime and disorder is a means to develop logical crime reduction strategies which enjoy public support and which are put into practice.

8.2 **Responsible Authorities**

The definition of what a responsible authority is under legislation is quite specific and broad, in an attempt to include as many agencies as possible. Section 5(1) of the Crime and Disorder Act 1998 defines responsible authorities for each local government area as:

- The council for that area and, where the area is a district and the council is not a unitary authority, the council for the county, which includes the district (i.e., in a two-tier authority both district and county councils are responsible).
- Every chief officer of police where any parts of their police area lies within the local government area.

- Every police authority where any part of their police area lies within the local government area.
- Every fire and rescue authority where any part of their area lies within the local government area.
- In Wales, every health authority where the whole or part of their area lies within the local government area.

KEY POINT—RESPONSIBLE AUTHORITIES

Responsible authorities under the Crime and Disorder Act include:

- local authorities
- police authorities
- health authorities and trusts
- chief officers of police
- fire authorities

8.2.1 **Role of responsible authorities**

Responsible authorities are required to work in partnership to identify the extent of these problems in their community and to develop strategies to deal effectively with these problems. In Wales, responsible authorities are issued guidance in respect of their duties by the National Assembly for Wales.

Their main roles can be summarized as follows:

- To review levels and patterns of crime and disorder, taking into account the knowledge and experience of persons in their area.
- To act in association with cooperating bodies.
- To invite the participation of others (invitees to participate).
- To prepare an analysis of the results of the review.

The Crime and Disorder Act also identifies those authorities that must cooperate with community safety partnerships. These are called cooperating bodies.

8.3 **Cooperating Bodies**

Section 5(2) of the Crime and Disorder Act 1998 states that responsible authorities must act in cooperation with every probation board and any part of whose area lies within the area. It is also a requirement that responsible authorities work in cooperation with the following in each local government area:

- parish councils in England
- community councils in Wales
- NHS Trusts
- schools' governing bodies

- independent schools' proprietors
- further education governing bodies.

Cooperating bodies represent local groups or agencies that can provide significant contributions to tackling crime and disorder in the local area. The Crime and Disorder Act 1998 places a legal obligation on cooperating bodies to cooperate fully in the work of strategy-setting process and also to help deliver the objectives set out in the crime and disorder strategy.

Cooperating bodies should be able to provide data or information to improve the understanding of local crime and disorder problems, and to contribute to the benefit of the local community as well as benefiting the core functions of the respective agencies.

It is hoped these bodies will introduce their knowledge and expertise as well as their abilities to support partnerships' initiatives.

8.3.1 The role of cooperating bodies

Cooperating bodies represent local groups or agencies that can provide a significant contribution to local crime reduction. In formulating a strategy, the Act requires that objectives must be set for the cooperating bodies and other contracted agencies.

To achieve this, cooperating bodies should be a key element of strategy development process, and important partners in the implementation and ongoing development of the strategy. Cooperating bodies should be able to provide salient data or information to improve the understanding of local crime and disorder problems, contributing to the benefit of the local community as well as deriving benefit to the core functions of their respective agencies.

It is believed that these bodies should be able to bring the benefit of their knowledge and expertise and details of their ability to help support partnerships' initiatives through early interventions, either as part of their core work or working together with other constituent partnership agencies.

The roles and requirements of these other agencies should be identified to establish what they can contribute in terms of information, resources, and ideas. Similarly, they need to understand what benefits they can reap from partnership working in terms of their work and core functions.

The Act also places a legal obligation on cooperating bodies to:

- cooperate fully in the work of and strategy-setting process
- help deliver the objectives set out in the crime and disorder strategy.

A further group identified as being significant for crime and disorder partnerships are a group called 'invitees to participate'.

8.4 Invitees to Participate

Invitees to participate represent a range of local groups and organizations that are involved and engaged in the community. Section 5(3) of the Crime and

Disorder Act 1998 includes a list of invitees to participate, and whilst this list is by no means exhaustive it is fairly comprehensive in scope. However, community safety partnerships are encouraged to contact local groups and communities in order to actively engage them in the audit process. Many of these groups have a large amount of information gathered during their day-to-day activities and can provide a fuller picture and understanding of the causes of crime and disorder in the local community. The local experience and knowledge of dealing with victims and perpetrators these agencies have is invaluable in helping to understand local problems and helping in finding solutions, and implementing strategies.

KEY POINT—INVITEES TO PARTICIPATE

These include:

- social landlords
- Training and Enterprise Councils
- Crown Prosecution Service
- magistrates' court committees
- Neighbourhood Watch committee
- religious bodies
- Drug Action Teams/Drug and Alcohol Teams
- youth voluntary organizations
- Crown Court managers
- victim support services
- medical practitioners
- trade unions.

In summary, Table 8.1 illustrates the main bodies termed responsible authorities, cooperating bodies, and invitees to participate.

Table 8.1 Parties involved in crime and disorder reduction audits

Responsible authorities	Cooperating bodies	Invitees to participate
Police	Probation committee	Secretary of State directs at least one
Local authority	Parish councils and	representative from:
Police authority	community councils	Social landlords
Fire authorities	(Wales)	Drug Action Teams/Drugs and Alcohol Teams
Health authorities in Wales	NHS Trusts	Training and Education Councils
	Governing bodies of	Voluntary organizations—Youth
	schools	Crown Prosecution Service
	Proprietors of	Crown court manager
	independent schools	Magistrates' court committee
	Governing bodies—	Neighbourhood Watch committee
	further education	Victim support service member

8.5. **Strategic Intelligence Assessments**

The Home Office has stated that every partnership will use an adapted version of the National Intelligence Model used by the police which will result in an intelligence-led problem-solving and outcome-orientated approach to community safety. This involves routinely analysing data and intelligence to inform strategic decisions and accurately direct resources and manage risk. These strategic assessments have to be undertaken at least every six months, and are used by all partners providing strategic and operational community safety functions. This replaces the three-year audits which were undertaken by community safety partnerships previously. There is now a six-monthly strategic intelligence assessment used to inform the new requirements to produce annual rolling three year community safety plans.

This approach depends heavily upon good quality data being produced by analysts and on good information being shared amongst partner agencies. Consequently, the previous requirement for a three-year audit has been removed and replaced by a rolling annual three-year community safety plan, underpinned by the six-monthly strategic assessments already discussed.

8.6 **The Strategy Document**

A strategy can also be described as a plan, an evaluation of the crime and disorder problems in the community, together with an action plan of what is going to be undertaken to tackle the relevant issues, the outcomes to be achieved, and the resources involved.

As we have seen, every three years the community safety partnership must produce a rolling annual three-year community safety plan, underpinned by the six-monthly strategic assessments, for its area. This must include anti-social behaviour. Data must be gathered from all partners to establish the nature, frequency, and hotspot locations of the problem. Following the production of the audit the crime and disorder reduction partnership must then consult with the public about their priorities for tackling disorder and crime. A Crime and Disorder Strategy is then produced for the following three years that takes into account both the audit and consultation findings.

A strategy needs to be based upon the needs of the local communities in the area and therefore based on what the real issues are. For example, if begging or street drinking is not an issue in the area or for the community then it does not need to be part of the strategy. Information about what is happening in the area can be obtained from the crime and disorder reduction partnership, local community groups, police statistics and local authority departments, and through the consultation process. The strategy should contain what the plan of work is for tackling the anti-social behaviour issues in the area and the range of interventions that are available.

This should include the following major points:

- Prevention such as provision for young people, supported housing, incentive schemes, strong civic message.
- Interventions such as multi-agency case conferencing and support for those that are struggling; mediation, family group conferencing, community conferencing, Acceptable Behaviour Agreements/Contracts, Parenting Contracts.
- Enforcement such as injunctions, possession proceedings, Anti-Social Behaviour Orders, Parenting Orders.
- Victim and witness support that will be offered.

Finally, there must be a mechanism for communicating with the public and informing them about the strategy in place and the progress that has been made.

8.6.1 What should a strategy look like?

In general terms a strategy document should have three clear and broad areas or headings. These are an introduction, a summary of the findings of the audit which helps develop the priorities, and a performance measurement structure to ensure the strategy is being delivered correctly.

Introduction

Here an opportunity exists for the partnership to give a brief overview of the structure of the partnerships strategy whilst also making people aware of the mission statement or vision. It is good practice for a partnership to have a mission statement and people should be made aware of it. An example of a mission statement could be as simple as this:

'To work together for a just, tolerant, and safe place to live.'

This section also contains the purpose of the strategy and how it is linked to the crime and disorder process. For example, it should give a description of the strategy cycle, and state that partnerships are required to tackle both crime and anti-social behaviour; this section should describe how the strategy will highlight priorities, aims, and objectives against which its success will be judged, and how the partnership will make best use of resources in tackling the priorities.

An opportunity also exists to discuss the partnership structure and any other plans of partners in the particular area. For example, one could give an explanation of how the accountability process works, and emphasize that feedback from communities will be identified within the strategy.

Summary of findings

This section of the document can be used to summarize the findings of the strategic assessments and develop priorities for attention. There is usually a discussion surrounding these issues, whereby a link between the analysis of the data and the priorities has been reached. The main issues or themes identified can be many and complex. However, some of the main issues and themes that are regularly identified can be seen in the following box.

KEY POINT—MAIN ISSUES AND THEMES IDENTIFIED FROM THE STRATEGIC ASSESSMENT

Crime related—focused on particular crimes such as theft of or from vehicles.
Disorder related—focused on particular disorder such as youth annoyance.
Geographical issues—identification of geographical hotspots.
Demographic issues—priorities focused on particular groups of people, such as the young or elderly.
Cross-cutting themes—where priorities cross a number of issues.

Performance management of priority areas

This section should be used to clarify the priorities that have been identified. Each priority should have an aim and a clear and meaningful objective attached to the aim with objectives having been considered using the SMART process, including targets, appropriate timescales, and performance measurements to enable effective monitoring.

An *aim* is a simple statement that sets out the purposes of the priority. It is important that aims are not confused with objectives—an *objective* is a specific statement that can be measured. It is a statement that describes something that you want to achieve, and relates to the overall aim. Put simply, an objective is a statement that describes something you want to achieve—the desired outcome of the priority. Objectives must be clear, meaningful, and measurable, i.e., they must be SMART. This is a mnemonic for the following:

Specific—it must have specific outcomes.
Measurable—you must be able to measure the outcome of an objective.
Achievable—it must describe something that can be achieved within the timescale and resources available.
Realistic—it must describe something that can be done.
Time-bound—a timescale must be set for when the objective is to be achieved.

Having identified the priority from the data and assessment process each priority must be allocated a target. Targets are the measurable parts of objectives. There must be a balance between setting challenging objectives and being realistic about what it is actually possible to achieve in a given time with the available resources.

Targets do not have to be focused on 'reductions' if this is not appropriate. If crime trends are showing an increase across an area, a target to maintain crime rates at current levels may be more appropriate.

Crime and disorder targets are an important method for partnerships to manage performance on their key crime priorities. It is, of course, important that realistic timescales are set for when the objective is to be achieved.

8.7 **Target-setting**

One way of ensuring that targets are set correctly is to follow a checklist. This could include the following:

- Targets should reflect the actions planned and what the partnership is trying to achieve.
- Targets must specify what must actually *happen* for the desired outcome to be achieved, for example, inputs (e.g., resources in terms of staff or cash), processes (e.g., the activities for which staff will have responsibility), target outputs (e.g., the immediate consequences of these activities), and milestones (stages to be reached by given dates).

These detailed targets may not need to be included in the strategy, but having them defined helps partners be clear about the level of investment and activity needed to achieve the desired result. It also helps managers to check that projects are on course. Setting targets for, and monitoring, inputs as well as outputs is vital for assessing the cost-effectiveness of particular initiatives and understanding why a project may not have achieved its intended results.

- Start from good baseline information. Meaningful targets and good project design depend on having good information on the scale and nature of the problem. Where there are gaps in the baseline information, set a target date by which the data will be obtained.
- Estimate the impact that the activities will have. Estimating impact is easier for some crimes than for others. Examples of good practice can help to give a feel for the expected impact from taking a similar course of action in similar conditions.

8.7.1 **Targets: where to start?**

Running through a list of questions can help in judging where to set a target:

- What is the starting position?
- What is the scale of the problem?
- What is the trend?
- How do these compare with other areas?
- What has a similar activity achieved elsewhere?
- Are we planning to tackle the problem in the same way?
- Are the conditions the same?
- Are we putting in the same resources?

- What else is going on that may affect performance?
- How might the target(s) be affected by other local or national initiatives?
- How does the local target relate to national targets?
- Has the staff providing services been consulted on the target?
- Does the target set take account of their input?
- How will staff commitment be secured?
- Is the target worthwhile? For example, will the public regard it as acceptable and will achieving it be satisfying?

Where possible an individual person should be responsible for delivering and reporting on each target.

- Consider how the target might be met. Could the target be met in ways *other* than those you intend? If so, how will you check for/guard against this?
- Consider setting targets that reflect the role of different partners. Targets that reflect different partners' objectives can help in tracking and acknowledging contributions made by different agencies.
- Consider how the targets will be communicated to people who need to know about them. When, and how, will targets be built into work plans? How will the targets be shared with a wider audience?
- Review progress at regular intervals. Checks against the targets will help to highlight where projects need adjusting or where targets need revising to reflect a changing situation. The action plan may also need revising to take account of new developments.

It is very easy, once a crime and disorder audit has been accomplished, priorities agreed, and strategies published, to be complacent. However, perhaps the most important part of the process is often overlooked—that of evaluation and monitoring. Organizations appear very good at putting into place new policies, procedures, or (in the case of crime and disorder prevention partnerships) audits and strategies, but it is another matter when it comes to evaluating or monitoring the plan. This is a vital part of the whole procedure if there is to be any credibility attached to the whole idea of crime and disorder reduction strategies. It is an important point for those involved in crime and disorder reduction partnerships.

8.8 **Evaluation and Monitoring**

This is the process of assessing whether or not a plan or a project is achieving or has achieved its stated objectives (impact evaluation). Evaluation can also be used to measure whether the processes being used to help achieve the objectives are working properly (process evaluation). Whatever type of evaluation is undertaken, the major point is that evaluation is about measuring progress against objectives. Further, evaluation is not an absolute science and can only ever give an approximation of how successful the project or strategy has been. The difference between evaluation and monitoring is that monitoring is the process of continually assessing whether or not a project is achieving its objectives, whereas evaluation seeks to identify the success or otherwise of a project once it has ended.

8.8.1 Why evaluate?

There are several good reasons why the process of evaluation should be used. These are:

- Many partnerships are funded by a variety of sources, including public and private revenue. Evaluation illustrates how effectively resources have been allocated, and may be part of the funding process that demands that costs and benefits are properly measured.
- In this era of 'what works', a well-conducted evaluation will illustrate what worked well and what did not. This will help when it comes to planning any future strategies as it allows for any improvements.
- It can be useful for others who wish to conduct similar work, as it will help to spread new ideas.
- The impact of crime and disorder strategies on differing parts of the community can be unexpected, and evaluation is often the only way of establishing this.

8.8.2 Different types of evaluation

As can be seen, when used properly evaluation is a useful management tool for controlling projects. It can be implemented at any preplanned point during the lifetime of a project or strategy. When an evaluation is carried out in the early stages of a project it is called a pre-evaluation or sometimes an appraisal. The idea behind this type of appraisal is to see whether the proposed project, etc., is feasible. However, a useful type of evaluation is when it is conducted at different points in the lifetime of the project so as to enable changes to be made if required. These can be referred to as key stage evaluations. Post-project evaluation is designed to see whether the objectives of a project or strategy have been achieved and can take place, either immediately after the project has ended or some time after the end of the project to see if the effects are still in place. Therefore, evaluation should be seen as an ongoing process, not just kept until the end of a project.

8.8.3 Levels of evaluation

It is not only at the temporal level that evaluation should be considered. Evaluation can take place at different levels.

Project-level evaluation

This is the basic level of evaluation and evaluates the specific objective, normally one that is clearly defined and addresses a single problem. An example may be increased street lighting to prevent thefts from vehicles. The idea of evaluation in this instance would be to see whether the increased lighting initiative has achieved its objective.

Programme-level evaluation

At this level, the evaluation is concerned with a group of projects that have a common theme and are being used to achieve a number of objectives that are linked together. For example, an initiative to reduce domestic burglary may involve several projects such as target hardening of vulnerable premises, leaflet circulation, and the introduction of a Neighbourhood Watch system. This level of evaluation is to measure whether the individual projects have achieved the objective.

Strategy-level evaluation

This is a fairly high level of evaluation and means evaluating many projects and programmes. The crime and disorder reduction strategies have to be evaluated every three years to see if they have met their objectives. The idea behind this level of evaluation is to measure the long-term objectives across a wide range of departments, organizations, agencies, and their activities.

8.8.4 The evaluation cycle

Evaluation, in many senses, can be seen as a project in its own right: it must be planned and organized and have clear methods of achieving its objectives. However, practitioners should not be overawed by this process. Reference to the evaluation cycle flow chart (Figure 8.1) and the accompanying examples should make the process easier to understand.

Setting objectives for the evaluation

Here the evaluation process starts by asking what exactly is the aim of the evaluation, what are the targets and the objectives, and against what baseline are the results to be measured. Objectives are a key tool for evaluation and project management and they often cause problems for people who have to write them and use them. Put simply, an objective is a statement that describes something you want to achieve—the desired outcome of a project or an evaluation study. A good evaluation should be able to compare the actual results of a project against the desired results. For this to take place it is important that objectives are written so that they can be measured. In order for this to take place objectives should be SMART produced.

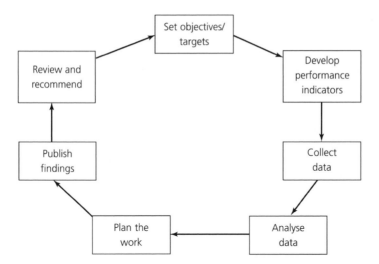

Figure 8.1 An evaluation cycle

It is important that project teams set a realistic number of objectives. For most crime reduction initiatives three or four objectives are enough. A larger number of objectives makes a project unwieldy to manage and very difficult to evaluate.

The baseline is the situation at the start of a project, before any preventative work has been carried out, i.e., the information that helps to define the nature and extent of the problem. The first step is to define the nature and extent of the problem.

Using baseline data to help formulate the objectives is an important part of all projects and vital to any evaluation. For example, an initial analysis of theft from cars in a town centre car park might show twelve offences per week. An evaluation of the situation at the end of the project shows that the number of thefts has reduced by a third, to eight per week. Having the baseline information available during the evaluation helps to measure the effects of any work carried out. Whether you are involved in a project from the start, or just in the evaluation stages, you should make sure that there is enough baseline information to help you measure the achievement of any action.

Develop performance indicators

A performance indicator (PI) is the means by which you know whether or not you have achieved your targets and objectives. A PI is any information that indicates whether a particular objective has been met. The two examples below illustrate this point.

A project to tackle theft from cars in a car park has an objective to reduce the number of thefts by 20 per cent over a six-month period. One of the performance indicators would be whether there had been a rise or fall in the number of reported incidents.

In this example, the number of recorded crimes is a direct indicator of whether the initiative has worked or not. A second project has an objective to reduce the fear of crime on a housing estate. The fear has been caused by several incidents of youth disorder and residents are too frightened to leave their homes. Several indicators could be used here:

- Has there been a rise in income for traders in local shops?
- Are local facilities such as libraries or a community centre being used more often?
- Have there been fewer calls to the police to attend potentially problem situations?
- Do local residents, when interviewed, feel safer and more confident when living in an area?

In this example, the first three indicators are indirect indicators. On their own none of them are conclusive proof that the initiative has worked, but taken together they would indicate whether the initiative had worked. You can also use PIs that measure whether the inputs and outputs in a project are working. For example, if a project is using public meetings as one of its inputs, a PI could be used to measure the number of meetings held and the number of people who attend each meeting. These kind of PIs are called process PIs. Performance indicators are only pointers towards success or failure, they are not conclusive proof. In both examples there are a number of other things that could happen to ease the problem. They may have nothing to do with the crime reduction measures. The answer is to choose indicators that support each other. For instance, in the second example none of those indicators alone would provide sufficient evidence. But taken together as a 'basket' of indicators they provide good evidence of the project's success or failure.

Collect and analyse data

This section is covered in depth in a separate chapter. However, the main points to remember briefly are:

- What data are needed?
- How much detail is required?
- Where do the data come from?
- Are they accurate, detailed, and reliable?
- How are the data to be collected?
- What problems can be expected in collecting the data?

As a rule-of-thumb approach it should be remembered that nothing should be collected unless it can be analysed. Some data such as crime figures do not need a great deal of analysis if any, but others might need analysis and interpretation to ensure that it is in the right format to apply to performance indicators, for example.

Planning the work

Having thus far decided on objectives, performance indicators, and data collection there is the important decision about who does what to be considered. For example, who will collect and analyse the data? Who will act as liaison between the different agencies? Who will write the final report? All these questions need answering. Usually, the first place to look is within the partnership organizations for people with specialist knowledge or those who are willing to do the work. The advantages of this are:

- they are usually more cost effective
- they already have access to a certain amount of data
- it helps to develop skills in existing staff.

However, there are occasions where external organizations are more beneficial for the evaluation exercise. The reason for this is quite simple: the more involved in a project someone is, the more chance that they will inadvertently meddle and skew the results. Using external expertise also provides more credibility to the final results. Whoever is used externally for the evaluation process, there are several points that need to be considered:

- the budget available for the use of external agencies
- the size of the task in hand
- the impact of the likely results.

Having thus decided who does what, a project plan including dates by which work should be completed, what resources should be made available, and who needs to be involved should be constructed. This will include critical dates for the completion of work, and could be as simple as entries on a calendar in the office.

Publish findings

Publishing the findings of the evaluation is an exciting and important part of the whole evaluation process. In general written reports are the most common method of publishing evaluation findings, but there are several points that practitioners need to consider before publication of the final document. These are:

- The audience—the intended audience will have a major effect upon how the information within the report is presented. For example, there may be several differences in a report for a technical expert and one intended for members of the public.
- The skills and knowledge of those receiving the report—a written report would probably need a summary of the main findings so that individuals can make a decision as to how much of the report is relevant to them.
- Presentation of the findings—although written reports are the most common, they can include many different ways of presenting results such as the use of tables, graphics, charts, photographs, etc. These should be clear and easy to read.

Review and recommend

Recommendations are included in the final evaluation document. Once the evaluation document has been published then any work carried out as a result of it should be reviewed. This is normally carried out by management teams, community groups, or crime and disorder reduction partnerships.

8.9 Glossary of Terms

There is often a bewildering range of terms and phrases used in the process of evaluation. Many have been used within the text of this chapter and have been defined for the police practitioner. However, in the course of the crime and disorder audit and evaluation process, individuals may come across several words not already covered, or words that mean the same as those already discussed. Therefore, to assist in this, an additional glossary of terms commonly used has been included. The definitions are arranged alphabetically so that as well as helping you to understand what they mean, this part can also be used as a reference.

For each word or phrase, there is a definition and, in most cases, an example. Where phrases or words are linked to each other these links have been emboldened.

Aim a simple statement that sets out the purpose of the project or evaluation. An example of an aim is: 'The aim of this evaluation is to measure the effects of the Burglary Reduction Initiative.' It's important not to confuse aims with objectives. An objective is a specific statement that can be measured. It states exactly what you want to achieve in your evaluation.

Benchmark a measure of performance in similar organizations against which the performance of your organization can be compared. Benchmarks can be used to measure how successful you are in dealing with a particular aspect of work and to set standards for performance in your own organization. For example, if an organization was looking at how effectively it dealt with telephone enquiries, it might compare its performance with other organizations doing similar work. The benefit of benchmarking for evaluation is that you can measure the success of a particular project by comparing it with other, similar projects. The important thing to remember is that the benchmarks you use must be for similar work in similar areas.

Evaluation the process of assessing, at a particular point in time, whether or not particular projects are achieving or have achieved their objectives. We have already looked at a definition of evaluation in some depth in this book. Evaluation is about measuring the outcomes of a particular project. An outcome is the overall result of a project. Evaluation can also be used to measure whether the processes used in a project are working properly. This is called process evaluation and it measures the inputs and outputs of a project.

Goal another term sometimes used for **targets**.

Initiative an alternative term often used to describe a **project**.

Inputs the resources put into a project to carry out the work. Resources can be financial, material, or human. For example, in a project to reduce the incidence of crime in a town centre by installing a CCTV, some of the inputs would be: money to buy equipment; the CCTV equipment itself; staff time to install it; staff time to monitor the system; and publicity material to launch the start of the system. From a project management point of view it is important to be aware of exactly what resources are available to carry out the work. When resources are limited, it can affect the objectives of a project and the scope of the work carried out. Being aware of the inputs used on a project is vital to its evaluation. As well as measuring the success of a project, you could be measuring the cost-effectiveness of any input and whether any specific methods were particularly useful. It could be that a project or method was effective because of the level of resources available.

Milestones key points during the life of a project. They are decided at the planning stage and can be time-based or event-based.

Mission the overarching reason why an organization exists. This is often described in a mission statement, which describes the overall aim(s) of the organization. It's useful to be aware of any mission or aims that an organization has set itself. Part of the process of evaluation might be to measure the success of a project, programme, or strategy by measuring it against the organization's mission. Another term often used for mission is **vision**.

Monitoring the process of continually assessing whether or not particular projects are achieving or have achieved their objectives. Monitoring is also used to check whether the processes being used are working effectively. Monitoring is carried out throughout the life of a project, while evaluation is only carried out at specific points in time. Monitoring is used to check whether specific targets have been met, how inputs are being used, and whether specific outputs have been achieved.

Outcome the overall result of applying the inputs of a project and achieving the outputs. In other words, by using resources to complete specific pieces of work you will achieve some results. To use the town centre CCTV example again: inputs were equipment, money, and staff time. Outputs were the installation of equipment, the monitoring centre, and the publicity material. The outcomes were a 15 per cent reduction in disorder offences. In this example the evaluation could measure the outcomes by comparing the 15 per cent reduction against the target reduction set out in the objective to establish whether the outcome is a direct result of the outputs—the installation of CCTV assessess whether the scheme has been cost effective by measuring the inputs (the costs of the project) against any savings made.

Output a piece of work produced for a project. For example, the installation of CCTV in a town centre, the establishment of a monitoring centre, and the production and distribution of publicity leaflets are outputs. It is important to realize that an output is not necessarily the final purpose of a project. Outputs are usually things that need to be done in order to produce the desired result. During the life of a project outputs are monitored to make sure they are being achieved on time and with the resources available.

Process evaluation the systematic measurement of the **inputs** and **outputs** of a **project**.

Programme a group or collection of projects designed to achieve particular objectives. The projects in a programme are usually linked to a particular problem or a particular area and fall under a common aim.

Project a series of activities that need to take place in order to achieve specific objectives. Projects have: specific objectives they are meant to address, a clearly defined timescale, a set of linked activities designed to produce specific outputs and outcomes, and clearly identified resources.

Qualitative performance indicators any information enabling the measurement of qualities, which are usually quite intangible things, such as the perceptions and feelings of individuals and groups. For example, changes in the level of fear of crime in the elderly would be a qualitative performance indicator.

Quantitative performance indicators any information enabling the measurement of tangible things, such as the number of burglaries, or percentage of homes burgled, in an area.

Resources the **inputs** to a **project**.

Targets the measurable parts of objectives (see **aims**). For example in this objective 'By the end of the project (in six months' time), the number of violent disorders in Anytown town centre will have been reduced by 20 per cent', the target is a 20 per cent, reduction in six months' time.

Vision the overarching reason why an organization exists. You may come across this term or others which mean the same thing, such as **mission**.

8.10 Summing Up

8.10.1 Responsible authority

Section 5(1) of the Crime and Disorder Act 1998 identifies responsible authorities. These include local authorities, police authorities, health authorities and Trusts, fire authorities, and chief officers of police. They are required to work together in carrying out crime and disorder reduction audits every three years.

8.10.2 **Cooperating body**

Section 5(2) of the Crime and Disorder Act 1998 specifies that some responsible authorities must act in cooperation with important bodies within their areas. These include community and parish councils, National Health Service Trusts, and further and higher education establishments, amongst others. Their role is to contribute to the local crime and disorder reduction process.

8.10.3 **Invitee to participate**

Section 5(3) of the Crime and Disorder Act specifies that some groups should be invited to participate, because of their local knowledge and activities within the community, in the crime and disorder reduction audit process. These include such bodies as social landlords, youth organizations, drug action teams, medical practitioners, and Neighbourhood Watch committees, amongst others.

8.10.4 **Strategy**

This is a plan that is produced as a result of the crime and disorder audit process. It includes an action plan of what is going to be undertaken to tackle the important issues raised, the outcomes to be achieved, and the resources allocated to tackle them. It is produced every three years.

8.10.5 **Targets**

Targets are the measurable part of an objective. For example, if our objective is to reduce domestic burglary by 30 per cent within six months in the BCU, the target is a 30 per cent reduction in six months' time.

8.10.6 **Monitoring and evaluation**

Monitoring is the continuous process of seeing whether or not particular projects are achieving their objectives. This process, for example, checks to see that crime and disorder reduction targets are being met. This process is carried out throughout the life of a project.

Evaluation on the other hand is the process of assessing, at a particular point in time, whether or not particular projects are achieving or have achieved their objective. It is about measuring the outcomes of a particular project.

8.10.7 **Local application**

Obtain a crime and disorder reduction partnership local crime audit. See if you can identify within its contents the following:

(1) Local needs and information.
(2) What types of information were used in the make-up of the audit.
(3) What the overall strategy of the document is.
(4) What targets are included in the local crime audit.
(5) How the targets are to be monitored and evaluated.
(6) Consider how you could improve any of these issues.

The following websites offer a variety of assistance in the form of reports, downloads and advice regarding local crime audits, strategies and similar documents:

http://www.audit-commission.gov.uk/
http://www.homeoffice.gov.uk/crime/communitysafety/index.html#3
http://www.crimereduction.gov.uk/
http://www.homeoffice.gov.uk/hmic/hmic.htm
http://www.nacro.org.uk/publications/index.htm
http://www.wales.gov.uk/subicsu/index.htm
http://www.youth-justice-board.gov.uk/YouthJusticeBoard/Prevention/
http://www.homeoffice.gov.uk/rds/index.html
http://www.drugs.gov.uk/Home

8.10.8 **Useful websites**

http://www.sholland.gov.uk/NR/rdonlyres/506347D3-820B-4789-AA74-
    3934D0DC5BBA/0/ReviewofPartnerships.pdf
http://www.idea.gov.uk/idk/core/page.do?pageId=8789291

Information and Consultation

9.1 **Introduction**

The rolling annual community safety plan underpinned by the six-monthly strategic assessments is a vital part in ensuring that partnerships are on target and are effective in tackling local problems. However, this can never be satisfactorily achieved unless the consultation process leading up to the introduction of the plan is effective. The Crime and Disorder Act 1998 provides quite specific guidance and information regarding this process, including a directive in section 17 that imposes a duty on all local authorities, the police, and others to ensure that crime and disorder reduction forms part of all their duties. This important section acts as a driver for agencies to come together in an attempt to tackle these problems, a move that is reinforced by section 115 of the Act which covers the exchange of information between agencies and has been strengthened by the Review of the Partnership Provisions of the Crime and Disorder Act 1998 published in 2006.

Both sections overarch the very important function of the consultation process leading up to the production of the rolling annual three-year community safety plan. The idea of consultation may appear to some to be quite a simple process. However, this function can be quite complex, and deserves to be discussed as a stand-alone idea. For example, who should be consulted and when are two important questions. Further, having decided on whom to consult and what kind of consultation is best suited for the purpose, how is this to be achieved? The most frequent of consultation methods is that of a local crime and disorder survey, and this approach is discussed at length.

In order to underpin the knowledge required for this type of consultation the preparation of questionnaire-type surveys is explored including the formulation of question types. The chapter ends by looking at the sampling process involved when deciding who to send postal questionnaires to, and some of the problems inherent in this process.

9.2 **Section 17 of the Crime and Disorder Act 1998**

Section 17 of the Crime and Disorder Act 1998 requires, by imposing a legal duty on all local authorities, including joint authorities, police authorities, National Park authorities, and the Broads Authority, and other agencies designated by the Home Secretary, to consider crime and disorder implications while exercising their duties. It also places a duty on responsible authorities to do all that they reasonably can to prevent crime and disorder in their area. It has been broadened by the Review of the Crime and Disorder Act 2006, which requires agencies to take into account anti-social behaviour, behaviour adversely affecting the environment, and substance abuse.

KEY POINT—SECTION 17 OF THE CRIME AND DISORDER ACT 1998

'Without prejudice to any other obligation imposed on it, it shall be the duty of each authority to which this section applies to exercise its various functions with due regard to the likely effect of the exercise of those functions on, and the need to do all that it reasonably can to prevent, crime and disorder in its area.'

This duty to do all that it can to prevent crime and disorder in all its dealings normally extends to any cooperating person or organization, where they have agreed to cooperate in the exercise of the functions on behalf of a responsible authority. This should ideally be in the form of a written agreement and, where the exchange of personal information is envisaged, a suitable information-sharing protocol, clearly outlining compliance with common law and relevant statutory restrictions, such as the Data Protection Act 1998 (Home Office 1998c).

9.2.1 **Protocols**

A protocol is a formal agreement or memorandum of understanding between partners within a crime and disorder reduction partnership which sets out the responsibilities regarding the exchange of information. They will often include clear statements to the effect that each of the partners who have signed up to the agreement understands the limits and constraints of information exchange for that particular agreement. It also acknowledges the relevant legal considerations and requirements, including common law duty of confidence, the Data Protection Act 1998, the Crime and Disorder Act 1998, and any other legislation that could be relevant.

The protocol may also include the following stipulations:

- That all information used between partnerships will be done so in strict compliance with conditions agreed and laid down in the protocol.
- Information exchanged will be used strictly for the purposes expressed within the protocol.
- Requests and exchanges for information are carefully recorded and that an audit trail is established should any future enquiries into information exchange be required.
- Procedures should be subject to strict quality control and where there is doubt about the exchange of certain information, legal advice is sought to safeguard the partners.

The Crime and Disorder Act 1998 does not allow for the blanket disclosure of personal information for crime and disorder purposes. It is a requirement of the Data Protection Act that the minimum amount of personal information should be exchanged, where this is necessary to fulfil a specific objective which requires it (for example, preparing an Anti-Social Behaviour Order). Non-personal or depersonalized information should be exchanged for general crime and disorder analysis. This should constitute the bulk of cross-departmental information-sharing activity.

As can be seen, the Crime and Disorder Act 1998 requires local authorities and others to consider crime and disorder reduction while exercising *all* of their duties. This reflects the reality that there are crime and/or disorder implications in decisions made across the full range of local authority services, and to correct the current situation under which these implications are often not recognized at the time decisions are taken, with expensive consequences.

9.2.2 The implications of section 17

The Crime and Disorder Act 1998 provided local authorities, the police, and a number of other key partners with a new legal framework to reduce crime and disorder. Within this, section 17 of the Act requires local authorities, police authorities, and other agencies to consider crime and disorder reduction and community safety in the exercise of all their duties and activities. Potentially this is a powerful tool, requiring authorities to look at the crime reduction potential of all their policies, budgetary and other decisions, and service provision. The recent introduction of a more performance-driven regime for crime and disorder reduction partnerships, supported by reporting structures introduced in the Police Reform Act 2002, is likely to further highlight the variation in responses to section 17.

Crime and disorder reduction partnerships' activities touch the work of most departments and service areas. Through section 17, officers and elected members of local authorities, etc., have an opportunity to consider how each can contribute to reducing crime and disorder, addressing the social, community, and physical 'drivers' of crime, and also enhancing quality of life for local communities.

Taking this approach will also help achieve 'best value' in the delivery of local services. Recognizing these links, many local authorities are using their best-value review process to help drive continuous improvement in tackling community safety issues.

Local authorities should also be aware of the legal consequences of not considering section 17, i.e., the risk that individuals or groups who feel that authorities are in breach of their duty may challenge their actions and decisions in the courts.

Local planning authorities in particular have started to use section 17 as a material consideration when determining planning applications. This has occurred, for example, where there has been concern about the growth of licensed premises in town and city centres, and a corresponding increase in late-night alcohol-related disorder. In a number of cases authorities have rejected applications for licensed premises on the grounds that this could lead to a further increase in crime and disorder.

9.3 **Section 115 of the Crime and Disorder Act 1998**

Section 115 of the Crime and Disorder Act 1998 provides for the supply of information from outside agencies in order for the necessary completion of the crime and disorder audit.

Public bodies can only disclose information if they have the power to do so. Section 115 provides a power to exchange information where disclosure is necessary to support the local crime and disorder strategy or objectives outlined within it, which must be primarily aimed at reducing crime and disorder in accordance with the Act's provisions.

KEY POINT—SECTION 115 OF THE CRIME AND DISORDER ACT 1998

'Any person who would not have power to disclose information to a relevant authority or to a person acting on behalf of such an authority, shall have power to do so in any case where the disclosure is necessary or expedient for the purposes of any provision of this Act.'

The police have an important and general power at common law to disclose information for policing purposes, which includes the prevention, detection, and reduction of crime. However, some other public bodies, which collect information, may not previously have had power to disclose it to the police and others. This section puts beyond doubt the power of any organization to disclose information to chief officers of police, police authorities, local authorities, probation committees, or health authorities, or to persons acting on their behalf. These bodies also have the power to use this information.

It should also be noted that section 115 provides a power to share information— it does not contain an overriding requirement to disclose. Nor does this power override other legal obligations such as the common law duty of confidence, the requirements of the Human Rights Act 1998 (Home Office 1998b), compliance with the Data Protection Act 1998, or other relevant legislation governing disclosures. However, as a result of the Review of the Crime and Disorder Act in 2006, there is now a duty on responsible authorities to share depersonalized data which is relevant for community safety purposes and which is already held in a depersonalized format.

9.3.1 **A wide range of information**

The awareness of local needs requires an understanding both of the nature of crime and disorder and its causes, in order to develop an effective programme to help deal with it. Therefore, the audit should look to develop the wider perspective of how crime impacts on the community and how the community can help impact on the crime. The audit should not rely on only one or two sources of information but must instead look to a range of sources from local organizations, community groups, and national sources.

The Act makes it clear that the duty to ensure that the work of tackling crime and disorder locally gets under way rests jointly on the police and local authorities or, as the Act entitles them, the 'responsible authorities'. But the Act also provides the ability for partnerships to be inclusive of the full range of agencies and individuals in their area.

9.3.2 Different sources of information

Information gathered by partnerships when formulating their strategies is referred to as data. Data can be defined as being primary or secondary. Primary data are collected for a specific purpose (e.g., information from local fear-of-crime surveys) whilst secondary data are data already collected by other agencies or individuals for their own use.

KEY POINT—DIFFERENT TYPES OF DATA

Primary data—collected for specific purpose by researchers, e.g., local crime surveys.
Secondary data—includes personal documents and official statistics.

It is important to note from the outset that too much reliance upon police data may result in insufficient attention being given to under-reporting of some types of crime, and that the crime audit may just reflect current police priorities. Data from a wide variety of sources should be considered. It must be remembered that secondary data, usually gathered by a particular agency for its own purposes, are designed for their own needs. It may therefore be difficult to incorporate such data in the crime and disorder audit. Some sources of data, which is not a definitive list, are shown in the box below.

KEY POINT—SOURCES OF DATA

- Recorded crime figures
- Service calls (including anti-social behaviour calls)
- Local authority housing data
- Data from social services
- Exclusion and truancy data from education departments
- Details of noise complaints from environmental health departments
- Probation data on offenders
- Data on drug treatment from health authorities

- Accident and emergency records on assaults
- Police authority data
- Fire service statistics on arson
- Hoax calls to the fire service
- Data from local voluntary sector organizations.

9.4 **Consultation**

The local assessments should produce a consultation document which can be widely circulated. The main aim of consultation is to ensure that the audit has interpreted problems accurately, to check that it has not missed crucial points, and to seek opinions about the proposed priorities and decisions.

9.4.1 **What is consultation?**

Consultation is defined as a process of dialogue that leads to a decision. This is a useful working definition as it brings into play four important points relating to what consultation should be.

Firstly, it is about sharing, publicizing, informing, and promoting interest so that all relevant persons, bodies, organizations, agencies, and groups are encouraged to take part in the process. Secondly, it is an ongoing activity not just a one-off function. This means that the consultation process is more than something that has to take place every three years. It should be seen as a regular activity that should become a core function of crime and disorder reduction partnerships. Thirdly, consultation involves people. It should include a wide range of individuals from within the community, including social groups and stakeholders, and these should represent the composition of the population of the local area. Finally, consultation is about producing action and outcomes.

KEY POINT—DEFINITION OF CONSULTATION

Consultation—a process of dialogue that leads to a decision.

It should be: inclusive, ongoing, participatory, and action- and outcome-oriented.

9.4.2 **Why consult?**

The benefits of consultation are:

- It helps to inform, publicize, and promote interest in the work of the crime and disorder reduction partnership. It also informs the community of the levels of crime, disorder, victimization, and perceptions of fear of crime. The benefit here, therefore, is educative.

- Consultation can bring together views about crime, disorder, and perceptions about crime, amongst other important issues. It can therefore in terms of local problems and issues of concern verify and identify these major experiences.
- Research has shown that consultation has a significant impact on strategies by confirming, narrowing, and ordering priorities for tackling crime and disorder, identifying priorities among hard-to-reach groups, and facilitating cooperation and communication between partners.

The best people to talk with on how to consult with specific communities are members of communities themselves. Local advice from community leaders, advocacy groups, faith leaders, etc., should be sought on approaches as well as targeting and methodologies. This should be done in the early planning stages. Accessibility of the crime and disorder reduction partnership to others is also important. Where possible and appropriate partnerships should, for example, provide (or offer) documentation in Braille, audiotape, or a relevant language. Many local authorities have umbrella organizations for disability groups, which may be able to offer Braille/audio translations.

There are three main groups who should be considered in the consultation process, namely persons or bodies specified by the Home Secretary and other relevant bodies, the public at large, and hard-to-reach groups. The last group will be considered first.

9.5 **Hard-to-reach Groups**

Hard-to-reach communities are not necessarily geographically compact. Targeting may be assisted through using existing agency databases. Confidentiality and the aims and objectives of differing organizations should be considered and respected. Many groups may be more willing to send things out on your behalf than to hand over mailing lists (e.g., many local gay and lesbian societies may be pleased to send out information/surveys on behalf of the crime and disorder reduction partnership). It must also be remembered that there may be mistrust between agencies (e.g., police and offender support groups) but if it is clear what the purpose of the consultation is (gathering information, informing, or enabling active participation), then cooperation is more likely to be forthcoming.

Crime and disorder impacts on different sectors of the community in different ways. Some sectors, for various reasons, are inaccessible to standard consultative mechanisms. Partnerships need a strategy to elicit the participation of locally appropriate hard-to-reach groups. The term 'hard-to-reach groups' is not very helpful, however, as groups may be considered as such for a variety of different reasons. For example, a hard-to-reach group may be considered as such because they are small and difficult to contact, or they may be hostile to the police or their needs are not understood or even acknowledged.

However, partnerships need to consider experiences that hard-to-reach groups may have had as victims or offenders, on their perceptions of fear of crime. A hard-to-reach group can be any group that is difficult to access for any reason, such as:

- physical inaccessibility (e.g., older frail people)
- language (e.g., first-generation immigrants to the UK)
- cultural perceptions and traditions (e.g., disadvantaged young people)
- social expectations (e.g., children and young people who are often not considered as appropriate consultees and who also do not often consider themselves as likely to be taken seriously).

KEY POINT—HARD-TO-REACH GROUPS NOT SPECIFIED BY THE CRIME AND DISORDER ACT 1998

These groups could include:

- homeless people
- children and young people
- drug users
- gay men, lesbian women, and transsexual and transgender people
- minority ethnic communities (particular sections of)
- victims of domestic abuse
- older people (especially older frail people and isolated older people)
- travellers
- asylum seekers
- people with learning difficulties
- people with disabilities
- people with mental health problems
- faith communities
- people who travel or commute into the area
- small businesses
- rural communities
- tourists.

Crime and disorder reduction partnerships are required to involve groups that may be considered to be hard-to-reach groups in the consultation process. Whilst the reasons why a group of people is hard to reach may be complicated, the fundamental idea is to make the process more inclusive by obtaining the views of marginalized or disadvantaged groups within the wider population. The guidance provided by the Crime and Disorder Act 1998 specifies the following groups as hard to reach. These can be seen in the following box:

KEY POINT—HARD-TO-REACH GROUPS SPECIFIED BY THE CRIME AND DISORDER ACT 1998

- Young men
- Homeless people
- Drug users
- Gay community
- Minority ethnic communities
- Children
- Older people.

Other hard-to-reach groups not mentioned might include travellers, tourists, and non-residents.

9.5.1 Defining locally appropriate hard-to-reach groups

It is essential that partnerships identify hard-to-reach groups specific to their area. For example, some partnerships have large numbers of older frail people (e.g., some seaside resorts) whereas others do not. Demographic information will help establish the degree of emphasis that is appropriate to place on consulting this group within a particular locality.

However, individual sections of the community should not be neglected simply because they represent a small proportion of the population in that area. It should be established whether, despite being a small proportion, certain groups experience a disproportionate incidence of crime.

9.5.2 Minority ethnic communities

Defining 'minority ethnic communities' as a whole as hard to reach is misleading. In many areas, specific sectors of minority ethnic communities are well integrated into society and therefore not difficult to access. Partnerships should distinguish the local population into specific sectors and assess whether each poses particular issues. As an example, a Pakistani community may be generally well integrated with society, but there may be specific sectors, such as first-generation immigrant Muslim women, who are not so well integrated and whose views and experiences are not catered for in existing consultative mechanisms. In this case, 'first-generation immigrant Muslim women' is the group for which specific targeting should be made.

Identifying and agreeing locally specific hard-to-reach groups has proved difficult for some partnerships. The following points may help to ensure that greater consideration is given:

- Nationally identified trends that are causing concern, e.g. homophobic crime, should be highlighted. Acknowledging the existence of these groups and their problems through national statistics is a reasonable beginning.

- The local area should be considered within the wider context of regional or national trends.
- Consideration of potential hard-to-reach groups (see examples above) with community representatives should be carried out, and then they should be consulted about the local representation and local issues.
- Partner organizations may have already undertaken work to identify the needs and concerns of particular groups.
- Consultation with many local agencies and organizations should be undertaken (see box below).

KEY POINT—LOCAL ORGANIZATIONS THAT COULD BE CONSULTED

- Ethnic minority businesses (may have umbrella organizations)
- Disability organizations
- Citizens' Advice Bureau
- Lesbian and gay societies
- Racial Equality Council
- Rape crisis centres
- Local religious centres and faith groups
- Chamber of Commerce
- Help the Aged and Age Concern.

9.6 **Methods of Consultation**

There are several main methods employed by crime and disorder reduction partnerships. These include postal questionnaires, meetings, panels, and other ways of consulting people. The information or data obtained in this manner generally fall into one of two areas, known as secondary and primary data.

9.6.1 **Secondary data collection**

One of the main benefits of undertaking a review of all existing sources of data is that it is low cost, and can provide a rich source of information useful for the crime and disorder reduction partnership. However, if the information obtained is of poor quality or is of limited use, other methods of obtaining this information should be considered.

Some possible sources of local data are:

- Minutes of public meetings: a review will show you what issues come up regularly. Choose a variety of groups, e.g., tenants' groups or Neighbourhood Watch.
- Minutes of individual organizations and agencies, both public sector and private sector, which may provide information about the important issues faced by their customers or users.

- Environmental scanning through the use of newspaper articles will provide a review of local feelings in the press, especially readers' letters, and may provide clues about what local people see as key issues.
- Many statutory agencies undertake local customer and employee surveys. This may be a useful source of information particularly if they include questions that may be useful, e.g., local authorities, tourist information centres, health organizations.
- The use of focus groups provides opportunities to ask agencies, voluntary groups, and private businesses if they have established why people may or may not use services, visit certain places, or undertake particular activities.
- Importantly, police and/or partner agency data on calls for service provide a good indication of local incidents and concerns.

This type of information is very important for crime and disorder reduction partnerships. The more information like this that can be put into context the more accurate and valuable it will be for establishing solutions to the problems highlighted. Some of the more common approaches are discussed further below.

9.6.2 Discussion-based methods

Discussion groups and similar approaches are almost exclusively qualitative in focus and allow for the raising and exploration of a number of diverse issues. Consequently they are not so dependent on the overall numbers of people involved. However, they can be quite demanding both of the people taking part and in their administration, and can easily become unrepresentative.

KEY POINT—ADVATAGES OF DISCUSSION GROUPS

Targeted discussion groups or focus groups have many of the same advantages and requirements of the face-to-face survey. A higher response rate (and avoidance of consultation fatigue) is more likely if the interviewer goes to the participants, for example by contacting existing local groups and attending their meetings.

Some considerations of discussion group consultation

Sometimes this type of discussion or consultation takes place away from the home and it may be necessary to make provision for participants, such as arrangements for transport and child care. It is also important to give consideration to the size and length of the focus group. An average focus group would include six to ten participants and it would last about 45–90 minutes. Participants may be asked to prepare for the focus group by reading background material or thinking about their experiences and priorities.

An atmosphere must be created in which participants feel free and safe to express their views. For example, agencies such as the police or the local authority must be prepared to accept criticism. A potential disadvantage of focus groups is that group dynamics may prevent the less confident from speaking, or reduce overall discussion time. This type of consultation process is more effective when a trained facilitator is available to ensure the group meets its objectives and that participants have an equal say in the discussions.

Keeping the focus group fairly small may also encourage greater participation. The session should be recorded, after seeking the group's permission and tapes transcribed, coded, and analysed. It might sometimes be appropriate to video discussion groups, particularly if body language and interaction between participants is likely to be of interest.

There are other types of discussion groups that are used throughout the country to assist in the consultation process, such as citizens' juries and panels.

9.6.3 Citizens' juries

Citizens' juries are small groups of people brought together usually to discuss specific issues. However, they can be recalled if needs be to rediscuss the matter. They will often comprise local specialists or interested parties alongside some more representative individuals. They can be particularly useful when trying to determine specific multi-agency responses to local problems, i.e., in taking the audit and strategy forward to action planning and implementation. It may be advisable to reconvene the jury throughout a three-year period as this can enable learning to develop and a monitoring and evaluation process to be established.

9.6.4 Panels

Some areas may have ongoing panels made up of local people, which are convened at intervals to consider local issues. These may be specifically geared to dealing with crime prevention or they may be more general, such as a citizens' panel. Consultation can then be presented in a wider context, as crime prevention issues may have been considered on a number of previous occasions.

Some problems with discussion groups

Sometimes the nature of discussion groups may mean that they have a strong relationship with agencies, which may impact on their independence and their appeal to some hard-to-reach groups. They also rely on a longer-term voluntary commitment, which may discourage some representatives from attending, such as people in full-time paid employment or young mothers. Some of these problems may be dealt with through 'booster samples', whereby participants from hard-to-reach groups are particularly sought to take part in the panel.

There may also be specialist local panels such as those dealing with domestic violence or racial harassment, which could be accessed for the purpose of consultation.

9.6.5 **Public meetings**

Public meetings have the advantage of being local and allow oral presentations, which may suit individual styles. However, there are many associated problems: attendance is commonly very low, and those people who do attend may also participate in the process by other means as well. Public meetings can be difficult to focus and very often localized interests dominate discussions. Again, agencies should be prepared to accept criticism of their work at meetings such as these. However, partnerships should not dismiss public meetings but be very clear about the objectives, trying to ensure that proceedings are recorded and focused on identifying priorities. What should be remembered is that public meetings should not be relied on alone as the source of consultation.

9.6.6 **Technology as means of consultation**

Increasingly, police and partners are utilizing the many forms of social networking that new technology affords. The rise in the use of such technology offers opportunities for the public to not only be informed about crime and disorder in their area, but also to be consulted. For example, the 'contact us' link on the website of the Metropolitan Police contains numerous links to other agencies as well as how to contact the police by traditional and newer technology. This approach is replicated by police and partners across England and Wales and enhances the ability to maintain and improve contact and information both for the public and for partnerships.

Most police and their partners can now be contacted on the following:

- YouTube
- Twitter
- Facebook
- Crimestoppers
- Web chat rooms.

Another way in which the public can be informed and consulted regarding crime and disorder in their areas is through the new crime-mapping websites that allow for information to be disseminated, sometimes at quite a low level of geographic location. For example the following website, <http://www.police.uk/>, requires an individual to merely enter their post code to see not only the crime levels in their area but also the contact details for the police and other useful agencies involved in community safety partnership work.

9.6.7 **Confidentiality**

Where possible, people who assist in the consultation process should not be identified in the information collected. However, for checking purposes, it may be necessary to record the names or other details that could be used to identify individuals. It is important, if collecting names, to be clear that these will not go beyond the people who are responsible for collecting the information. This will have to be made clear to those involved and to reassure the respective respondents. For discussion groups, it is more difficult to conceal identities from others within the group, although it should still be possible to prevent wider access to such information.

9.6.8 **Primary data collection**

Primary data are gathered specifically for the purposes of the assessments. They can supplement and enrich the secondary data that may be available to crime and disorder reduction partnerships. There are, however, some issues that need to be considered before embarking on primary data collection.

The crime and disorder reduction partnership needs clearly to have considered the following points:

- What are the specific issues to be addressed and what kind of information is needed on these?
- Who is the source of the information?
- What is the available budget? (For example, postal questionnaire surveys can be expensive to administer.)
- What expertise is available within the partnership? (For example, the partnership may be in a position to use existing staff or may be reliant upon an external company/higher education establishment to design the research and collect the information.)

There is a variety of methods that could be used for collecting primary data when undertaking assessments. Decisions on which methods to use should be based on the answers to the above questions.

Methods for collecting primary data

The different methods of collecting data vary in terms of their cost, the quality and depth of information they supply, and the level of response they are likely to secure. For example, face-to-face surveys should result in a higher response rate than a general postal questionnaire, but they are time-consuming and need a team of trained researchers. They may also allow people to give more considered answers, and this manner of collecting data is useful for those who are non-literate. They may therefore be more cost-effective for some purposes. The first thing one needs to consider is the kind of information that is needed. This is important as it dictates the method you use to gather your data. There are two basic approaches to gathering data: qualitative and quantitative.

Qualitative data

Qualitative approaches do not require such large numbers of responses for their results to be useful as it is less dependent on numbers. What they do require is the person answering the questions to provide thoughtful answers. However, they can be more demanding in terms of the analysis required to extract the required information. It is possible and quite common to combine both approaches in a single data-collection exercise.

Qualitative methods are less focused on numbers and offer the opportunity to explore issues and gain more in-depth information about them, particularly where the range of possible answers is not known beforehand. They will supply you with information about such matters as:

- what the experiences of a particular group of people are
- how people deal with particular issues
- why people feel unsafe in a certain area.

Quantitative data

Quantitative methods are centred on the quantity or numbers of certain responses, for example, the number of people who answer 'yes' to a particular question. This will enable the researcher to gather information about such matters as:

- the extent of victimization
- the proportion of people with a particular experience
- the strength of certain attitudes.

These are most appropriate when the potential range of answers you can expect to each question is known in advance, and typical questions involve ticking boxes or filling in numbers. Quantitative data are also particularly useful for measuring change, because it is relatively easy to ask the same questions again at a later date and to compare the results. For quantitative information to be reliable (and especially when measuring change), it needs to be based on relatively large numbers of responses.

Questionnaire surveys

Surveys are generally based around questionnaires, either completed by the respondent or filled in by an administrator. Common approaches include postal, telephone, or face-to-face questionnaires. They can provide valuable indicators on a range of measures. In relation to crime, their main advantage is that they include unreported crime. They are often (though not invariably) quantitative in focus, and therefore need large samples in order to provide robust findings.

Surveys are not good at measuring sensitive crimes, such as sexual assault, but can be particularly effective in assessing issues such as business crime. A major disadvantage to surveys is that people may be ill-informed about crime and disorder reduction issues, and may not have given significant consideration to identifying different priorities. The questionnaire used in such surveys is commonly referred to as a research instrument.

9.7 Designing a Survey Questionnaire

The design and ordering of questions in surveys is a specialist task, and in general where possible the employment of individuals who are experts in this field is recommended. Questionnaires should always be piloted or tested on individuals before being used to see whether respondents understand what is being asked of them, and (in the case of face-to-face interviews) whether interviewers find the questionnaire easy to use.

The first step in designing any question or instrument is to define exactly what it is you want to find out about, and what information you need about it. This is not always easy. Some of the considerations involved in designing an appropriate questionnaire are discussed below. A typical local crime and disorder reduction questionnaire, in this instance researching the implementation of an alley gate scheme, is given in Appendix 1.

9.7.1 What is a good questionnaire?

In general a good questionnaire is one that is understood by the person filling it in. This means that they are able to do so in the manner that they are intended to by the researcher. The person filling it in must be told how to complete this task, what questions to answer, what to miss out, and even how to answer them, for example, a tick in the appropriate box. Lastly the questionnaire should consider that the respondent has actually taken time to provide the information and complete the questionnaire. Therefore it should be as clear and easy to complete as possible, as well as looking as professional as possible in its layout.

Questionnaires take longer to complete than people think, so it is wise to allow plenty of time for its formulation and construction. As a general rule, a short questionnaire contains about five to ten questions, a medium-length questionnaire will have around fifteen to twenty questions, and a more complicated and lengthy questionnaire will contain more than twenty questions.

However, what must be remembered when considering the length of the questionnaire is simply this: the questions must be pertinent to the research and must be justified for their inclusion. Questions should not be included merely because the researcher thinks they are interesting or on mere whims. They must be included to produce a useful finding in terms of the research problem.

9.7.2 **Types of questions**

In general, there are three types of questions that are used in questionnaire design. These are open-ended, fixed choice, and checklist-type questions.

Open-ended questions

Open-ended questions allow the individual completing the questionnaire to answer in whatever way he or she chooses. They are simply questions with a space left on the questionnaire for the answer to be written in by the person answering the question. The best way to use them in your instrument is by describing something or illustrating examples.

KEY POINT—EXAMPLE OF AN OPEN-ENDED QUESTION

If a respondent answers either 'poor' or 'very poor' to a question relating to police efficiency in their area, then an open-ended question in follow-up that would illustrate the answer might be a simple 'Why do you say that?' This will allow the respondent to provide a detailed answer and probes deeper into the facts.

Fixed choice questions

Fixed choice questions restrict the respondent's answers by providing a list of categories for the respondent to choose from. These can be quite extensive or as simple as a Yes/No response. This type of question is quite simple and quick in terms of answering, and therefore is preferred by most crime and disorder reduction partnerships. The results can also be summarized quite quickly.

KEY POINT—EXAMPLE OF A FIXED CHOICE QUESTION

Would you say crime prevention advice was…

| Very useful | ☐ | Fairly useful | ☐ |
| Not very useful | ☐ | Not useful at all | ☐ |

Checklist-type questions

Checklist-type questions are similar to fixed choice questions in that they provide a fixed or limited number of responses for an individual to choose from. The difference between this type of question and a fixed question is that the respondent can choose as many categories as they think apply.

KEY POINT—EXAMPLE OF A CHECKLIST-TYPE QUESTION

Which of the following departments have you worked in since joining the police service? Please tick as many as apply to you.

Traffic department	☐	Plain clothes department	☐
CID	☐	Family support unit	☐
Community safety unit	☐	Research	☐
Drugs squad	☐	Training department	☐
Underwater unit	☐	Dog section	☐
Mounted section	☐	Air support	☐
Other (please specify)_____			

Whichever choice of question it is decided to use, each has its advantages and disadvantages. Table 9.1 lists these for ease of reference.

Table 9.1 Advantages and disadvantages of different types of questions

Question type	Advantage of use	Disadvantage of use
Open-ended questions	(1) Do not constrain the respondent; they can answer what they like (2) Allow the researcher to keep an open mind because of the potential for numerous types of responses	(1) These are difficult to analyse because of the types and numerous differences that can occur in responses (2) If the question is misunderstood by the respondent, answers may be misleading
Fixed choice and checklist-type questions	(1) These are quick to answer so encourage responses (2) They are speedily answered (3) Analysis is much easier as they invariably contain one-word responses	(1) There could be a tendency to constrain the respondent—whatever they think has to fit into a predetermined box

9.7.3 Things not to include in the questions

When one considers how to write questions it may appear at first to be an easy exercise. However, there are some difficulties, some obvious and some not so. To obtain the best results, the questionnaire designer should follow some simple rules. Firstly, before the question is asked, consider: *What exactly is this question asking?* And then: *Why do I need to know the answer?* This helps to get a clear idea of what you are trying to measure. Does the question sound right and will it provoke a response that can be measured correctly?

Some of the more common faults in designing questions are discussed below.

Leading questions

A leading question is one that suggests a particular answer to the respondent. For example, you could ask within the local crime audit the following question:

How good a job do you think the police do around here?

Because the question contains the word 'good', it suggests that the police do a good job not a bad one. This type of question may lead to respondents giving you what you want to hear not what is actually happening. Here, to avoid this problem, we could employ a closed-question approach such as the one below.

KEY POINT—EXAMPLE OF A CLOSED-QUESTION APPROACH

What do you think of the way the police do their job in this area?

(Please choose your answer from the list below)

A very good job	☐	Bad job	☐
Good job	☐	A very bad job	☐
Neither a good nor a bad job	☐		

Vague questions

This type of question includes words or phrases that are vague or whose meaning is unclear. When reading your questions, if you are able to ask yourself the question 'It depends what you mean by...?' then the question is probably vague. For example, consider the question below:

Do you often see a police community support officer around here?

Yes ☐
No ☐

The person answering the question will start to consider what is meant by often. Could it mean once a week, once a month, or a year? Does it mean in a vehicle or on foot? What is meant by the term around here? My street, my village, my town? This illustrates the problem of vagueness in these types of questions. Again this problem can be solved by providing precise responses for the respondent to answer:

On average, how often do you see a police community support officer on foot in your housing estate?

Every 1–2 days	☐
Every 3–5 days	☐
About once a week	☐
About once a fortnight	☐
About once a month	☐
Other (please specify)_____	

Double-barrelled questions

This question is one that asks two questions at once. This will cause confusion for the person answering the questions, as they will not know which part of the question to answer. For example:

> Do you ever worry that you or a member of your family might suffer from a theft?

This asks two questions, one about the respondent and the other about members of the respondent's family. It means that when answered the answer will be unreliable. If the respondent stated yes in answer to the question, does he/she mean that they are worried for themselves, or that they are not worried about themselves but are worried about their families?

It also introduces another factor to consider, the use of technical language. Whilst the definition of theft can probably be recited word-perfect by most police officers, for non-police personnel this may actually be a term that encompasses robbery, deception, and all other acquisitive crime. This could be an important distinction when conducting a local crime and disorder survey. The matter can be resolved by asking two shorter, simpler questions, which will make it easier for the respondent to answer.

9.7.4 Important steps in questionnaire construction

Some of the major problems and points about questionnaire design for use in assessments and surveys have been discussed briefly above. Table 9.2 illustrates some of the important steps that need to be taken in its construction.

9.8 Sampling for Surveys

The questionnaire having been successfully designed, it has to be administered to the people who are to be asked their views, etc. Sampling is the term used to denote the collection of information and the drawing of inferences about a population. A population is the target or group of people that researchers are interested in. This is usually defined in terms of having something in common, for example a job, or perhaps more importantly in terms of assessments, where people live. It is rare indeed that researchers can ask everyone in a locality their views in a crime survey, so in most circumstances a smaller proportion of people is selected from the population for the purposes of the research. This group is called the sample.

Table 9.2 Construction of a questionnaire

Stage	Comments
Stage One Define the problem and establish what you want to find out	Start a list of the things you want to find out about, e.g., the attitude of the public to the police, to crime, to disorder, etc.
Stage Two List some rough questions you may want to ask	For example, you may want to ask about contact with the police so you could consider the following: 'When was the last time you saw a police officer?'
Stage Three Decide on the format the questions will take	How will the question be asked? Open-ended, fixed choice, or checklist-type questions
Stage Four Rephrase the questions	The question must represent what you want to find out about and it must be clear, simple, and understandable
Stage Five Check the questions	Check for any revision. Ask the following: What is this question asking? Why do I need to know the answer?
Stage Six Get the questionnaire typed up	Check it for omissions, mistakes, and badly worded questions; being careful here can save you work later on
Stage Seven Pilot the questionnaire	Having checked and amended the first draft, get some friends or colleagues or members of the public to try and complete the questionnaire; tell them to let you know of any problems or anything they found difficulty with
Stage Eight Check it again	This is a repeat task but a necessary one. Check for any minor changes and make any amendments following the pilot stage
Stage Nine Write up a covering sheet	If you are using a postal survey, it is important to ensure that a covering letter accompanies the questionnaire along with a prepaid reply envelope. It should be emphasized to the respondent how important their views are and stress the confidentiality of the data provided. Always thank them for their time
Stage Ten Final version check prior to distribution	One final check of the instrument for typing or layout errors before it is distributed

> ### KEY POINT—SAMPLING TERMINOLOGY
>
> **Population**—the general group of people a researcher is interested in.
> **Sample**—a smaller group of people taken from the population for the purposes
> of the research.

9.8.1 Why sample?

As can be seen, it is a rare occasion when a researcher can measure everything about or everyone in a population. The cost of administering such a scheme would be prohibitive, whilst the time involved in doing so would also be a major factor. If certain rules about sampling are followed, however, it is not necessary to do this. Indeed, the measurements taken from a sample from the population will give you more or less the same results as you would get by measuring the whole population. They will never be exactly the same but within reasonable acceptable limits of error.

9.8.2 A sampling frame

A sampling frame is a formal representation of the population. For example, if we are sampling people this will usually be a numbered list of all the individual members of the population. The easiest sampling frames are the types of records that are kept by organizations. For example, if a survey was to be undertaken of all police officers working in a police force, a list could be provided by the Human Resources or Personnel departments. This list could then be numbered consecutively from number 1 upwards. If on the other hand the research only affected inspectors then they could be extrapolated from the list and renumbered. A sampling frame often used is the electoral roll. Whilst this is supposed to contain details of all people over the age of 18 in a particular area there are some drawbacks with its usage. For example, it does not include people under the age of eighteen, or those who have not registered to vote.

9.8.3 The sampling process

Figure 9.1 illustrates the sampling process from a general population, into a sampling frame, and then into the sample itself.

Once the sampling frame has been drawn up, the sample must be selected. The most important thing is to reduce bias in the sampling process, otherwise the results will not be representative. There are many methods for doing this but for the purposes of conducting local public surveys of areas covered by BCUs the following methods are likely to be of benefit.

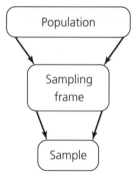

Figure 9.1 The sampling process

Interval sampling

This approach involves selecting a sample at regular intervals from the whole of the sampling frame. For example, if the research required a 10 per cent sample, then every tenth number or individual in the list would be chosen. It is best to use this method in a sampling frame that is not organized or structured to prevent bias.

Scenario—Simple random sampling

A questionnaire survey was being carried out by a police service with 2560 police staff. The sampling frame would be a list of all the names listed consecutively from 0001 to 2560. Having decided how many you are going to sample, say in this case 200, you would select the first 200 numbers from the computer-generated list of numbers and select those numbers from the sampling frame. These would be the numbers that identify the police staff for inclusion as your sample.

Simple random sampling

This is the basic method for selecting a sample from a sampling frame. This involves referring to the sampling frame and determining how many entries there are, then using random numbers to select as many individuals as are needed for the sample. This method generally uses a random number table that is generated by a computer.

Scenario—Interval sampling

A police force wanted to know how well the public were dealt with by front-desk staff at a particular busy police station. Rather than ask every person who went to the front desk, they selected every third person who came out from the office for an interview. This avoided bias because the interviewer could not select people he/she thought might be cooperative or pro-police.

Stratified sampling

This approach limits the process of selection to make sure that certain groups in the population are represented in the right proportions. For example, in the general population of England and Wales, there are more women than men, roughly 52 per cent female and 48 per cent male. This means that in a selection of 200 individuals the number of females for sampling purposes should be 104, whilst the number of males should be 96.

Scenario—Stratified sampling

There are, in general, fewer female police officers than male officers. For argument's sake, let us assume the ratio of female to male officers is 3:7, or out of every ten officers three are female. A police force wished to survey a random selection of 200 officers. This means that to get the right representative proportions, they would need a female to male ratio of 60:140. If they used a simple random sampling process they might end up with far too many male officers in their sample. Therefore the sampling frame needs to be divided into two groups, and the sample would be drawn in two stages in the right proportions. In our scenario, the researchers would need a random sample of 60 female officers and a random sample of 140 male officers to achieve a representative stratified sample.

The process of questionnaire design and the sampling process should assist those police practitioners and others who are engaged in the consultation process. The idea is to ensure that the consultation process is representative, clear, and objective, whilst actually attempting to address the problems identified through the whole process.

9.9 **Summing Up**

9.9.1 **Section 17 of the Crime and Disorder Act 1998**

Section 17 of the Crime and Disorder Act 1998 requires all local authorities, including joint authorities, police authorities, National Park authorities, and the Broads Authority, to consider crime and disorder implications while exercising their duties. It also places a duty on responsible authorities to do all that they reasonably can to prevent crime and disorder in their area.

9.9.2 **Section 115 of the Crime and Disorder Act 1998**

Section 115 of the Crime and Disorder Act 1998 provides for the supply of information from outside agencies in order for the necessary completion of the crime and disorder audit.

9.9.3 **Protocol**

A protocol is a formal agreement or memorandum of understanding between partners within a crime and disorder reduction partnership which sets out the responsibilities regarding the exchange of information.

9.9.4 **Consultation**

Consultation is defined as a process of dialogue that leads to a decision.

9.9.5 **Hard-to-reach groups**

The term 'hard-to-reach groups' is not very helpful, as groups may be considered as such for a variety of different reasons. For example, a hard-to-reach group may be considered as such because they are small and difficult to contact, or they may be hostile to the police, or their needs are not understood or even acknowledged.

9.9.6 **Citizens' juries**

Citizens' juries are small groups of people brought together usually to discuss specific issues. However, they can be recalled if needs be to rediscuss the matter. They will often comprise local specialists or interested parties alongside some more representative individuals.

9.9.7 Panels

Some areas may have ongoing panels made up of local people, which are convened at intervals to consider local issues. These may be specifically geared to dealing with crime prevention or they may be more general, such as a citizens' panel.

9.9.8 Primary data

Primary data are gathered specifically for the purposes of the audit.

9.9.9 Secondary data

These data are information that has already been collected by individuals/ agencies, and can be of benefit to crime and disorder reduction partnerships. Examples include minutes of meetings, private company information on customers, etc.

9.9.10 Qualitative data

Qualitative approaches do not require such large numbers of responses for their results to be useful as they are less dependent on numbers.

9.9.11 Quantitative data

Quantitative methods are centred on the quantity or numbers of certain responses, for example, the number of people who answer 'yes' to a particular question.

9.9.12 Sampling

A smaller group of people taken from the population for the purposes of the research.

9.9.13 Sampling frame

A sampling frame is a formal representation of the population. For example, if we are sampling people this will usually be a numbered list of all the individual members of the population. The easiest sampling frames are the types of records that are kept by organizations.

9.9.14 **Population**

The general group of people a researcher is interested in.

9.9.15 **Local application**

Obtain a copy of the local crime and disorder reduction plan. Try to establish the following information:

(1) What evidence can you find of information-sharing by different agencies within the partnership?
(2) Can you tell if most of the information used is primary or secondary data?
(3) What evidence is there of any protocols having been used in gathering information?
(4) What evidence is there of consultation with hard-to-reach groups?
(5) Is the report based mainly on qualitative or quantitative data?
(6) How do you think the report could have been improved?
(7) Using the methodology chapter of the report can you establish the following:
   (a) What sampling method was used in the collection of the data?
   (b) Was there any use of citizens' juries, panels, or other secondary data?

Primary Legislation and Quality of Life Issues

10.1 **Introduction**

In addition to the general powers available to the police practitioner, such as powers to arrest for theft, etc., there has been an increase in the amount of legislation passed to support community safety. These are available not just to police officers but to the wider police family, and are focused on community safety and addressing many quality of life issues.

Underpinning all crime and disorder reduction partnerships lies the legislation that drives it forward. Practitioners must at least have a working knowledge of the powers available to them if the partnership approach is to be totally successful. However, legislation is also subject to amendment and change as different incidents can occur that challenge the law, whilst social and political changes can influence government approaches to certain offences which lead to amendments.

One would not expect to hire a plumber to mend a leak if the plumber did not know how to use the tools at his/her disposal. Neither would you expect a police practitioner or anyone engaged in dealing with crime and disorder reduction not to know their powers or, at least, the main Acts of Parliament that support their work.

This chapter, therefore, highlights the main Acts of Parliament that underpin successful community safety work. Many have been discussed and referred to in more depth elsewhere in this book. It will briefly describe the main elements of the Acts in order for the practitioner to have a basic understanding of their aims and content, and will then explore in a little more depth the more commonly found 'quality of life' issues that affect the working partnership.

10.2 **Important Legislation**

The Environmental Protection Act 1990

This is an Act to make provision for the improved control of pollution arising from certain industrial and other processes; to re-enact the provisions of the Control of Pollution Act 1974 (Home Office 1974) relating to waste on land with modifications as respects the functions of the regulatory and other authorities concerned in the collection and disposal of waste and to make further provision in relation to such waste; and to restate the law defining statutory nuisances and improve the summary procedures for dealing with them. It also provides for the termination of the existing controls over offensive trades or businesses and to provide for the extension of the Clean Air Acts (Home Office 1956, 1968a) to prescribed gases; it amends the law relating to litter and makes further provision imposing or conferring powers to impose duties to keep public places clear of litter and clean, as well as many other areas where the police practitioner may become involved. The provisions of this Act are extremely useful as they underpin the manner in which individuals can be dealt with for a variety of offences including excess noise, litter, noxious waste, etc.

The following sections will consider areas that appear to be common problems for the police practitioner and include such considerations as domestic disputes, dogs, harassment, and the illegal use of fireworks. All of these are areas which the crime and disorder reduction partnership regularly becomes involved in. This Act can be found in full at the following website: <http://www.legislation. gov.uk/ukpga/1990/43/contents>.

The Housing Act 1996

The Housing Act 1996 (Home Office 1996b) is quite an important Act of Parliament as it makes provisions about housing, including provisions about the social rented sector, houses in multiple occupation, landlord and tenant matters, the administration of housing benefit, the conduct of tenants, the allocation of housing accommodation by local housing authorities, homelessness, and related matters. It is a useful Act for police practitioners and partnership workers to be aware of. In particular the areas of starter tenancies, eviction, injunctions, and particularly witness and victim intimidation are important areas to be aware of. This Act can be found in full at the following website:
<http://www.legislation.gov.uk/ukpga/1996/52/contents>.

The Protection from Harassment Act 1997

The Protection from Harassment Act 1997 (Home Office 1997c) was introduced following a number of highly publicized cases of stalking. It has been applied far more widely than just for this purpose. It appears that the Act was originally intended to address the relatively small number of cases of harassment as it contains a very simple one-line preamble:

> An Act to make provision for protecting persons from harassment and similar conduct.

This Act can be found in full at the following website:
<http://www.legislation.gov.uk/ukpga/1997/40/contents>.

The Crime and Disorder Act 1998

The Crime and Disorder Act 1998 (Home Office 1999a) imposes new statutory duties on local authorities to form 'community safety partnerships' and Youth Offending Teams (YOTs). Partnerships are required to carry out a rolling consultation process and to develop strategies based upon their findings.

The Act also sets out certain conditions under which specified offences will be deemed to be 'racially aggravated' and increases the powers available to the courts in the punishment of racist offences. Sections 28 to 32 of the Crime and Disorder Act 1998 took existing offences and set out circumstances under which those offences were deemed to be aggravated. These offences are:

- Section 20 of the Offences Against the Person Act 1861 (Wounding or grievous bodily harm)
- Section 47 of the Offences Against the Person Act 1861 (Causing actual bodily harm)
- Section 39 of the Criminal Justice Act 1988 (Common assault)
- Section 1(1) of the Criminal Damage Act 1971 (Criminal damage)
- Section 4 of the Public Order Act 1986 (Causing fear/provocation of others)
- Section 4A of the Public Order Act 1986 (Intentional harassment, alarm, or distress)
- Section 5 of the Public Order Act 1986 (Causing harassment, alarm, or distress)
- Section 2 of the Protection from Harassment Act 1997 (Harassment to others)
- Section 4 of the Protection from Harassment Act 1997 (Putting in fear of violence).

Part 5 of the Anti-Terrorism Crime and Security Act 2001 (Home Office 2001b) amended the Crime and Disorder Act 1998, extending 'racially aggravated' to include 'racially or religiously aggravated' offences.

This Act was reviewed during 2006 and has been amended slightly in some important areas. More details on this can be found at the following website:
<http://www.sholland.gov.uk/NR/rdonlyres/506347D3-820B-4789-AA74-3934D0DC5BBA/0/ReviewofPartnerships.pdf>.

The main provisions of this important Act have been discussed at some length in Chapters 3 and 9. This Act can be found in full at the following website:
<http://www.legislation.gov.uk/ukpga/1998/37/contents>.

The Police Reform Act 2002

One of the most influential Acts of Parliament to have been passed in recent times is the Police Reform Act 2002 (Home Office 2002a). This Act is part of the government's wider plan to modernize many public services, and seeks to address such issues as the structure of the police as well as to introduce the capacity for use of a wider policing family. This Act has major implications for the delivery of crime and disorder reduction within communities. The long title of the Act succinctly sums up its main objectives.

KEY POINT—LONG TITLE OF THE POLICE REFORM ACT 2002

'An Act to make new provision about the supervision, administration, functions and conduct of police forces, police officers and other persons serving with, or carrying out functions in relation to, the police; to amend police powers and to provide for the exercise of police powers by persons who are not police officers; to amend the law relating to anti-social behaviour orders; to amend the law relating to sex offender orders; and for connected purposes.'

This Act can be found in full at the following website:
<http://www.legislation.gov.uk/ukpga/2002/30/contents>.

The Anti-Social Behaviour Act 2003

The Anti-Social Behaviour Act 2003 (Home Office 2003a) is designed to ensure that there are appropriate powers to deal with serious anti-social behaviour. It introduces new powers for tackling the problems of premises used for drug dealing and for dispersing intimidating groups, and enables the police to tackle the nuisance that can be caused by young people with air weapons. It also supports action against gun crime by banning the possession of imitation guns and air guns in public without good reason.

Two key areas of the legislation impacting upon the police are:

(1) Powers to close down premises being used for the supply, use or production of Class A drugs, where there is associated serious nuisance or disorder. This power has been promoted in the media as the power to close 'crack houses'. However, the definition of premises is so wide as to include pubs and clubs.

(2) Another area within the legislation relates to the dispersal of groups of two or more and also to return young people under sixteen who are unsupervised in public places after 9 p.m. to their homes. This is a controversial area and currently subject to judicial review. Therefore police practitioners are urged to seek the latest position regarding this subject prior to implementation of any initiative based on this part of the Act.

At the time of writing the present government is looking to substantially alter this legislation and this has been discussed in full elsewhere in this book. This Act can be found in full at the following website:
<http://www.legislation.gov.uk/ukpga/2003/38/contents>.

The Drugs Act 2005

This Act makes provision in connection with controlled drugs and for the making of orders to supplement anti-social behaviour orders in cases where behaviour is affected by the misuse of drugs. This Act can be found in full at the following website:
<http://www.legislation.gov.uk/ukpga/2005/17/contents>.

The Serious Organised Crime and Police Act 2005

This Act established the Serious Organised Crime Agency and sets out its constitution, functions, general powers and its relationship with ministers. It also gives investigating authorities new powers to compel individuals to answer questions or produce relevant documents; formalizes and adds to the existing arrangements relating to 'Queen's Evidence'; makes all offences arrestable; makes search warrants more flexible; and gives community

support officers more powers. This Act can be found in full at the following website:
<http://www.legislation.gov.uk/ukpga/2005/15/contents>.

The Prevention of Terrorism Act 2005

This Act allows the Secretary of State to make 'control orders' to restrict the movements or behaviour of suspected terrorists who cannot be prosecuted or deported, or impose obligations on them. This Act can be found in full at the following website:
<http://www.legislation.gov.uk/ukpga/2005/2/contents>.

The Violent Crime Reduction Act 2006

This Act contains a variety of measures designed to combat alcohol-related violence and disorder, including new 'drinking banning orders' and 'alcohol disorder zones'. It amends licensing laws to promote the objectives of crime prevention and child welfare. It also tightens the law on airguns, imitation firearms, and the purchase of knives and introduces a new power for school staff to search pupils for weapons. This Act can be found in full at the following website:
<http://www.legislation.gov.uk/ukpga/2006/38/contents>.

The Racial and Religious Hatred Act 2006

This Act made it illegal to threaten people because of their religion, or to stir up hatred against a person because of their faith. It was designed to fill gaps in existing laws, which already protected people from threats based on their race or ethnic background. This Act can be found in full at the following website:
<http://www.legislation.gov.uk/ukpga/2006/1/contents>.

The Terrorism Act 2006

This Act created a number of new offences: acts preparatory to terrorism; encouragement to terrorism; dissemination of terrorist publications; and terrorist training offences.

It also amended the Terrorism Act 2000 and other legislation. This Act can be found in full at the following website:
<http://www.legislation.gov.uk/ukpga/2006/11/contents>.

The Police and Justice Act 2006

This Act established the National Policing Improvement Agency, a new body to replace Centrex (the Central Police Training and Development Authority) and PITO (the Police Information Technology Organisation). It also amended the Police Act 1996 regarding the composition and functions of police authorities.

Originally the reorganisation was intended to prepare for the amalgamation of police forces but this was not taken forward. It standardizes the powers of Community Support Officers (CSOs) and provides a new power in relation to dealing with truancy. It also gives police powers to track the movements of suspected terrorists and serious criminals within Britain. This Act can be found in full at the following website:
<http://www.legislation.gov.uk/ukpga/2006/48/contents>.

The Offender Management Act 2007

This Act allows for the establishment of probation trusts; supports the development of the commissioning of probation services; and enables greater partnership working with providers in the voluntary, charitable, and private sectors. This Act can be found in full at the following website:
<http://www.legislation.gov.uk/ukpga/2007/21/contents>.

The Counter-Terrorism Act 2008

This Act introduces a system of control orders designed to disrupt and prevent terrorist activity. This Act can be found in full at the following website:
<http://www.legislation.gov.uk/ukpga/2008/28/contents>.

The Criminal Justice and Immigration Act 2008

This Act covers a wide area including: a new criminal offence of incitement to hatred on the grounds of sexual orientation; new civil penalties for serious breaches of data protection principles; abolishing the common law offences of blasphemy and blasphemous libel; ending automatic discounts for offenders given an indeterminate sentence after the initial sentencing decision has been judged unduly lenient; powers for courts to make dangerous offenders given a discretionary life sentence serve a higher proportion of their tariff before being eligible for parole; a new offence of possession of extreme pornographic images; non-dangerous offenders who breach the terms of their licence to be recalled to prison for a fixed 28-day period; creating a Youth Rehabilitation Order for children and young offenders; bringing compensation for those wrongly convicted broadly into line with compensation for victims of crime; and providing for special immigration status for terrorists and serious criminals who cannot currently be removed from the UK for legal reasons. This Act can be found in full at the following website:
<http://www.legislation.gov.uk/ukpga/2008/4/contents>.

The Policing and Crime Act 2009

This Act introduces a wide range of measures including: a mandatory code of practice for alcohol retailers; the creation of a new offence of paying for sex with a prostitute who has been coerced or deceived; the power for police and local authorities to apply for injunctions against people involved in gang-related violence; increasing the effectiveness and public accountability of policing; regulation of lap dancing clubs; enhancing airport security; strengthening the arrangements for recovery of assets obtained through criminal means; and improving the efficiency of arrangements for judicial cooperation between the UK and its international partners. This Act can be found in full at the following website:

<http://www.legislation.gov.uk/ukpga/2009/26/contents>.

The Police Reform and Social Responsibility Act 2011

This Act introduces wide ranging changes to the accountability process of the police by allowing for the introduction of Police and Crime commissioners instead of Police Authorities outside of London and for the Mayor's Office for Policing and Crime within the Metropolitan Police area. It also introduces changes to the Licensing Act 2003 by the introduction of the Night Time Levy as well as provisions regarding licensing of premises. In addition it introduces changes to the structures of two tier authorities in England with regard to community safety. This Act can be found in full at the following website:

<http://www.legislation.gov.uk/ukpga/2011/13/contents>.

10.3 Quality of Life Issues

10.3.1 Domestic disputes and violence

On many occasions police staff may become involved in dealing with domestic disputes. These disputes usually involve partners or relatives of the individuals involved in the dispute and need careful handling. The police have a positive duty to protect the rights of individuals, as the Human Rights Act 1998 (Home Office 1998b) supports individuals' rights.

Whilst domestic disputes could involve a whole range of breaches of the criminal law from breach of the peace or even murder, on many occasions police officers will be called to domestic disputes where court orders are in being. Court orders are made under section 42 of the Family Law Act 1996 (Home Office 1996c).

Non-molestation order

Section 42 of the Family Law Act 1996 provides for the issue of a non-molestation order which will contain one or both of the following provisions:

- Prohibiting a person (the respondent) from molesting another person who is associated with the respondent.
- Prohibiting the respondent from molesting a child.

KEY POINT—MEANING OF MOLESTATION

Molesting includes conduct which does not have to be actual physical violence and includes conduct which intentionally causes such a degree of harassment that the intervention of the courts is required.

The court may make a non-molestation order if:

- An application for the order has been made by a person who is associated with the respondent
- In any family proceedings to which the respondent is a party the court considers that the order should be made for the benefit of any other party to the proceedings or any relevant child, even though no such application has been made.

Power of arrest for breach of order

Section 47 of the Family Law Act 1996 states that if a court makes an order and it appears that the respondent has used or threatened violence against the applicant or a relevant child, it can attach a power of arrest to one or more specific provisions of the order. If this is so, then a constable may arrest without warrant a person whom he/she has reasonable cause to suspect to be in breach of any such provision.

The person arrested in accordance with any breach of a provision under this section must be brought before the relevant judicial authority within a period of twenty-four hours beginning at the time of arrest. However, for the purposes of the twenty-four-hour time period, Christmas Day, Good Friday, and Sundays are not to be taken account of. This process is illustrated in Figure 10.1.

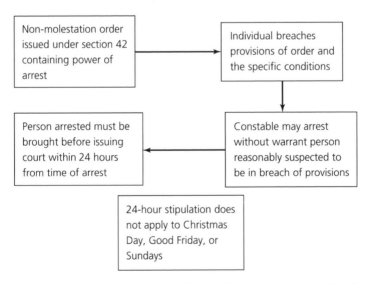

Figure 10.1 Power of arrest for breach of non-molestation order issued under the Family Law Act 1996

10.3.2 **Domestic violence**

Police may become aware of domestic violence through contact with other partnership agencies either as part of a documented process or through informal methods such as word of mouth. Whatever way this information comes to the notice of the police, there is a duty of positive action placed upon the police. The Human Rights Act 1998 (Home Office 1998b), for example, provides safeguards for the rights of victims. The right to life and the right not to be subjected to torture or to inhuman or degrading treatment make it clear that the police have this duty to fulfil. Both the European Convention on Human Rights and other legislation, such as the Race Relations Act 1976 (Home Office 1976) (as amended by the Race Relations (Amendment) Act 2000 (Home Office 2000b)), place a clear responsibility on public authorities to fulfil these obligations without discriminating on any grounds.

KEY POINT—DEFINITION OF DOMESTIC VIOLENCE

The ACPO definition of domestic violence is:

'Any incident of threatening behaviour, violence or abuse (psychological, physical, sexual, financial or emotional) between adults, aged eighteen and over, who are or have been intimate partners or family members, regardless of gender and sexuality.'

(Family members are defined as mother, father, son, daughter, brother, sister, and grandparents, whether directly related, in-laws or step-family.)

All victims of domestic violence should receive the appropriate quality of service according to their individual needs. Therefore all allegations should be properly investigated and offenders held accountable through the criminal justice system, without discrimination.

Action taken by the police should ensure the protection of victims and children while allowing the criminal justice system to hold the offender to account. If an effective and proactive procedure is to be carried out, then this will mean that where a power of arrest exists it should normally be exercised to allow the investigation to continue and to prevent any further offences being committed.

Should a power to arrest exist but the officer investigating believes that an arrest is not necessary, he/she should take the action shown in the following box.

KEY POINT—ACTION WHEN NO ARREST IS MADE AT DOMESTIC INCIDENT

- Record reasons why an arrest not made.
- Explain to the victim the reason why an arrest has not been made.
- Give consideration to issuing a warning under the Protection from Harassment Act 1997.
- Record details on the police IT recording system and gather evidence to support any future prosecutions, either civil or criminal.
- Refer the victim to relevant agencies for support and assistance (e.g., Victim Support, solicitor, Citizens' Advice Bureau).

KEY POINT—POWERS OF ENTRY

- Common law gives powers to prevent or deal with a breach of the peace.
- Section 17(1)(b) of the Police and Criminal Evidence Act 1984 provides for a constable to enter any premises for the purposes of arresting for an arrestable offence, which includes assaults occasioning actual bodily harm, grievous bodily harm, or criminal damage.
- Section 17(1)(e) of the Police and Criminal Evidence Act provides for a constable to enter a premises for the purposes of saving life or limb or preventing serious damage to property.
- Section 48 of the Children Act 1989 (Home Office 1989b) provides for the issue of a warrant to search for children who may be in need of emergency protection.
- Entry is authorized where there has been a breach of a civil injunction with a power of arrest attached.

The priorities of the police service in responding to domestic violence are as follows:

- To protect the lives of both adults and children who are at risk as a result of domestic violence.
- To investigate all reports of domestic violence.
- To facilitate effective action against offenders so that they can be held accountable through the criminal justice system.
- To adopt a proactive multi-agency approach in preventing and reducing domestic violence.

Domestic violence forums

The police practitioner should be aware that the police service is usually well represented at every level of partnership working. For example, the BCU commander should represent the police force at a strategic crime and disorder reduction level, and should have responsibility, together with partners, for allocating resources and providing the strategic direction to ensure delivery of the main objectives. Part of the strategy of the crime and disorder reduction partnership should be the formation of domestic violence forums, which can assist in meeting crime and disorder reduction targets.

This forum, as with any other, should be regarded as a means to an end and must not be regarded as the end itself. There should therefore be clear policies and guidelines available, along with plans for tackling the problem. It is recommended that each domestic violence forum develop a policy statement, keep details of victims of domestic violence, and provide training for service deliverers in meeting the needs of victims and ensuring the accountability of offenders.

10.3.3 Dogs

Many research documents and crime audits regularly ask people what the main problems are in their community. One of the major problems highlighted by communities revolves around animals and in particular the issue of dogs. This involves the control of dangerous dogs as well as the problems associated with dogs fouling pavements and other public areas. Because of the importance that appears to be placed upon these problems by communities, the police practitioner needs to have an understanding of the legislation surrounding these offences.

The Litter (Animal Droppings) Order 1991 enabled by the Environmental Protection Act (1990) (Home Office 1990b) places a duty on local authorities to keep the following areas clear of dog faeces:

- Any public walk or pleasure ground.
- Any land laid out as a garden or used for the purpose of recreation.
- Any part of the seashore which is frequently used by large numbers of people, and managed by the person having direct control of it as a tourist resort or recreational facility.
- Any esplanade or promenade.
- Any land not forming part of the highway or, in Scotland, a public road, which is open to the air, which the public are permitted to use on foot only, and which provides access to retail premises.
- A trunk road picnic area.
- A picnic site.

The Dogs (Fouling of Land) Act 1996 (Home Office 1996d) allows authorities to designate any land in their area as 'poop scoop' areas without any requirement to provide signs or dog waste bins. The land must be publicly accessible and open to the air; however, the following areas are not included:

- Carriageways with a speed limit of more than 40 mph.
- Land used for agriculture or woodlands.

- Land which is predominantly marshland, moor, or heath.
- Rural common land.

The penalty for not clearing up dog fouling can be up to £1000 if taken to court, but there is also provision for a fixed penalty scheme with a fine of £50 in England and Wales.

In England and Wales the main legislation relating to dog fouling is dealt with under the Environmental Protection Act 1990 (Part IV) (Home Office 1990b).

Exceptions to the offence are:

- the person in charge of the dog has a reasonable excuse for not clearing up (being unaware of the fouling or not having the means to clean up is not an excuse)
- the owner or occupier of the land has consented to the faeces being left
- the person puts the faeces in a bin on the land
- the person in charge of the dog has a registered visual impairment.

Dog warden schemes

Many crime and disorder reduction partnerships have a direct input into these schemes. This is one of the most effective ways of tackling the dog fouling problem. The dog warden has three important roles in the community:

- Enforcement—enforcing the legislation relating to dog fouling, dogs in general, and local by-laws.
- Educational—promoting responsible attitudes to dog ownership, and developing an understanding of the role of the dog warden and how the public can be supportive.
- Practical—handling and securing stray dogs, dealing with problems relating to noisy and nuisance dogs.

Stray dogs

Much time and effort can be expended when dealing with stray dogs. Individuals will deliver dogs to police stations or contact responsible authorities to report them. This will probably continue until the provision of section 68 of the Clean Neighbourhoods and Environment Act 2005 (Home Office 2005b) comes into force which will transfer responsibilities of stray dogs completely from the police service to the local authority.

Crime and disorder reduction partnerships are frequently aware of environmental problems caused by these incidents and it is important that police officers, as well as other persons involved in this area, are aware of the roles and responsibilities of each other. The following list explains and describes the common procedures used when dealing with the problem of stray dogs.

Common procedures for dealing with stray dogs

(1) Every local authority shall appoint an officer (under whatever title the authority may determine) for the purpose of discharging the functions imposed or conferred by this section for dealing with stray dogs found in the area of the authority.

(2) The officer may delegate the discharge of his functions to another person but he shall remain responsible for securing that the functions are properly discharged.

(3) Where the officer has reason to believe that any dog found in a public place or on any other land or premises is a stray dog, he shall (if practicable) seize the dog and detain it, but, where he finds it on land or premises which is not a public place, only with the consent of the owner or occupier of the land or premises.

(4) Where any dog seized under this section wears a collar having inscribed thereon or attached thereto the address of any person, or the owner of the dog is known, the officer shall serve on the person whose address is given on the collar, or on the owner, a notice in writing stating that the dog has been seized and where it is being kept, and stating that the dog will be liable to be disposed of if it is not claimed within seven clear days after the service of the notice and the amounts for which he would be liable under subsection (5) below are not paid.

(5) A person claiming to be the owner of a dog seized under this section shall not be entitled to have the dog returned to him unless he pays all the expenses incurred by reason of its detention and such further amount as is for the time being prescribed.

(6) Where any dog seized under this section has been detained for seven clear days after the seizure or, where a notice has been served under subsection (4) above, the service of the notice and the owner has not claimed the dog and paid the amounts due under subsection (5) above, the officer may dispose of the dog—

(a) by selling it or giving it to a person who will, in his opinion, care properly for the dog;

(b) by selling it or giving it to an establishment for the reception of stray dogs; or

(c) by destroying it in a manner to cause as little pain as possible.

However, no dog seized under this section shall be sold or given for the purposes of vivisection.

(7) Where a dog is disposed of under subsection (6)(a) or (b) above to a person acting in good faith, the ownership of the dog shall be vested in the recipient.

(8) The officer shall keep a register containing the prescribed particulars of or relating to dogs seized under this section and the register shall be available, at all reasonable times, for inspection by the public free of charge.

(9) The officer shall cause any dog detained under this section to be properly fed and maintained.

(10) Notwithstanding anything in this section, the officer may cause a dog detained under this section to be destroyed before the expiration of the period mentioned in subsection (6) above where he is of the opinion that this should be done to avoid suffering.

Failure to keep dogs under control

Crime and disorder reduction partnerships, and in particular the police, have, on many occasions, to respond to complaints from within communities regarding the lack of control of dogs. The Dangerous Dogs Act 1991 (Home Office 1991b) deals with the duties imposed on owners of dogs and introduces several offences.

Section 3(1) of the Dangerous Dogs Act 1991 states that:

(1) If a dog is dangerously out of control in a public place—
 - the owner; and
 - if different, the person for the time being in charge of the dog
   is guilty of an offence, or, if the dog while so out of control injures any person, an aggravated offence, under this subsection.

(2) If the owner or, if different, the person for the time being in charge of a dog allows it to enter a place which is not a public place but where it is not permitted to be and while it is there—
 - it injures any person; or
 - there are grounds for reasonable apprehension that it will do so,
   he is guilty of an offence, or if the dog injures any person, an aggravated offence, under this subsection.

KEY POINT—WHO CAN COMMIT THE OFFENCE?

The offence can be committed by both the owner and the person in charge in the case of section 3(1), whilst the second set of circumstances applies to either the owner or the person in charge.

Whether someone is in charge of a dog is a matter for the courts to decide.

A person who is the owner of a dog but was not with it at the material time in charge of it shall have the defence for the accused to prove, that the dog was at the material time in the charge of a person whom he reasonably believed to be a fit and proper person to be in charge of it. However, to avail himself/herself of this defence, there must be evidence to show that the owner had for the time being divested himself/herself of responsibility for the dog in favour of an identified person.

10.3.4 **Truants**

Children and young people who fail to attend school are often blamed for anti-social behaviour and criminal activity besides not being subjected to the long-term socialization effects of schooling. It is therefore important for police practitioners to be aware of the powers available to them for dealing with this problem.

KEY POINT—WHAT IS UNLAWFUL ABSENCE FROM SCHOOL?

A child or young person is deemed to be absent from school unlawfully unless the reason for absence falls within one of the following:
- official leave
- unavoidable cause or delay
- a day set aside for religious observance.

Truancy sweeps

Every day over 50,000 pupils miss a day of school without permission and an estimated 7.5 million school days are missed each year through truancy. Research shows that these children who are not in school are most vulnerable and are easily drawn into crime and anti-social behaviour, and are more likely to be unemployed after leaving school. The 2002 MORI Youth Justice Survey of young people showed that those who play truant are more likely to offend than those that do not, with two-thirds (65 per cent) of truants having offended compared to less than a third (30 per cent) of those who have not played truant. The link between truancy and crime was also stated in the 2004 MORI Youth Justice Survey.

The government's determination to reduce unauthorized absence and tackle truancy saw the start of national coordinated truancy sweeps in May 2002. Since then there has been a determination to maintain the momentum of truancy sweeps by conducting national exercises twice a year.

Data from the previous sweeps show that, of 91,778 pupils stopped, 40 per cent were truanting and 42 per cent of those truants were accompanied by an adult.

Truancy sweeps are carried out by partnerships of police officers and education welfare officers. Truancy sweeps are also a good way of bringing together a number of agencies in a joint effort to tackle the truancy. Under the Crime and Disorder Act 1998, the police have powers to pick up (but not arrest) children playing truant and take them to a designated area or, sometimes, back to school. Generally this power will be used through occasional 'sweeps' where police and education welfare officers join forces for a day and target particular areas, for example in shopping centers.

Truancy sweeps are now a regular feature in local education authorities. In order to make best use of the truancy sweeps education welfare officers, connections personal advisors, learning mentors, and school pastoral staff are encouraged to work together to create an individual reintegration plan for each child picked up on a sweep. It is important that good monitoring information is collected, to gain a national picture on truancy in order to inform future policy.

Section 16 Crime and Disorder Act 1998

Section 16 of the Crime and Disorder Act 1998 empowers a police officer to take a child or young person whom she/he has reasonable cause to believe is of compulsory school age, and is absent from school without lawful authority, back to school or to another place designated by the local education authority. The child or young person must be in a public place.

This power can be used when:

- the local education authority has designated a place for the purpose of this provision
- the local education authority has notified the chief officer of police for that area
- a police officer of superintendent rank or above has specified an area and time period in which this power can be used.

The power applies only to those children and young people who are pupils registered at a school. It does not apply to children and young people educated at home who, quite lawfully, are out and about, alone or accompanied, during school hours.

Scenario—Good practice in tackling truancy

In some areas, local beat officers work jointly with school staff in the delivery of breakfast clubs and learning mentors to reinforce the importance of school attendance, learning, and relationships between the police and students.

Bus advertising campaigns and posters are sometimes used in media campaigns aimed at anti-truancy. Campaigns such as these are often run in conjunction with the local education welfare service.

'Pupil Watch' hotline services run via the local authority's call centres in some areas encourages public/corporate vigilance of young people not in school and provides a formal reporting mechanism.

10.3.5 Public nuisances

Whilst perhaps not falling into the classification of more serious offences, there are many forms of activity that are a constant source of annoyance to the public and also a source of many calls for police and partnership intervention. There is a common law offence of a person creating or being responsible for a public nuisance, an offence that exists alongside and sometimes overlapping certain aspects of criminal behaviour. The common law concept of nuisance can be separated into two, namely a public nuisance and a private nuisance. Private nuisance is usually dealt with as a tort or wrongdoing under the civil law, but public nuisance can be dealt with in accordance with the criminal law.

KEY POINT—A PUBLIC NUISANCE

A public nuisance is an unlawful act or an omission to discharge a duty which in either case obstructs or causes inconvenience or damage to the public in the exercise of their common rights.

This offence is triable either way and the courts have unlimited powers of sentence on indictment. This is an arrestable offence.

An important point to note for this offence to be proved is the fact that the act or omission affected the public in general as opposed to a small number of people (such as the people who work in a particular location).

Scenario—Public nuisance

A group of young people entered the premises of a school with the intention of sniffing glue. In this case it was argued that they committed a public nuisance by unduly interfering with the comfortable and convenient enjoyment of the land, even though the school was empty.

The courts have unlimited sentencing power in relation to this offence so there may well be some advantage to considering its use to cases where there are only minor summary offences involved.

KEY POINT—EXAMPLES OF A PUBLIC NUISANCE

Allowing a rave to take place in a field
Selling meat that was unfit for consumption
Contaminating houses with dust and noise from a quarry
Making hundreds of nuisance telephone calls to several women

Defence to public nuisance

The defence available for this offence is that of statutory authorization. For example, the building of a new railway line tunnel will be covered by statute and therefore the defence is available.

Enforcement

Besides the power of arrest and the sentences available for public nuisances using the criminal courts, there is always the use of a court injunction as a preventative measure available. Local authorities have the power to apply for a public nuisance injunction under the Local Government Act 1972 (Home Office 1972) and there should be no reason why crime and reduction partnerships, through the office of the chief of police, should not do the same.

Another area where the demand for police and partnership intervention is called for and appears to seriously disrupt the quality of life for individuals within the community is in the indiscriminate use of fireworks. Use of fireworks is not limited to one specific time of the year by any means, and there is an increasing use of fireworks by individuals throughout the year. However, there is legislation in place that enables crime and disorder reduction partnerships to tackle these incidents.

10.3.6 The Fireworks Act 2003

Previous legislation regarding fireworks tended to focus upon the supply of fireworks rather than the use, whilst much of the existing legislation was severely dated and needed updating. The Fireworks Act 2003 (Home Office 2003c) regulates the sale and use of fireworks under certain circumstances and makes provision for regulations, in particular the Fireworks Regulations 2004.

KEY POINT—THE MEANING OF FIREWORKS

'Fireworks' means fireworks for the purposes of the British Standard Specification published on 30 November 1988 or any British specification replacing it. The regulations categorize specific types of fireworks according to the danger they present, and range from caps and party poppers to intricate devices used in pyrotechnic displays.

Possession of fireworks

Regulation 4 of the Fireworks Regulations 2004 introduces the offence of possession of fireworks under the age of eighteen years of age in a public place, whilst regulation 5 stipulates that no person shall possess a category 4 firework.

> ## KEY POINT—PUBLIC PLACE AND ADULT FIREWORK
>
> For the purposes of these Regulations, a public place means any place to which at the material time the public have or are permitted access, whether on payment or otherwise.
>
> Adult firework is any firework which does not comply with the relevant requirements of part 2 of BS 7114 (except a cap, cracker snap, novelty match, party popper, serpent, sparkler or throwdown).
>
> A category 4 firework is one specified by the Regulations as such in BS 7114.

The regulations contain exemptions to cover people who have such fireworks in the course of their work or business or who are properly authorized to conduct displays. Sections 4 and 5 of the Act allow for regulations which prohibit the sale of fireworks in certain circumstances. Supplying includes selling, exchanging, and giving fireworks, but does not include supplying when done so in the course of business.

Prohibition of certain fireworks at night

Regulation 7 of the Fireworks Regulations 2004 stipulates that no person shall use an adult firework during night hours. The definition of 'night hours' is the period beginning 11 p.m. and ending at 7 a.m. the following day. Exceptions to this regulation are shown in the following box. It can be seen that this legislation has taken into account traditional festivals and celebrations that involve the use of fireworks.

> ## KEY POINT—EXCEPTIONS TO USE OF FIREWORKS AT NIGHT
>
> (1) Beginning at 11 p.m. on the first day of the Chinese New Year and ending at 1 a.m. the following day.
> (2) Beginning at 11 p.m. on 5 November and ending at 12 a.m. the following day.
> (3) Beginning at 11 p.m. on the day of Diwali and ending at 1 a.m. the following day.
> (4) Beginning at 11 p.m. on 31 December and ending at 1 a.m. the following day.
> (5) A firework display by a local authority.
> (6) A national public celebration/commemorative event.

Breach of fireworks regulations

Section 11 of the Fireworks Act 2003 creates an offence of breach of the Fireworks Regulations. There is no specific power of arrest for this summary offence. The section has three specific subsections attached to it, namely:

- Any person who contravenes a prohibition imposed by fireworks regulations is guilty of an offence.
- Any person who fails to comply with a requirement imposed by or under fireworks regulations to give or not to give information is guilty of an offence.
- Where a requirement to give information is imposed by or under fireworks regulations, a person is guilty of an offence if, in giving the information, he makes a statement which he knows to be false in a material particular or recklessly makes a statement which is false in a material particular.

In relation to the supply of fireworks to a child or young person there is a defence available to the defendant to show that he/she had no reason to suspect that the person was under the relevant age.

Throwing of fireworks

Currently, it is an offence contrary to section 80 of the Explosives Act 1875 to throw, cast, or fire any fireworks in or into any highway, street, thoroughfare, or public place. This is triable summarily, and has no specific power of arrest attached to it. However, it is anticipated that the Fireworks Act 2003 will repeal this offence when the relevant section of it comes into force.

10.4 Summing Up

10.4.1 Domestic violence

The ACPO definition of domestic violence is: 'any incident of threatening behaviour, violence or abuse (psychological, physical, sexual, financial or emotional) between adults, aged eighteen and over, who are or have been intimate partners or family members, regardless of gender and sexuality.' (Family members are defined as mother, father, son, daughter, brother, sister and grandparents, whether directly related, in-laws or step-family.)

10.4. 2 Breach of injunctions

The role of the police in this instance is to bring the defendant before the courts so that they can explain their behaviour. There is generally no need for an investigation or prosecuting function on the part of the police.

10.4.3 **Unlawful absence from school**

A child or young person is deemed to be absent from school unlawfully unless it falls within one of the following: official leave, unavoidable cause or delay, or a day set aside for religious observance.

10.4.4 **Public nuisance**

A public nuisance is an unlawful act or an omission to discharge a duty which in either case obstructs or causes inconvenience or damage to the public in the exercise of their common rights.

This offence is triable either way and the courts have unlimited powers of sentence on indictment. It is an arrestable offence.

10.4.5 **Fireworks**

'Fireworks' means fireworks for the purposes of the British Standard Specification published on 30 November 1988 or any British specification replacing it. The regulations categorize specific types of fireworks according to the danger they present, and range from caps and party poppers to intricate devices used in pyrotechnic displays.

10.4.6 **Local application**

(1) Obtain a copy of the local crime and disorder reduction strategy for your area. Identify what Acts of Parliament have been used as a basis for the formulation of the document.
(2) Contact the local education authority and establish how many truancy sweeps have taken place in your area and examine the results.
(3) Speak to your local BCU or force research office and obtain a list of the breakdown of calls made to the police. Establish how many of the calls can be placed in the quality-of-life issues discussed in this chapter.
(4) Contact your local domestic violence forum and obtain a copy of their policy and procedures document. What training is being provided for this unit?

10.4.7 **Useful websites**

http://www.homeoffice.gov.uk/rds/index.htm
http://www.youth-justice-board.gov.uk/YouthJusticeBoard/Prevention/
http://www.nacro.org.uk/who-we-are/
http://www.opsi.gov.uk/acts.htm

Appendix

Typical Questionnaire Used in a Local Crime and Disorder Survey

Alley Gate Research
Primary Questionnaire

The Local Crime and Disorder Reduction Partnership are involved in a scheme whereby gates are to be installed at the end of the rear lanes situated behind houses in this area. This is commonly called 'alley gating'. Part of this evaluation is to interview people before the gates are installed. We are asking selected people to take part in this important questionnaire survey to help us with this task. Please spare a few moments of your time in order for it to be completed. Your views really are very important.

Please tick the box that nearest represents your answer.

1. Location of dwelling in relation to the proposed nearest alley gate

Near the end of the row of houses nearest to the gate ☐₁
Situated in the middle of the row of houses ☐₂

(PLEASE REFER TO INSTRUCTIONS RE LOCATION ON SEPARATE SHEET)

2. Ownership/type of house

Privately owned ☐₁   Local authority owned ☐₂
Privately rented ☐₃   Housing association ☐₄
Other (please specify)——————————————————☐₅

3. Number of residents in dwelling house

1 person living alone ☐₁   2–3 people living together ☐₂
4–6 people living together ☐₃   7 and over living together ☐₄

4. Do you consider yourself to be the head of the household?
(Mortgage payer, rent payer, etc.)

Yes ☐₁

No ☐₂

5. Please indicate your age group

Under 18 years of age	☐₁	18–30	☐₂
31–40	☐₃	41–50	☐₄
51–60	☐₅	61 years and over	☐₆

6. Please indicate your gender

Male ☐₁
Female ☐₂

7. Do you think the introduction of the gates is ...?

A good thing ☐₁
A bad thing ☐₂
Not sure ☐₃

8. Which ONE of the below is the main problem that you have in your back lane?

Graffiti on walls, etc.	☐₁	Drug abuse	☐₂
Burglary	☐₃	Youths congregating	☐₄
Litter/dogs fouling paths	☐₅	Noise	☐₆
Other (please specify) _____			☐₇

9. Do you think the alley gates will reduce this problem?

Yes ☐₁
No ☐₂
Not sure ☐₃

10. Do you use the rear lane of your house during the daytime?

Yes ☐₁
No ☐₂
If No, please explain why _____

_____

11. Do you use the rear lane of your house during the hours of darkness?

Yes ☐₁
No ☐₂
If No, please explain why _____

_____

12. Do you think that the amount of crime and disorder in the area where you live has changed in the past year?

It is about the same	☐₁	There is more now	☐₂
There is less now	☐₃	Not sure	☐₄

13. How safe do you feel in your own home at night?

Very safe	☐₁	Fairly safe	☐₂
Unsafe	☐₃	Very unsafe	☐₄

14. How safe do you feel in your own home in the daytime?

Very safe	☐₁	Fairly safe	☐₂
Unsafe	☐₃	Very unsafe	☐₄

15. Would you be prepared to be re-interviewed some months following the installation of the gates?

Yes ☐₁
No   ☐₂

16. How long have you lived at this address?

Under 1 year	☐₁	1–5 years	☐₂
6–10 years	☐₃	11–15 years	☐₄
16–20 years	☐₅	Over 20 years	☐₆

17. If you have any other issues you would like to mention, please include them here:

_____
_____
_____

Once again many thanks for your time.

References

The list below contains details of all the references to the literature and to legislation that are made within the text. For more information on books from Blackstone's go to: http://www.blackstonespolicemanuals.com or email police.uk@oup.com.

ACPO (2005a), *Practice Advice on Core Investigative Doctrine 2005*, Cambridge, NCPE.

ACPO (2005b), *Practice Advice on Professionalizing the Business of Neighbourhood Policing 2005*, Cambridge, NCPE.

Alderson, J. (1984), *Law and Disorder*, London, Hamish Hamilton.

Alderson, J. (1998), *Principled Policing: Protecting the Public with Integrity*, Winchester, Waterside Press.

Allat, P. (1984), 'Residual Security: Containment and Displacement of Burglary', *Howard Journal of Criminal Justice*, vol. 23, pp. 99–116.

Anderson, D., Chenery, S., and Pease, K. (1995), *Biting Back: Tackling Repeat Burglary and Car Crime*, Police Research Group Crime Detection and Prevention Paper 58, London, Home Office.

Anderson, R. W. (1976), *The Economics of Crime*, London, Macmillan.

Audit Commission (1996), *Tackling Patrol Effectively*, London, Audit Commission.

Audit Commission (1998), *A Fruitful Partnership*, London, Audit Commission.

BBC (2010), *David Cameron launches Tories' 'big society' plan*, Available: <http://www.bbc.co.uk/news/uk-10680062>, [Accessed [26/08/10].

Becker, G. S. (1968), 'Crime and Punishment: An Economic Approach', *Journal of Political Economy*, vol. 76, pp. 169–217.

Beckett, I. (1998), 'Command and Patrol', *Police Review*, 2/1/1998, pp. 24–25.

Bennett, T., and Durie, L. (1999), *Preventing Residential Burglary in Cambridge: From Crime Audit to Targeted Strategies*, Policing and Reducing Crime Unit Police Research Paper 108, London, Home Office.

Benyon, J. (1984), *Scarman and After*, Oxford, Pergamon Press.

Benyon, J., and Solomos, J. (1993), *The Roots of Urban Unrest*, Oxford, Pergamon Press.

Blair, T. (1998), 'Blair Delivers Zero Tolerance', *BBC News Online*, 29/9/1998, <http://news.bbc.co.uk>.

Blunkett, D. (2004), 'Blunkett Heralds Return of "Local Bobbies"', *Guardian*, 9/11/2004.

Bowling, B. (1996), 'Zero Tolerance: Cracking Down on Crime in New York City', *Criminal Justice Matters*, vol. 25, pp. 11–12.

Brantingham, P. J., and Faust, F. (1976), *Juvenile Justice Philosophy: Readings, Cases, Comments*, London, The West Group.

Bratton, W. J. (1998), 'Crime is Down in New York City: Blame the Police', in Dennis, N. (ed.), *Zero Tolerance, Policing a Free Society*, London, IEA, pp. 29–43.

Bridgeman, C., and Hobbs, L. (1997), *Preventing Repeat Victimisation: The Police Officer's Guide*, Police Research Group, London, Home Office.

Bright, J. (1991), 'Crime Prevention: The British Experience', in Stenson, K., and Cowell, D. (eds.), *The Politics of Crime Control*, London, Sage, pp. 62–86.

Bright, J. (1996), 'Preventing Youth Crime in High Crime Areas: Towards a Strategy', in Bennett, T. (ed.), *Preventing Crime and Disorder: Targeting Strategies and Responsibilities*, Cambridge, Institute of Criminology, pp. 365–383.

Bright, J. (1997), *Turning the Tide: Crime, Community and Prevention*, London, Demos.

Bright, J. (1999), 'Preventing Youth Crime', in Francis, P., and Fraser, P. (eds.), *Building Safer Communities*, London, Centre for Crime and Justice Studies, pp. 96–103.

Brown, C. (1997), *Dwelling Burglaries: The Need for Multi-Agency Strategies*, Police Research Group, London, Home Office.

Cabinet Office (2010), *Building the Big Society*, London, Cabinet Office.

Cameron, D. (2010), *Big Society Speech*, London, Press Office.

Chartered Institute of Housing (1995), *Neighbour Nuisance: Ending the Nightmare*, Good Practice Briefing Guide No. 3, Coventry, CIH.

Choongh, S. (1997), *Policing as Social Discipline*, Oxford, Oxford University Press.

Clarke, C. (1999), 'Charles Clarke Underlines Partnership Approach to Delivering Safer Communities', Home Office News Report 372/99, London, Home Office, 24/11/99.

Clarke, R. V. (ed.) (1997), *Situational Crime Prevention: Successful Case Studies*, 2nd edn., New York, Harrow and Heston.

Clarke, R. V., and Felson, M. (1993), *Routine Activity and Rational Choice, Advances in Criminological Theory*, Vol. 5, New Brunswick, NJ, Transaction Publications.

Clarke, R. V., and Mayhew, P. (eds.) (1980), *Designing out Crime*, London, HMSO.

Cohen, S. (1985), *Visions of Social Control*, Cambridge, Polity Press.

Coleman, A. (1985), *Utopia on Trial*, London, Shipman.

Coote, A. (2010), *Cameron's 'big society' Will Leave the Poor and Powerless Behind*, Available: <http://www.guardian.co.uk/commentisfree/2010/jul/19/big-society-cameron-equal-opportunity>, [Accessed [26/08/10].

Crawford, A. (1998), *Crime Prevention and Community Safety: Politics, Policies and Practices*, Harlow, Longman.

Crawford, A. (1999), *The Local Governance of Crime: Appeals to Community and Partnerships*, Oxford, Oxford University Press.

Crawford, A., and Lister, S. (2004), *The Extended Police Family: Visible Patrols in Residential Areas*, York, Rowntree Foundation.

Della Porta, D., and Reiter, H. (1998), *Policing Protest*, Minneapolis, University of Minnesota Press.

Dennis, N., and Mallon, R. (1998), 'Zero Tolerance: Short Term Fix, Long Term Liability?', in Dennis, N. et al (eds.), *Zero Tolerance: Policing a Free Society*, London, IEA, pp. 44–62.

Eaton, G. (2010), 'The "big society": new doubts emerge', London, *New Statesman*, Available: <http://www.newstatesman.com/blogs/the-staggers/2010/07/society-bank-reserves-cameron>, [Accessed 16 July 2012].

Ehrlich, I. (1973), 'Participation in Illegitimate Activities: A Theoretical and Empirical Analysis', *Journal of Political Economy*, vol. 81, pp. 521–564.

Ehrlich, I. (1975), 'The Deterrent Effect of Capital Punishment: A Question of Life and Death', *American Economic Review*, vol. 65, pp. 397–417.

Ehrlich, I. (1977), 'Capital Punishment and Deterrence: Some Further Thoughts and Evidence', *Journal of Political Economy*, vol. 85, pp. 741–788.

Ekblom, P. (1992), 'The Safer Cities Programme Impact Evaluation: Problems and Progress', *Studies on Crime and Crime Prevention*, vol. 1, pp. 35–51.

Elliot, R., and Nicholls, J. (1996), *It's Good to Talk: Lessons in Public Consultation and Feedback*, Police Research Group Paper 22, London, Home Office.

Felson, M. (1998), *Crime and Everyday Life*, 2nd edn., Thousand Oaks: Pine Forge Press.

Felson, M., and Clarke, R. V. (1998), *Opportunity Makes the Thief: Practical Theory for Crime Prevention*, Police Research Series 98, London, Home Office.

Fielding, N. G. (1995), *Community Policing*, Oxford, Oxford University Press.

Flanagan, R. (2008), *Her Majesty's Inspectorate for the Constabulary: Serving Communities and Individuals*, HMIC. London: Central Office of Information.

Forrester, K., Chatterton, M., and Pease, K. (1988), *The Kirkholt Burglary Prevention Project, Rochdale*, Home Office Crime Prevention Unit Paper 13, London, Home Office.

Forrester, K., Frenz, S., O'Connell, M., and Pease, K. (1990), *The Kirkholt Burglary Project: Phase II*, Home Office Crime Prevention Unit Paper 23, London, Home Office.

Friedman, R. R. (1992), *Community Policing, Comparative Perspectives and Prospects*, New York, St. Martin's Press.

Garland, D. (1996), 'The Limits of the Sovereign State', *British Journal of Criminology*, vol. 36, pp. 445–471.

Gilling, D. (1997), *Crime Prevention: Theory, Policy and Politics*, UCL, London.

Goldstein, H. (1990), *Problem Oriented Policing*, New York, McGraw-Hill.

Graham, J., and Bowling, B. (1995), *Young People and Crime*, Home Office Study 145, London, HMSO.

Gravelle, J., and Rogers, C. (2009a), *The Economy of Policing: The Impact of the Volunteer*, Policing: A Journal of Policy and Practice 2009, Oxford University Press.

Gravelle, J., and Rogers, C. (2009b), *Your Country Needs You: The Economic Viability of Volunteers in the Police, Safer Communities: A Journal of Practice, Opinion, Policy and Research*, Pavilion Publishing, Volume 8, Issue 3 July 2009.

Griffiths, W. (1997), *Zero Tolerance: A View from London*, IEA Conference Papers, London, IEA.

Her Majesty's Inspectorate of Constabulary (1997), *Policing with Intelligence: A Thematic Inspection*, London, Home Office.

HMSO (2004), *The Bichard Inquiry Report*, London, HMSO.

Holdaway, S. (1984), *Inside the British Police: A Force at Work*, London, Blackwell.

Home Office (1956), *The Clean Air Act 1956*, London, HMSO.

Home Office (1968a), *The Clean Air Act 1968*, London, HMSO.

Home Office (1968b), *The Licensing Act 1968*, London, HMSO.

Home Office (1971), *The Misuse of Drugs Act 1971*, London, HMSO.

Home Office (1972), *The Local Government Act 1972*, London, HMSO.

Home Office (1974), *The Control of Pollution Act 1974*, London, HMSO.

Home Office (1976), *The Race Relations Act 1976*, London, HMSO.

Home Office (1978), *The Refuse Disposal and Amenity Act 1978*, London, HMSO.

Home Office (1980a), *The Magistrates' Court Act 1980*, London, HMSO.

Home Office (1980b), *The Highways Act 1980*, London, HMSO.

Home Office (1984a), *Police and Criminal Evidence Act 1984*, London, HMSO.

Home Office (1984b), *Crime Prevention Circular 8/1984*, London, HMSO.

Home Office (1988), *The Road Traffic Act 1988*, London, HMSO.

Home Office (1989a), *Tackling Crime*, London, HMSO.

Home Office (1989b), *The Children Act*, London, HMSO.

Home Office (1990a), *Circular 44/90 Crime Prevention: The Success of the Partnership Approach*, London, HMSO.

Home Office (1990b), *The Environmental Protection Act 1990*, London, HMSO.

Home Office (1991a), *Safer Communities: The Local Delivery of Crime Prevention through the Partnership Approach (The Morgan Report)*, London, HMSO.

Home Office (1991b), *The Dangerous Dogs Act 1991*, London, HMSO.

Home Office (1994a), *Partners against Crime*, London, HMSO.

Home Office (1994b), *The Police and Magistrates' Court Act 1994*, London, HMSO.

Home Office (1996a), *The Police Act 1996*, London, HMSO.

Home Office (1996b), *The Housing Act 1996*, London, HMSO.

Home Office (1996c), *The Family Law Act 1996*, London, HMSO.

Home Office (1996d), *The Dogs (Fouling of Land) Act 1996*, London, HMSO.

Home Office (1997a), *Getting to Grips with Crime: A New Framework for Local Action—Examples of Local Authority Partnership Activity*, London, HMSO.

Home Office (1997b), *The Confiscation of Alcohol (Young Persons) Act 1997*, London, HMSO.

Home Office (1997c), *The Protection from Harassment Act 1997*, London, HMSO.

Home Office (1998a), *Reducing Offending: An Assessment of Research Evidence on Ways of Dealing with Offending Behaviour*, Research and Statistics Directorate Research Study 187, London, Home Office.

Home Office (1998b), *The Human Rights Act 1998*, London, HMSO.

Home Office (1998c), *The Data Protection Act 1998*, London, HMSO.

Home Office (1998d), *The Public Interest Disclosure Act 1998*, London, HMSO.

Home Office (1999a), *Crime and Disorder Act 1998*, London, HMSO. (The review of this Act can be seen at the following address: <http://webarchive.nationalarchives.gov.uk/20100413151426/http://crimereduction.homeoffice.gov.uk/partnerships60.htm>, [Accessed 16 July 2012].)

Home Office (1999b), *The Youth Justice and Criminal Evidence Act 1996*, London, HMSO.

Home Office (1999c), *The Local Government Act 1999*, London, HMSO.

Home Office (2000a), *The Countryside and Rights of Way Act 1978*, London, HMSO.

Home Office (2000b), *The Race Relations (Amendment) Act 2000*, London, HMSO.

Home Office (2000c), *The Local Government Act 2000*, London, HMSO.

Home Office (2001a), *Policing a New Century: A Blueprint for Reform*, London, HMSO.

Home Office (2001b), *The Anti-Terrorism, Crime and Security Act 2001*, London, HMSO.

Home Office (2001c), *The Private Security Industry Act 2001*, London, HMSO.

Home Office (2002a), *The Police Reform Act 2002*, London, HMSO.

Home Office (2002b), *The Mobile Telephones (Reprogramming) Act 2002*, London, HMSO.

Home Office (2003a), *The Anti-Social Behaviour Act 2003*, London, HMSO.

Home Office (2003b), *The Licensing Act 2003*, London, HMSO.

Home Office (2003c), *The Fireworks Act 2003*, London, HMSO.

Home Office (2003d), *Drunk and Disorderly: A qualitative study of binge drinking among 18 to 24 year olds*, Home Office Research Study 262, London, HMSO.

Home Office (2004a), *Building Communities, Beating Crime: A Better Police Service for the 21st Century*, London, HMSO.

Home Office (2004b), *National Policing Plan 2005–2008: Safer, Stronger Communities*, London, HMSO.

Home Office (2004c), *Confident Communities in a Secure Britain: The Home Office Strategic Plan 2004–2008*, London, HMSO.

Home Office (2004d), *Criminal Statistics England and Wales 2004*, London, HMSO.

Home Office (2005a), *Neighbourhood Policing: Your Police, Your Community, Our Commitment*, London, Home Office.

Home Office (2005b), *The Clean Neighbourhoods and Environment Act 2005*, London, HMSO.

Home Office (2005c), *The Prevention of Terrorism Act 2005,* London HMSO.

Home Office (2006a), *The Violent Crimes Reduction Act 2006,* London, HMSO.

Home Office (2006b), *The Racial and Religious Hatred Act 2006,* London, HMSO.

Home Office (2006c*), The Terrorism Act 2006,* London, HMSO.

Home Office (2006d), *The Police and Justice Act 2006,* London, HMSO.

Home Office (2007), *The Offenders Management Act 2007*, London, HMSO.

Home Office (2008a), *The Counter Terrorism Act 2008*, London, HMSO.

Home Office (2008b), *The Criminal Justice and Immigration Act 2008*, London, HMSO.

Home Office (2009), *The Policing and Crime Act 2009*, London, HMSO.

Home Office (2011), *The Police Reform and Social Responsibility Act 2011*, London, HMSO.

Home Office (2010), *Radical reforms for Police Announced*, Available: <http://www.homeoffice.gov.uk/media-centre/press-releases/radical-reforms-police>, [Accessed 26/08/10].

Hough, M., and Mayhew, P. (1983), *The British Crime Survey: First Report*, Home Office Research Study 76, London, HMSO.

Hough, M., and Tilley, N. (1998), *Getting the Grease to the Squeak: Research Lessons for Crime Prevention*, Police Research Group Crime Detection and Prevention Paper 91, London, Home Office.

Hughes, G. (1998), *Understanding Crime Prevention*, Buckingham, Open University Press.

Independent (2010), *The Big Society: a Genuine Vision for Britain's Future – or Just Empty Rhetoric?*, Available: <http://www.independent.co.uk/news/uk/politics/the-big-society-a-genuine-vision-for-britains-future-ndash-or-just-empty-rhetoric-2030330.html>, [Accessed 26/08/10].

ITN (2010), *What is the "Big Society" initiative?*, Available: <http://itn.co.uk/59eb147bcb73391305d1226c9945aa69.html>, [Accessed 26/08/10].

Jacobs, J. (1962), *The Life and Death of Great American Cities*, New York, Vintage Books.

Jeffery, C. R. (1971), *Crime Prevention through Environmental Design*, Beverly Hills: Sage.

John, T., and Maguire, M. (2004), *The National Intelligence Model: Key Lessons from Early Research*, Home Office Online Report 30/04, Available: <http://www.homeoffice.gov.uk/rds/pdfs04/rdsolr3004.pdf>.

Jones, T., and Newburn, T. (2006), *Plural Policing: a Comparative Perspective*, Abingdon, Routledge.

Kelling, G., and Cole, C. M. (1996), *Fixing Broken Windows*, London, Free Press.

Kuhn, T. S. (1996), *The Structure of Scientific Revolutions*, 3rd edn., Chicago, University of Chicago Press.

Labour Party (1994), *Partners against Crime*, London, Labour Party.

Labour Party (1997), *Because Britain Deserves Better*, London, Labour Party.

Leigh, A., Read, T., and Tilley, N. (1996), *Problem Oriented Policing: Brit Pop*, Police Research Group, Crime Detection and Prevention 75, London, Home Office.

Leigh, A., Read, T., and Tilley, N. (1998), *Brit Pop II: Problem Oriented Policing in Practice*, Policing and Reducing Crime Unit, Police Research Series Paper 93, London, Home Office.

Loveday, B. (2000), 'New Directions in Accountability', in Leishman, F., Loveday, B., and Savage, S. (eds.), *Core Issues in Policing*, 2nd edn., London, Pearson Education, pp. 213–231.

Lurigo, A. J., and Rosenbaum, D. P. (1994), 'The Impact of Community Policing on Police Personnel: A Review of the Literature', in Rosenbaum, D. P. (ed.), *The Challenge of Community Policing: Testing the Promises*, Beverly Hills, Sage, pp. 147–163.

Mallon, R. (1997a), 'Enough Is Enough', *Daily Telegraph Magazine*, April 1997, p. 22.

Mallon, R. (1997b), 'Mallon's Law', *Police Review*, 21/3/1997, pp. 16–18.

McLaughlin, E., and Muncie, J. (2001), *Controlling Crime*, London, Sage.

McLaughlin, E., and Muncie, J. (2006), *The Sage Dictionary of Criminology*. London, Sage.

Morris, S. (1996), *Policing Problem Housing Estates*, Police Research Group Crime Detection and Prevention Paper 74, London, Home Office.

Mulraney, S. (2000), 'Making Your Mind Up', *Police Review*, 16/9/2000, p. 22.

NCIS (2000), *The National Intelligence Model*, London, National Criminal Intelligence Service.

Newman, O. (1972), *Defensible Space: Crime Prevention through Urban Design*, New York, Macmillan.

Newman, O. (1976), *Design Guidelines for Achieving Defensible Space*, National Institute of Law Enforcement and Criminal Justice, Washington, DC, Government Printing Office.

Neyroud, P. (1998), 'Intelligent Zero Tolerance, an examination of police strategies and Performance', *Police Research and Management*, Spring 1998, vol. 2(2), pp. 3–11.

Office for National Statistics (2010a), *UK Government Debt & Deficit: Deficit 11.4 % of GDP*, Available: <http://www.statistics.gov.uk/CCI/nugget.asp?ID=277>, [Accessed 26/08/10].

O'Byrne, M. (2001), *Changing Policing: Revolution not Evolution*, Lyme Regis, Russell House Publishers.

Palmer, D. (1997), 'When Tolerance is Zero', *Alternative Law Review*, vol. 22(5), pp. 232–236.

Peak, K. J., and Glensor, R. W. (1996), *Community Policing and Problem Solving: Strategies and Practices*, London, Prentice Hall.

Pearce, D., and Harrison, J. (1997), '"Broken Windows"—NYPD Blues', *Police Magazine*, December, p. 11.

Pyle, D. J. (1995), *Cutting the Costs of Crime: The Economics of Crime and Criminal Justice*, IEA Hobart Paper 129, London, IEA.

Read, T., and Tilley, N. (2000), *Not Rocket Science? Problem Solving and Crime Reduction*, Crime Reduction Research Series Paper 6, London, Home Office.

Reiner, R. (2000), *The Politics of the Police*, 3rd edn., London, Harvester Wheatsheaf.

Rock, P. (1989), 'New Directions in Criminological Theory', *Social Studies Review*, vol. 5(1), pp. 2–6.

Romeanes, T. J. (1996), *Problem Oriented Policing: The Cleveland Approach*, Middlesbrough, Cleveland Constabulary.

Romeanes, T. J. (1998), 'A Question of Confidence: Zero Tolerance and Problem Oriented Policing', in Hopkins-Burke, R. (ed.), *Zero Tolerance Policing*, Leicester, Perpetuity Press, pp. 39–48.

Sadd, S., and Grinc, R. (1994), 'Innovative Neighbourhood Oriented Policing: An Evaluation of Community Policing Programmes in Eight Cities', in Rosenbaum, D. P. (ed.), *The Challenge of Community Policing: Testing the Promises*, Beverly Hills, Sage, pp. 27–52.

Sampson, A., Smith, D., Pearson, G., and Blagg, H. (1988), 'Crime, Localities and the Multi Agency Approach', *British Journal of Criminology*, vol. 28, pp. 478–493.

Scanlon, D. E. (1999), *The Crime and Disorder Act 1998: A Guide for Practitioners*, London, Callow.

Silverman, E. B. (1998), 'Below Zero Tolerance: The New York Experience', in Hopkins-Burke, R. (ed.), *Zero Tolerance Policing*, Leicester, Perpetuity Press, pp. 57–67.

Smith, M. J., and Tilley, N. (2004), *Crime Science: New Approaches to Preventing and Detecting Crime*, Cullompton, Willan.

Strathclyde Police (1996), *Spotlight Initiative*, Glasgow, Strathclyde Police.

Straw, J. (1999), 'Blair Zeros in on Crime', *BBC News Online*, 25/8/1999, <http://news.bbc.co.uk>.

Tilley, N. (1993), *The Prevention of Crime against Small Businesses: The Safer Cities Experience*, Police Research Group Crime Detection and Prevention Paper 45, London, Home Office.

Tilley, N. (1994), 'Crime Prevention and the Safer Cities Story', *Howard Journal*, vol. 32(1), pp. 40–57.

Tilley, N. (1997), *Problem Oriented Policing*, IEA Seminar Papers, London, IEA.

Tilley, N. (2000), 'The Evaluation Jungle', in Pease, K., Ballintyne, S., and McLaren, V. (eds.), *Key Issues in Crime Prevention, Crime Reduction and Community Safety*, London, IPPR.

Tilley, N., and Brooks, S. (1996), 'Popular Coppers', *Police Review*, 2/2/1996, pp. 24–25.

Tilley, N. (ed.) (2005), *Handbook of Crime Prevention and Community Safety*, Cullompton, Willan.

Tilley, N., Smith, J., Finer, S., Erol, P., Charles, C., and Dobby, J. (2004), *Problem Solving Street Crimes: Practical Lessons from the Street Crime Initiative*, London, Home Office.

Todd, T., Nicholas, S., Povey, D., and Walker, A. (2004), *Crime in England and Wales 2003/4*, London, HMSO.

Trojanowicz, R. C. (1983), 'An Evaluation of Neighbourhood Foot Patrol Programme', *Journal of Police Science and Administration*, vol. 11(4), pp. 410–419.

Trojanowicz, R. C. (1986), 'Evaluating a Neighbourhood Foot Patrol Programme: The Flint Michigan Project', in Rosenbaum, D. P. (ed.), *Community Crime Prevention*, Beverly Hills, Sage, pp. 258–262.

Trojanowicz, R. C. (1990), 'Community Policing Is not Police Community Relations', *FBI Law Enforcement Bulletin*, vol. 1, October 1990, p. 10.

Trojanowicz, R. C, and Bucqueroux, D. (1990), *Community Policing: A Contemporary Perspective*, Cincinnati, Anderson.

United Nations (1991), *8th United Nations Congress on the Prevention of Crime and the Treatment of Offenders*, Havana, August/September 1990, New York, United Nations Secretariat.

Waddington, D., Jones, K., and Critcher, C. (1989), *Flashpoints*, London, Routledge.

Wadham, J. (1998), 'Zero Tolerance Policing: Striking the Balance, Rights and Liberties', in Hopkins-Burke, R. (ed.), *Zero Tolerance Policing*, Leicester, Perpetuity Press, pp. 49–56.

Wainwright, M. (2000), '"Robocop" Hits Back as Zero Tolerance Policing Damned', *Guardian*, 23/6/2000.

Wilson, D., Ashton, J., and Sharp, D. (2001), *What Everyone in Britain Should Know about the Police*, London, Blackstone Press.

Wilson, J. Q., and Kelling, G. L. (1982), 'Broken Windows: The Police and Neighbourhood Safety', *Atlantic Monthly*, 29 March, p. 38.

Woolf, H., and Tumim, S. (1991), *Prison Disturbances April 1990: Report of an Inquiry*, CM 1456, London, HMSO.

Young, J. (1992), 'Ten Points of Realism', in Young, J., and Matthews, S. (eds.), *Rethinking Criminology: The Realist Debate*, Oxford, Oxford University Press, pp. 24–68.

Index